THE FUTURE OF LEARNING

The Future of Learning

Issues and Prospects

Edited by

Mario Tokoro

Sony Computer Science Labs Inc., Tokyo, Japan

and

Luc Steels

Sony Computer Science Laboratory, Paris, France and VUB AI Laboratory, Brussels, Belgium

Amsterdam • Berlin • Oxford • Tokyo • Washington, DC

ISBN 1 58603 319 0 (IOS Press)
ISBN 4 274 90577 2 C3055 (Ohmsha)
Library of Congress Control Number: 2002117405

Publisher
IOS Press
Nieuwe Hemweg 6B
1013 BG Amsterdam
The Netherlands
fax: +31 20 620 3419
e-mail: order@iospress.nl

Distributor in the UK and Ireland
IOS Press/Lavis Marketing
73 Lime Walk
Headington
Oxford OX3 7AD
England
fax: +44 1865 75 0079

Distributor in the USA and Canada
IOS Press, Inc.
5795-G Burke Centre Parkway
Burke, VA 22015
USA
fax: +1 703 323 3668
e-mail: iosbooks@iospress.com

Distributor in Germany, Austria and Switzerland
IOS Press/LSL.de
Gerichtsweg 28
D-04103 Leipzig
Germany
fax: +49 341 995 4255

Distributor in Japan
Ohmsha, Ltd.
3-1 Kanda Nishiki-cho
Chiyoda-ku, Tokyo 101-8460
Japan
fax: +81 3 3233 2426

PRINTED IN THE NETHERLANDS

Preface

This is the first volume in a new series on 'The Future of Learning'. The goal of this series is to publish multidisciplinary discussions that contribute to improving the education of children and adults of all ages anywhere on earth. These improvements must be founded on well thought out educational methodologies and policies and a better understanding of human learning. They can involve information technology (e-learning, Internet, broadband) but only as a support tool, not as an end in itself.

The discussions being brought together in this series are typically based on workshops, conferences, or international projects. They involve participants from the various sciences investigating learning, as well as practitioners involved in education at different age levels. The material is presented in a way that might be accessible to a broad audience.

The first volume of the series sets the scene. It identifies factors that contribute to the current crisis in education, which is now felt throughout the world. It reports on some innovative projects that give hope for the future, and surveys recent results in cognitive neuroscience, artificial intelligence, and educational psychology. This volume also examines the potential uses of broadband and mass media in supporting education.

Mario Tokoro and Luc Steels
Series editors

Contents

Theme V. Learning Must Be Fun

Theme VI. A Peek into the Future

motivations of individual students. This contrasts with teacher-centered learning which is now - by necessity - the main mode of education. In teacher-centered learning, learners are uniformly put through the same curriculum.

Recent advances in the neurosciences and cognitive sciences offer us insights which could help to significantly improve learning practices at all ages. Societies have always developed the educational systems they need and it is now up to us to do the same: to invent the future of learning. Solutions already exist or can be found, although putting them into practice will require important political and societal changes.

The new media are not a threat but constitute an enormous potential for education, if properly understood and used. They can help cope with the enormous demands, and support the new role of the teacher as a catalyst for learning processes rather than a source of knowledge.

This book brings together position papers and parts of the debates that took place at the workshop. Even though it is never possible to capture lively interchanges in a written document, we believe that the book reflects the spirit of what was said. The text is organised in terms of themes. For each theme, there are statements by workshop participants, followed by group discussion. This discussion does not necessarily stick exclusively to the given theme but weaves a rich web of ideas around it.

Themes

Here is a brief description of the five main themes and the different contributions within each theme.

Theme 1: Education Must Be Learner-Centered. Everybody agrees that topics and learning methods should ideally be chosen and organised in function of the learner. This contrasts with standardised curricula and uniform learning methods imposed in a top-down manner. Learner-centered education requires large amounts of resources which is why they could not be implemented in the past. But advances in information and communication technology give us a new instrument to help achieve this now: ubiquitous access to information. The World Wide Web is already showing what is possible, but this trend will accelerate with the spreading of broadband communication networks that allow unlimited access to text, sound and moving images from anywhere at any time. This new instrument might be the force that enables new methods of education, methods that are individualised, learner-centered, and support life-long learning.

The first contributor to this theme is Mario Tokoro, who sets the stage for the rest of the discussions. As a senior vice-president of the Sony Corporation, Mario Tokoro is a prime mover in the development of new technologies relevant for education, and as professor of computer science at Keio University in Tokyo he was highly regarded as a brilliant educator. Tokoro shares with us his optimistic vision that broadband will finally open up learner-centered learning and thus achieve the highest self-actualisation of human beings. The second contributor is Caroline Nevejan. She researches and investigates innovative educational processes for life-long learning in the information society at the 'Hogeschool' of Amsterdam. She is responsible for various real-world experiments in the integration of information technology in curricula, and reports concepts and ideas that have proven useful in actual practice. The group discussion that follows builds further on the enthusiasm for applying broadband networks to education but also stresses the need for a continued role of teachers to give guidance to the massive amount of information that is now available.

Figure 2: Every child has a unique constellation of talents and developmental trajectories. The challenge to our education system is to bring out the highest potential in each child. (mw)

Theme 2: The Well-Functioning Classroom. New technologies will not make the classroom obsolete. But innovation is possible and necessary in the classroom. The dominating educational practice needs to be questioned, for example, should education be planned in a top-down fashion, based on 'educational objectives' that teachers try to optimally satisfy or is a more creative bottom-up approach possible? Can the motivational development of learners be ignored, i.e. should schools focus exclusively on subject matter, or should they rather take the whole person into account? And if so, how should this be done? Should parents be barred from schools, or should they on the contrary participate heavily in the organisation and educational programs? Discussions around this theme pinpoint problems within current education systems and bring out new ideas based on concrete case studies ranging from toddler and pre-school education to education for secondary school children.

The first contributor to this theme is Carla Rinaldi, who presents results from the Reggio Emilia educational experiments, started by Loris Malaguzzi after the Second World War. Rinaldi explains the main ideas behind this enormously succesful educational project: a positive image of the child as a rich resource of skills and knowledge, participation of the complete community in schools, particularly the parents, a stimulating school environment, continuous documentation and reflection, and a technique called 'progettazione' which replaces the rigid top-down planning of the curriculum. The second contributor to this theme is Mariane Hedegaard, a professor of educational psychology in Denmark. She brings in the Vygotskyan perspective which emphasises a cultural-historical dimension into the development of children. She describes a new approach to education in the classroom, called the 'double move' approach, which not only concentrates on the subject matter taught, but also on the motivational development of children.

Theme 3: The Developing Brain. What can contemporary cognitive science and brain science teach us that is relevant for the future of learning? In the past decade, a growing body of solid evidence has been emerging on the development of the brain in co-evolution with the developing mind. New data are emerging about the importance of stimulation, self-activity, motivation, cognitive development and many other aspects of cognition that are relevant for learning. Although the cognitive neurosciences are far from mapping out the brain's developmental trajectories, it is obvious that the results of this research have growing importance for education.

The first contributor to this theme is Mark Johnson, a professor of psychology well known for his many contributions to the understanding of cognitive development, particularly in young children. Johnson defends the position that the growing child combines both innate capabilities and learning in a constructivist way. This implies that rich stimulation and active learning is important but it needs to take place knowing and exploiting optimally the constraints and critical periods imposed by genetics. The second contributor is Ken Mogi, a physicist and neuroscientist researching visual processes (in particular qualia) and consciousness in the brain. He focuses on the AHA-experience as a critical manifestation of a crucial step in learning. The group discussion that follows deepens the theoretical contributions and explores their relevance for learning.

Theme 4: Learning Must Be Social. The construction of autonomous robots has progressed so dramatically in the last decade that robots are becoming a potentially very important tool for investigating cognition and communication. Moreover they have reached a level of sophistication where it is becoming possible to use them as a new educational medium. The contributors to this theme are both involved in this novel usage of robotics and their case

Figure 3: How can we enrich educational activities so that they become as joyful as play? When learning is fun it motivates the learner and is much more effective and long lasting. (mw)

studies center on the importance of social learning.

The first contributor to this theme is Luc Steels, who has been doing intense research on early word learning and the origins of grounded communication. He describes robotic experiments he has carried out with his colleagues at the Sony Computer Science Laboratory in Paris, attempting to carefully reconstruct the early acquisition of visually grounded concepts and words. Steels argues for the importance of social and cultural learning, and shows through his experiments that individualistic, statistical learning is less effective. The second contributor to this theme is Kerstin Dautenhahn, a professor of computer science at the University of Hertfortshire (UK), who has been using robots as educational and therapeutic tools for autistic children. It appears that autistic children appreciate the predictability of robots, and that the robot can become a medium for inducing social interaction and the development of a 'theory of mind' - two capabilities autistic children to a large extent lack. Here again the social component of learning is emphasised. The group discussion expresses both astonishment at the level of performance of current robots and the ease with which children interact with them, as well as worries of overemphasising technology in education.

Theme 5: Learning Must Be Fun. The final theme focuses on the emotional and motivational aspects of learning and on the importance of intuition and creativity. Results of research into brain science leave no doubt that the developing brain needs a balanced emotional and motivational state to establish the proper connections and sustain their functioning. The brain is an organ that needs a healthy body and a healthy environment to function. It follows that educational environments can only be successful if they induce a positive attitude both in the learner and the teacher.

The first contributor to this theme is Olivier Coenen. He is a brain scientist, making computational models of the cerebellum. Coenen introduces the results of various animal experiments which study the impact of motivational factors on learning and memory. The second contributor is Eduardo Punset, a professor of economics at the University of Barcelona, who has been very active in diffusing science through mass media like television. His main message is that science teaching is not only of enormous importance, but that it can and must be delivered in a way that everybody finds interesting and fun. Finally, there is a contribution by Bernard Allien, a sociologist and media expert, who attempts to bring together many threads discussed earlier in the workshop. He stresses knowledge enjoyment, intuition and enhanced creativity as key ingredients for effective learning.

Marleen Wynants, a Belgian journalist who has published widely on the future of education, concludes the book with a playful story 'Brains at Play' on what this future might be like.

A Manifesto for the Future of Learning

At the risk of simplifying the enormous richness of the debates, it is worthwhile to extract six major take-home lessons:

1. MAKE LEARNING FUN. The evidence is clear: learning is easier when the learner is motivated and when the learning process is a joyful activity. The model of the disciplined child who passively absorbs whatever information is fed to them can no longer work. So a primary challenge is to permeate all educational programs and tools with excitement and enjoyment.

2. EVERYBODY CAN BE A TEACHER. Learning cannot be confined to the classroom, and everybody can and must play a role in teaching children. Parents, family members and citizens at large cannot leave education entirely to schools but must engage in it themselves - even if this is difficult due to the heavy demands contemporary society already places on them. This will require political and societal changes and a renewed valorisation of the importance of education in society.

3. EVERYBODY CAN BE A LEARNER. The need for life-long learning is now obvious to everyone and so we must all continue to foster the desire to learn and be open to new ideas and insights, including from children.

4. EXPLOIT THE POWER OF NEW MEDIA. The new information and communication technologies do not have to pose a threat but can be an enormous resource for education. This implies important responsabilities for technologists to develop the media so that they can be used optimally in education, but also for educators to maximally seize the opportunities by the development of new content. The use of new technologies should be as natural, and is as important, as books, pencils or clay, but should always be seen as complementary and never an end in itself.

Figure 4: People of all generations must get involved in education. Everybody can be a teacher and everybody can be a learner. (mw)

5. DIVERSITY NEEDS TO BE RESPECTED. Brain science and cognitive science are giving us new insights into learning that urgently need to be integrated into educational practices in our society. For example, the idea that everybody has exactly the same type of brain - and therefore that all children should go through the same curriculum at the same pace - is clearly wrong. There are many different types of brains, requiring that education becomes more individualised to bring out the best in each. Stock should be taken of this kind of insight and much more research should be carried out into how it can be translated into educational practice.

6. SET THE TEACHERS FREE. One of the most dangerous trends seen today is the use of bureaucratic optimisation procedures, developed for the management of manufacturing processes, in education. The excessive rules and regulations now streaming down on educators from centralised bureaucracies is stifling individual creativity and is a major cause of educational dysfunctioning. We argue that the heavy influence of educational bureaucracy should be diminished sharply. The initiative should be given back to the teachers - provided of course that they are given managable numbers of students, and adapted materials.

The discussions and articles in this book address crucial issues for society. They are full of optimism. If we adopt the right changes to current behaviors and societal priorities, we can rebuild environments in which all children can flourish to become participating citizens and in which life-long learning is a joy that propels our societies to greater harmony and well-being.

Acknowledgement

The organisation of a workshop requires many people working in the background. We are particularly indebted to Nicole Bastien who managed the practical organisation of the workshop, and the staff of the 'Chateau de Bagnols' for their great hospitality. Additional help was provided by members of the Sony Key project (Takahiro Sasaki, Bunya Kasai, Michinori Kawachi, Jerome Allien). Marleen Wynants took the pictures at the workshop marked with (mw). Additional photographs were supplied by Angus McIntyre (am), Francois Pachet (fp), and Takahiro Sasaki (ts). Marleen Wynants performed the basic transcription and editing of the dialogs. Ezra Belgrado (Marleen's daughter) did all the drawings. Alexandra Miranda has been of great help in improving the text. We are indebted also to the staff of IOS Press, particularly Einar Frederiksson, Anne Marie De Rover and the rest of the IOS team for their efficient production of the book.

Theme I.

Education Must Be Learner-Centered

Bears. Ezra, age 6

The 20th century was the century of reductionism. Reductionism worked well for the scientific discipline physics. So well that people started believing that reductionism was the only way to think. But when we apply it to biology or to a discipline like learning, it does not work. If we cut down living systems or cognitive systems to small pieces, we don't see anything at all. So I think the 21st century must be the century for synthesis.

I believe this will be a wonderful century. Mainly because we will understand more and more about our desire to learn, about the why. What is knowledge? Why do people want to obtain that? What we have learned at this workshop is that we are only touching the tip of the iceberg. We have to connect more each separate part into a coherent whole; and then the total will be larger than the sum of its parts.

Mario Tokoro

Chapter 1

The Knowledge Revolution

by Mario Tokoro

Mario Tokoro is a Corporate Executive Vice President and CTO of Information Technology of Sony Corporation, and the President and the Director of Research of Sony Computer Science Laboratories in Tokyo which he founded in 1988. Until 1997 he was a professor of computer science at Keio University. He is a leader in the field of Computer and Internet Technologies and known as a loving educator.

Education began in a primitive form thousands years ago and has undergone many changes due to evolutions in society. In particular, the Industrial Revolution had a great impact on the education system in various ways. Nevertheless the fundamental approach to education has been almost the same throughout history: it has been unidirectional (from teacher to learner) and homogeneous (the same for all). The current education system is still very much tied to the past, partly because teachers have grown up with this framework and partly because we have not had the appropriate tools for an ideal education.

At the moment we are experiencing an "Information Technology Revolution". The Internet and the World Wide Web have enabled people to obtain rich information about whatever they are interested in. These technologies have also made multi-directional or "personal-casting"-style communication very easy. We can say that the public has been liberated from information hardship. I believe therefore that information technologies can be reformed substantially to include the concept of "Learner-centered Learning" or "Interest-driven Learning", leading to a new revolution, the Knowledge Revolution.

Another important development that is currently taking place is driven by advances in cognitive science and neuroscience. Although a lot remains to be discovered, I believe that current insights already provide important ideas that could help realise learner-centered learning. In particular they show the enormous importance of very early educational stimulation, and motivation.

1.1 Phases in Educational History

We can distinguish three important phases in the history of education coinciding with important changes in society: the agricultural revolution, the industrial revolution and most recently the information technology revolution.

The Agricultural Revolution

The origin of schools dates back several thousand years, to the time of the agricultural revolution. Prior to this, as hunters and gatherers, people relied on nature for their own survival. Children acquired the necessary skills and understanding for survival through their daily interaction with parents and siblings. In such a primitive environment, institutionalized schools were not only unavailable, but deemed unnecessary.

This changed with the agricultural revolution. Following advancements in agricultural technology, the efficiency of food production rose, allowing people to settle down. As people began to live in larger numbers of groups or communities, more complex knowledge and skills became necessary to manage the community. A division of labour was introduced, creating a gap between the rich and the poor. Eventually, these communities developed into the ancient states.

Once communities had developed into states, written language was invented for the purpose of keeping records of taxes, contracts etc. Sheepskin, stone and papyrus were commonly used as writing materials. Originally, the characters were not elements of phonetic alphabets but were symbolic images. The privileged/ruling class used language as a means to pass down knowledge from one generation to the next, and schools were founded as places to train their children.

By the Middle Ages, the power of religious institutions, such as churches and temples, grew, and these began to play a prominent role in institutionalized education. However, education was still limited to the ruling/privileged class. As a matter of fact, education remained

Figure 1.1: The highest goal of education should be the self-actualization of the individual. This is not really possible when education is designed to form everybody in the same mold. (am)

a privilege until the Modern Age. Although the invention of printing technology by Johann Gutenberg did accelerate the spread of biblical knowledge, the ruling class was the only class that derived any benefit. The lower class was still required to perform physical labour. Education was not widely available, and schooling remained under the control of the ruling class.

In opposition to education/schooling being used as a tool to exercise control, people like Comenius began to pursue the development of "true education for the public" or "education for the individual" during the Renaissance. "Education for the individual" means allowing any individual with a desire to learn to have access to what they want to learn; in other words, provide individuals with the proper resources and tools for knowledge acquisition. These ideas were also part of the Enlightenment and the educational theories of Jean-Jacques Rousseau. Individualised education is more in tune with humankind's natural curiosity and desire to acquire new knowledge. It is also in line with Maslow's theory of the hierarchy of human needs. Maslow [4] identified a hierarchy of five levels: at the bottom are physiological desires, then we find safety, love, esteem and finally self-actualization as the highest amongst the five human needs. The movements towards individualised education never expanded into a large movement, and remained fairly localized because the means of communication were inadequate.

The Industrial Revolution

As we move forward in time into the late eighteenth century, the time of the Industrial Revolution, we find that the accepted norm of the school as a place for the privileged class was challenged. Prior to the invention of the steam engine, it was believed impossible to detach knowledge from the situation/place in which it was applied, or to communicate it using language (written or verbal). Hence, production know-how was passed down from one generation to the next, either from parent to child or from foreman to apprentice. To borrow the words of Polanyi: Knowledge was passed down in the form of "Tacit Knowledge" [7].

But because it was necessary to "program" steam engine-powered machines to perform certain tasks, it became crucial to transform this "Tacit Knowledge" into "Explicit Knowledge" and establish a scientific know-how that could be taught and transferred. This marked the beginning of the field of mechanical engineering. Moreover, workers no longer had to be experienced, but had to function as simple task laborers controlling machines. So we begin to see written language used to communicate everyday matters among the masses, not only among the heirs within the ruling class. And in the name of extending literacy, schools were opened up to the public.

But even though education was becoming widespread, what was taught in schools (the curriculum) lay in the hands of industrial capitalists. They were interested in maximizing production, and so schools taught knowledge and skills that would help to enhance labour output and sustain the social order. In other words, although the audience changed, schools were still used as an institution to help the members of the ruling class secure their status. The only difference is that the ruling class now comprised industrial capitalists rather than the aristocracy. Education for the royal heir may have been "education for the individual," but school education was nothing but a tool to accomplish the goal of the regime in the most efficient fashion. Today's education is still an emanation of this period. Even though there are obviously many teachers who share the Comenius ideal that education should be a means of self-fulfillment of the individual, the basic educational system is still a form of indoctrination to prepare individuals to become obedient citizens and efficient workers.

The Information Revolution

There is no doubt that the past two revolutions, agricultural and industrial, have had an impact on education. We are currently going through an important new change in society often characterised as the Information Revolution, and we now examine the effect on education and schools.

The Information Revolution, also known as the Digital Information Revolution, has its origin in the digitization of information, which itself was made possible through the invention of computers in the mid-twentieth century. The digitization of information has allowed information to be electronically manipulated, transmitted, stored and displayed.

Many other forms of information technology greatly influenced our lives prior to the era of the computer. The postal system enabled people to communicate over great distances by letter. The invention of the telephone allowed real-time communication by voice. The popularization of mail gave birth to correspondence courses, and the telephone enabled individuals to gather information quickly from other people. There is also the evolution of mass communication. The newspaper helped to deliver news/information to a large audience. Radio and television made possible the real-time broadcast of news, entertainment and educational courses. And these technologies helped lay the ground for the Digital Information Revolution during the latter half of the twentieth century.

The Information Revolution did not occur all at once, but developed in several phases. The first phase occurred between 1946 and 1960 with the invention of the computer. Machines acquired the ability to perform arithmetic and logic computing at very high speed. The second phase occurred between 1985 and 1990. Based on advancements in communication technology, information could now travel between different physical locations, almost in real-time. Personal computers appeared on the market around this time and helped shift power to individuals. The third phase occurred between 1990 and 1995, when the World Wide Web was invented and became widespread. The Web allowed a large a volume of information to be shared amongst an audience of unlimited size in real time. Currently we are entering the fourth phase (2000-2005/2010), characterized by the ubiquitous broadband network.

1.2 Learner-centered Learning

The Web and Broadband Networks

Technologies developed during the Information Revolution have had an enormous impact on society and people's lifestyles. There has of course also been an impact on education. One of the most distinctive characteristics of the 'Web' is the hyperlink. The word "Web" is derived from the fact that home-pages are linked to one another, forming a very dynamic web-like database of information. By forming a link between related items of information, a large database of the world's most up-to-date knowledge and ideas has been created in a staggeringly short amount of time. Anyone is able to access what they are looking for, by conducting a simple search.

The Web is different from conventional mass media such as books, newspapers, radio and TV because it allows large amounts of information to be exchanged in a bi-directional or even multi-directional manner. Books with text and graphics, radio with spoken information, and TV broadcasting with live video, are all radical inventions. However, in all these cases, the flow of information occurs in only one direction, from the sender to the receiver, so there is no interaction between the two. Of course some form of response can also be made by means of other media, such as telephone, but only one-on-one and in real-time. Using the Web, one is not only able to receive information, but also to publish one's response on the Web, or to send email. Anyone can create his/her own Web site, and send information. In other words, the Web has empowered individuals for the first time to acquire and provide information according to their desires.

I mentioned earlier that there have been efforts in the past to realize a kind of "education for the individual". But due to the lack of proper technology, none of these efforts was ever truly fruitful. Individuals did not have access to proper tools by which they could acquire their own information. The Web has finally given the individual the basic tool to acquire the information and thus engage in "Learner-centered Learning". He/she is now able to acquire information based on his/her interest or desire, and gain new knowledge accordingly.

The next phase in the development of the Information Revolution is the availability of vastly expanded communication bandwidth which gives a so-called broadband network. It will not only enable simple text, sound and graphics to be displayed, but will also enable high-quality video to be exchanged. Wireless technology will eliminate constraints caused by separation in time and place, allowing individuals to access information anywhere, any time. It will also become possible to receive and send moving images (video), even while travelling. Individuals can therefore easily acquire, transmit, and exchange information-rich content, and thus gain new knowledge.

From Information to Knowledge

Before going any further, it is necessary to define better what I mean by "knowledge", specifically by making a comparison with information. Data generally means a collection of symbols, for example a set of coded numbers. It becomes information when there are meanings or attributes attached to them. Information becomes knowledge when the relationships among particular items of information have been clearly defined and stored. Obviously, merely gathering information is not sufficient to form knowledge. Knowledge will not form unless the sender and receiver of information share a common context or situation, and the information is "grounded" in the common context, that is, they "share common ground". Let me give an example of what I mean, since the expression "common ground" is not easily understood.

Imagine reading a map of a town you have never visited. By looking at the map, you can gain some understanding of the layout of the roads and the location of landmarks. However, when you look at the map *after* you have visited the town, your experience is totally different. This is because by visiting the actual town, you have gained *grounded* knowledge as opposed to simply information.

Nonaka uses the Japanese word *ba* to explain how knowledge is created [6]. *Ba* refers to more than two individuals sharing a situation in a particular setting. The sharing of a situation usually requires the individuals to be in the same place, and to touch, feel, listen to, eat, and experience the same things. However, *ba* does not necessarily have to be a place in the real world. It can be a conceptual/abstract place, which is common in fields such as mathematics or philosophy, as long as the sender and receiver of information share the *ba* where information is given its meaning. With technological advancements brought about by broadband technologies, sharing a virtual situation/space that closely resembles reality will become more common, and the transformation of information into knowledge will become easier.

The desire to learn belongs on the same level as an individual's desire to fulfil their need for self-actualization. This desire cannot be fulfilled through indoctrination or unilateral education. Unlike the other four needs identified by Maslow, self-actualization is growth-oriented. The learner-centered acquisition of information through the Web and the instant acquisition of knowledge in a short time by means of the ubiquitous broadband network, will help individuals satisfy their needs more quickly. Once individuals are able to exercise learner-centered learning in the truest form, in the ubiquitous broadband network environment, the stage will be set for the next revolution, the so-called Knowledge Revolution.

Since the beginning of recorded history, a lack of appropriate tools and technologies has inhibited individuals from fully satisfying their innate desire to learn in an individualised manner. But as we move forward from the Information Age to the Knowledge Age, proper technology will help individuals to *enjoy* fulfilling their highest desire. We should definitely take some action to help make this a reality. But to do so, we also need a better understanding of the brain.

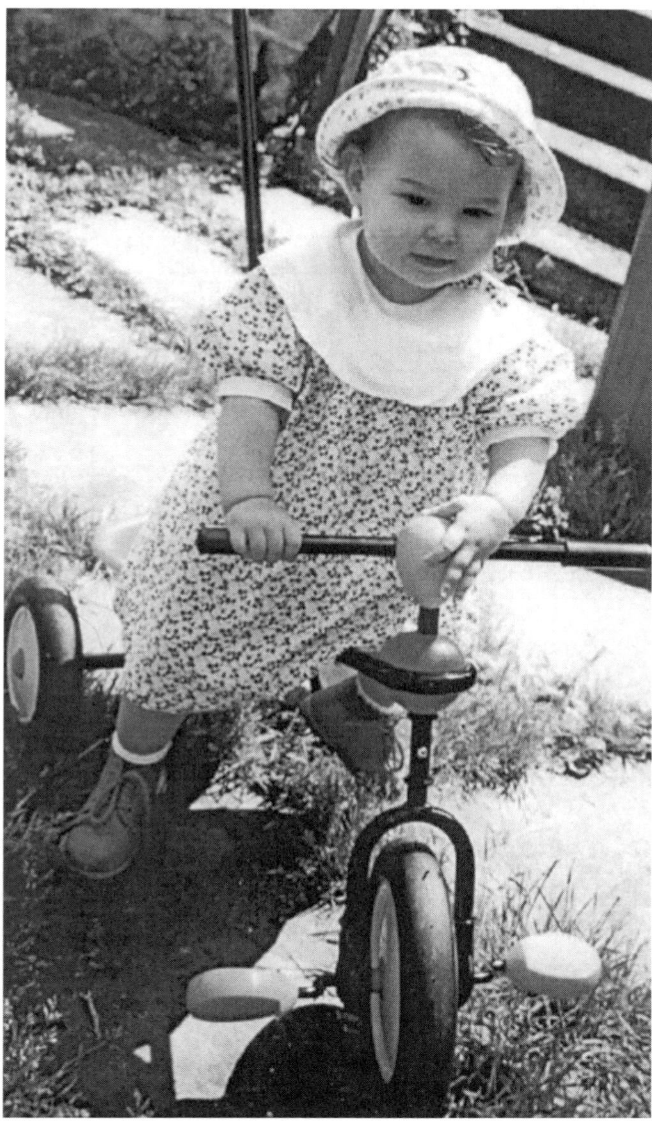

Figure 1.2: Knowledge only becomes grounded through experience with reality itself. This is particularly true for sensori-motor intelligence, developed in the first years of life. (fp)

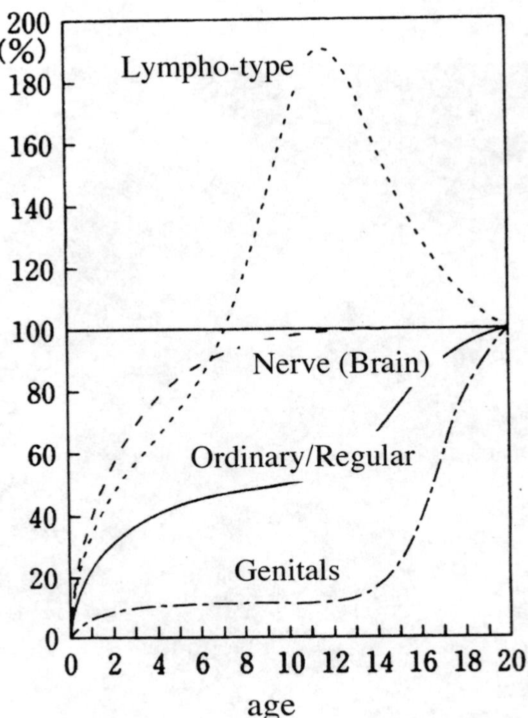

Figure 1.3: A comparison of growth curves for different types of cells.

1.3 Brain Development

Recent advancements in brain science have been remarkable, providing scientific support for education, and offering insights into why early childhood education is so important. In this section, I highlight some of the findings that I believe are very relevant for designing new learner-centered learning environments.

Critical Phases in Brain Development

Figure 1.3 displays Scammon's famous growth curve (from [9]). It breaks down cells of the human body into germ cells, ordinary cells, nerve cells and lymph cells, and compares their development over the course of years. This chart is often used to show how the brain develops more rapidly compared with other parts of the body. It is a classic chart in the sense that it only depicts qualitative characteristics. However, more accurate, quantitative data is beginning to be obtained following recent advances in measurement technology.

Figure 1.4 (from [9]) shows the development of the brain in more detail. The weight of the brain is merely 400 grams when a child is first born. Then it becomes 800 grams by the

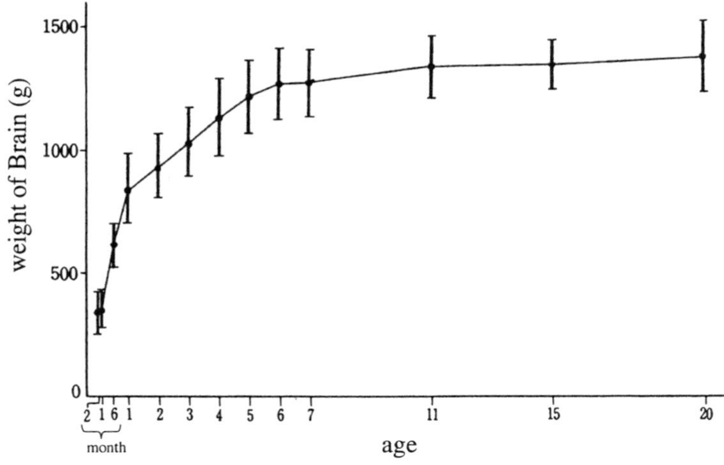

Figure 1.4: Growth curve of the brain (y-axis) over time (x-axis).

end of the first year, 1,100 grams by the third year and 1,200 grams by the fourth year. By the age of six or seven, the weight of the brain has stabilized.

Until recently, it was commonly believed that the human brain developed gradually over the course of several years. At birth, the neural areas involved in touch sensing and motor control are already highly active and they develop to almost the same level of activity as that of an adult within just a year after birth. For a long time, it was believed that the prefrontal cortex, where higher level thought takes place, would develop only gradually and at a later stage, after the individual was sufficiently grown. This is the Gradual Development Theory, first published in 1894 by Paul Felchsig [1]. But in 1985, Pasco Rakic and others [8] found that most of synapses in the cortex develop concurrently and at a relatively early stage. They introduced a new Synchronous Development Theory, opposing the Gradual Development Theory.

Figure 1.5 from [3] shows the trend in the number of synapses in the prefrontal cortex by age. The number of synapses peaks at 15,000 - 20,000 within eight to fifteen months after birth. This chart only depicts the number of synapses in the visual cortex, but it is gradually being discovered that the number of synapses increases in a similar pattern in all parts of the brain. Figure 1.6 from [2] shows the number of synapses and the density of neurons in the prefrontal cortex. Again, we see that the number of synapses peaks at between two and three years of age, and declines between the ages of 10 and 15.

When looking at behavioral development, it seems that the Gradual Development Theory is closer to reality. Babies are able to make only simple movements based on reflexes and instincts. Later, various modes of sensation such as touch, vision, smell, and so on, are integrated and begin to work cooperatively. Then they learn to act according to what they see and sense (feel). Lastly, we begin to observe advancements in the capacity for recognition, and then higher thought processes such as conceptual thinking and problem solving.

Contrary to these observations of gradual development, the Concurrent Development The-

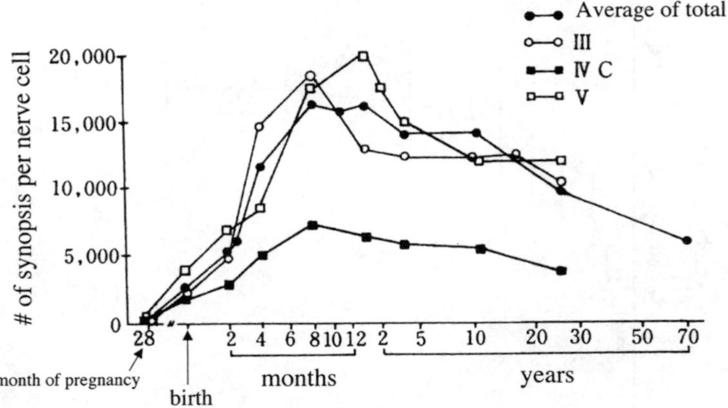

Figure 1.5: Growth in the number of synapses in the primary visual cortex (y-axis) related to age (x-axis).

ory assumes that the basic structure of the complete brain already develops stroke during very early phases of human growth. Some researchers even believe that if the brain cells or synapses in some area are not stimulated properly by the time a person turns twelve years of age, that part of the brain may actually begin to degenerate. For example, if the sense of sight is not stimulated by the age of two-and-a-half, it becomes almost impossible for that individual to ever become fully-sighted. Perhaps a set of neurons does not gradually develop, but gradually degenerates, which may be an anatomical or physiological interpretation of the Gradual Development Theory. There is no clear answer to the question of why synapses that have not been stimulated in a particular period degenerate. It may be because the secretion of hormones eliminates parts that have been judged "redundant" in order to conserve energy.

So, unless all parts of the brain are stimulated shortly after birth, the brain may never be able to exercise its full potential. In particular, applying stimuli to the synapses during the critical period is absolutely crucial to the development of the relevant capabilities. This does not necessarily mean that it is impossible for an adult to acquire new skills such as language, or playing an instrument, or sport. What I want to emphasise here is that there are periods during which the best results in learning can be obtained the most efficiently, and that these periods are limited. Knowledge about these critical periods appears to be very important in thinking about education.

Concentration and Motivation

Concentration and motivation, two important prerequisites for learning, are other aspects where brain science may help provide additional insight. Children can concentrate very well on one thing, blocking everything else out of their mind. When a child is preoccupied with a toy, it is very difficult to draw their attention away, even by making a loud sound or showing them something else that might gain their interest. Children often do the same thing with the toy repeatedly, and will not stop until they are satisfied. They will raise their head for

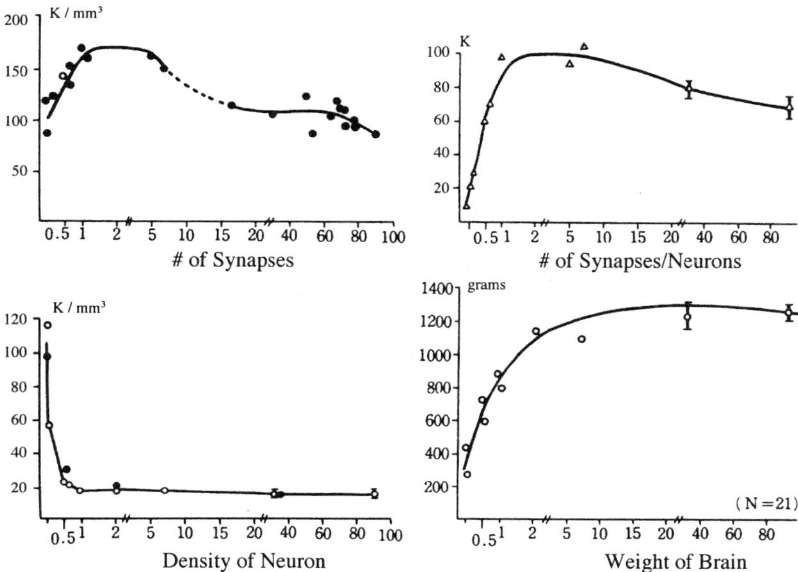

Figure 1.6: Number of synapses (top left), density of neurons (bottom left), synapses compared to neurons (top right) and brain weight. All plotted in relation to age (x-axis).

the first time only after they are ready to do something else. Maria Montessori, a famous Italian educational theorist, first pointed out this phenomenon [5]. Through research, it was later discovered that not only does this phenomenon commonly occur when a child is placed in a proper setting, but it also occurs whenever certain criteria are met. It would be very interesting to know if there is any difference between the brain activity of a child when in a familiar situation and that of the same child when exercising extreme concentration.

Children have a natural inclination to learn. It is important to let them pursue activities that they choose until they are fully satisfied. It would be ideal to place children in an open environment and provide various stimuli so that they can learn what they want to learn. If we are able to prove physiologically that interest-driven education enhances the formation of synapses, then we will be able to make a tremendous contribution to education, not only for children but also for all people. It will be an important step towards learner-centered learning.

I also hope that one day we will understand why people want to learn, what motivates them to seek personal fulfilment. These new insights will help to increase the credibility of Maslow's theory perhaps raising it to the level of universally accepted science.

1.4 Conclusion

If computers and the Internet were utilized according to a proper understanding of the development of the brain, a great opportunity for the advancement of humankind in general would exist. If learning were not enforced, but if individuals could be supported at each stage of

Figure 1.7: Computer and the Internet are not a substitute for physical contact and communication with parents, which is of enormous importance particularly in the first stages of life.

development according to their desire for learning, they could easily and naturally enhance a wide range of abilities.

I am not claiming, and I do not even believe, that computers and the Internet are all we need to improve education and learning. The (sensory) perception that occurs between birth and the age of two must be physically grounded, and in this sense, physical contact and communication with parents is extremely important. In the period between three and seven years of age the foundations of language develop, in addition to the ability to form a basic understanding of events before they actually occur. This requires interaction with rich environments and competent language speakers. Calculation and logic develop between the ages of eight and twelve, at the same time as the notion that one is a member of society. So at this age, it is most important to have direct interaction with different individuals. Between 13 and 15 years of age, one becomes aware/conscious of one's sexuality and identity. There is no doubt that the presence of members of the opposite sex is required.

I feel that it is important for us to discuss and build a future of learning that our predecessors could only imagine, because we now have the proper scientific support from brain science and broadband network technology. If it became accepted that learning is a life-long process that fulfils our desire to know, then the importance of providing the right tools and environment at the right time would multiply several fold. I believe that learner-centered learning will stimulate human creativity, lessen the chance of unnecessary fighting, and contribute to peace in general.

Bibliography

[1] Felchsig, P. (1894) Zur Entwickelungsgeschichte der Associationssysteme im menschlichen Gehirn.Neurol Cbl 1894; 13: 606-608

[2] Huttenlocher, P.R. (1997) Synaptic density in human frontal cortex. Development changes and effects of age. Brain Res., 163:195–205, 1979.

[3] Huttenlocher, P.R. (1990) Morphometric study of human cerebral cortex development, Neuropsychologia, 28, 517-527, 1990

[4] Maslow, A. (1968) Toward a Psychological Being. Wiley, New York.

[5] Montessori, M. (1964) The Montessori Method. Schocken Books, New York.

[6] Nonaka, I. and H. Takeuchi (1966) The Knowledge-Creating Company. Oxford University Press, Oxford.

[7] Polanyi M (1966) The Tacit Dimension. Routledge and Kegan Paul, London.

[8] Rakic P. (1985) Limits of neurogenesis in primates," Science, 227:1054-6, 1985.

[9] Scammon, R. E. (1930) The Measurement of Man. University of Minnesota Press, Minnesota.

Group Discussion 1: The Knowledge Revolution

From Information to Knowledge

Nevejan : Could you elaborate on when information becomes knowledge. And on the difference between information and knowledge based on sharing common ground, or common space.

Tokoro : Consider the bottle of water here in front of me. When I talk to you in another space about a bottle of water, you are not able to see this one. But if there is common ground, for example because we are in the same space, if I can show this bottle to you, then you know what it means. The information has become knowledge. It is no longer an abstract sense of a bottle of water but a real one. I don't have to say that the bottle is made out of glass, is standing on the table, with the cap still on it, not open, etc. A common ground allows a communication of various things that cannot be taught or communicated in the formal or logical way of transmitting information. Especially for young ages, we need to communicate everything in the grounded sense, so that afterwards, when I'm talking to you about a bottle of water, you can ask me wether it is open, whether it is made of glass, etc.

Steels: This grounding is not only important for children. When medical doctors learn about diagnosis, their knowledge has to be grounded in experience with live human bodies. When engineers design a robot, they need a very grounded way of thinking about how the sensors and actuators will behave. I think a lot of problems come from lack of grounding. For example, architects design buildings which do not function in a specific context because they did not take the time to have enough grounded experiences of the urban context or failed to imagine the future uses of the building. Their abstract thinking is not sufficiently grounded. Same thing for many laws and policies that are issued.

Dautenhahn: Here is how I think about this. Suppose you show me twenty different bottles of water. Although I've never seem them before or never touched them, I think I will be able to recognize the nature of a bottle because I know how it feels, I can use my imagination and my mental world to put myself in the mindset of touching the bottle. For adults it may be sufficient to just see visual data but for children who have never seen a bottle before, that is a totally different story.

Tokoro : I agree for 100 percent with that and more. It is not only vision but the touch, the smell, the taste. Kids try to eat and touch everything that comes in their way. That is very important during the first years. But afterwards they don't need to do that any more because they know. They know what the objects are, basically. Then we can introduce other things, then we can engage in abstract thinking and start to use the computer as a tool, but unless there is grounded knowledge of objects in the world, it's irrelevant. The correlation with the real world is important.

The Role of Broadband in Physical Grounding

Allien: To integrate, we need a lot of input. When children ride bicycles, they are not thinking they are riding bicycles but they are nevertheless doing very complex tasks. There is a lot of knowledge integrated unconsciously. It is so complex that is difficult to debrief it afterwards or recuperate it in the conscious sense.

Nevejan: That's exactly the issue we have to deal with for distance learning: How do you create grounding when you're not sharing the same space.

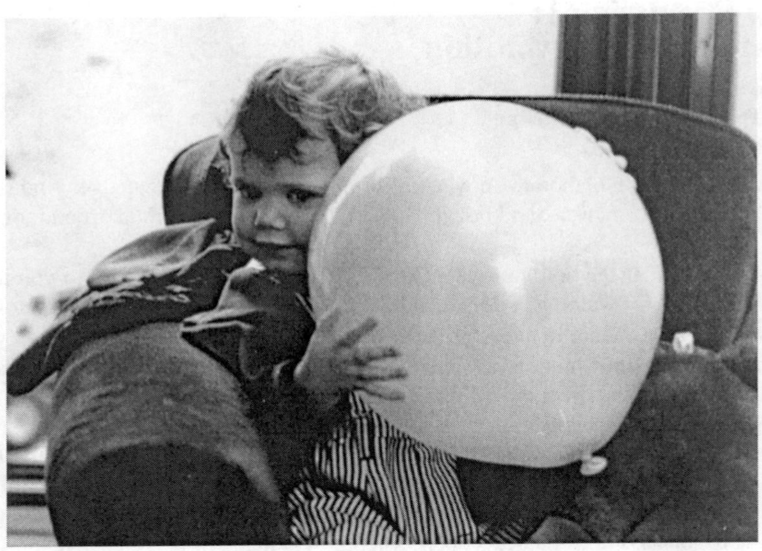

Figure 1.8: Learning about concepts, such as what a balloon is like, involves touching and manipulating it, listening to the sounds it makes when scratching it, and seeing a balloon fly in the air when it is let loose. (mw)

Tokoro: Exactly, that is why I believe broadband is so important. Images are very important. If I want to explain you something which you have never ever seen, then it is almost impossible. I cannot describe it in terms of symbols. But if I can show a picture, then it becomes easier for you to understand what I mean. This is necessary if information is to become knowledge. If I have a movie and I can show you the pouring out of the water and the sound that accompanies that movement, then you will see what it is. And when I drink it, you'll realize I'm not just talking about any kind of water, but drinking water. And that creates inspiration for the next and the next and the next questions. Internet or broadband can be used in an efficient way to help share common ground.

Steels : I think we all agree upon the importance of real world physical stimulation during the early ages. Virtual technologies are perhaps more important at a later age, because at the early age the physical stimulation and affection are so crucial. I see the opportunities of technology arise more at the moment when you already have a healthy learner, which should be established in the very early critical period. Once this is achieved, technology can be a fantastic medium to feed such a person's curiosity.

Tokoro: I completely agree with that. We have to understand better how the brain grows. And then we can use a computer safely from 6 or 7 or 8 years old, although you can start earlier for particular things.

The Role of Broadband in Social Grounding

Coenen: There's one thing we keep talking about, and I think it is very important, which is that we should allow students to come up with their own strategy and not inhibit their thoughts or intuitions, that there should be learner-centered learning. But I believe that you should also allow people who have already gone through a certain pad, to provide help, particularly by giving shortcuts. I remember when we were studying physics we had a lot of hard problems and often we would be in a little group and then we would work at it together. One student would find a shortcut and another would find another one and in the end it would all work out. But there are some students who worked only by themselves and they always had these 10 pages of solutions. They go up to the professor and he has a one page solution. I believe that is what the education process should be, it should transmit shortcuts and tricks so that you can get further.

Steels: Psychological studies have shown that if two children work together, they can solve a problem which none on their own could solve. We all have experienced in brainstorming sessions how solutions pop up from dialogs and interactions between people. So this is a major challenge for educational technologies based on information technology: How can they support collective learning. Right now the individual learner is very much alone with the computer screen. Perhaps broadband can help but we need to understand much better how computers can be used in a collaborative setting.

Mogi: Children are always inspired by other children. They enjoy learning something together rather than being told by adults. The behaviour of children is easily transmitted to other children. Perhaps we can create a new experiment: If we would have free use of broadband technology, we could transmit the behaviour of children in Reggio Emilia, Italy to a kindergarten in Tokyo. Japan. Hence children in Tokyo might be influenced by the way the children in Reggio behave and vice versa. It might be very interesting to watch that.

Nevejan: On a big screen.

Mogi: Yes, on big screens and without any interruption.

Nevejan: They could dance together.

Johnson: When we talk about technology and children and even young children, like the Reggio children communicating by broadband with Tokyo, we clearly have to bear in mind that we are shaping brains here. And we can start very early, this is possible, but we need to be careful because there are big risks in raising whole generations of differently shaped and specialized brains. That could be good but that could be very bad too. Starting early, you might also use formats that don't work so well with adults. So this would be a nice occasion perhaps to use new formats, to use some new type of interactional spaces.

Nevejan: There was this experiment by the National Institute of Technology in India where they face the problem that they have to educate a lot of children and have no schools and no money. So I know this professor who has his office in a very rich street but the backside gives out on a poor neighbourhood. He made a whole in the wall and stuck a computer screen through it. He installed a video camera above it and put touch pad on the side. He left it there. After a few days somebody touched the pad and saw that something on the screen moved. Very soon all the children were getting slightly excited over the fact that it moved and within a week they were downloading pictures, songs, they had developed a language about what it was about, because nobody had told them anything.

So this professor figured that we don't have to teach that kind of thing, we just put it there and people will explore with trial and error. I thought, no, no, it's just because it is near to your institute. But he repeated this in three locations in India, in rural India but also in another urban neighbourhood, and every time he had the same results. So he didn't know what to do

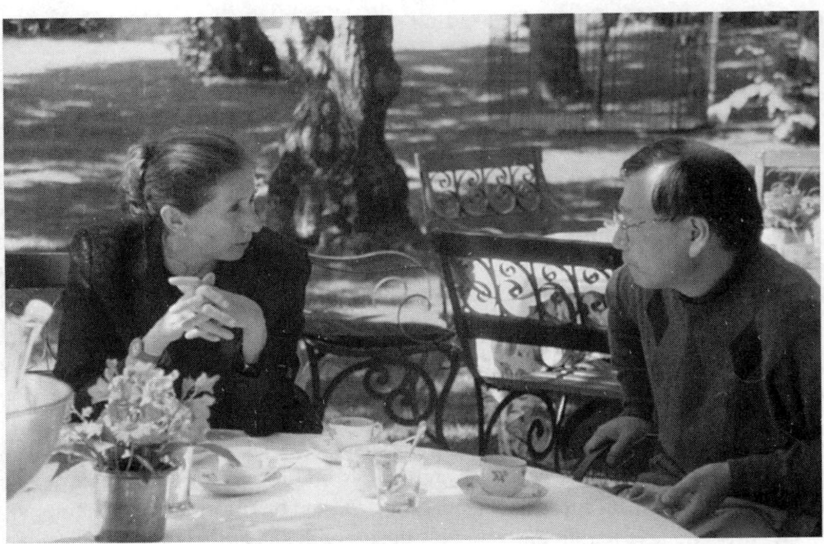

Figure 1.9: Caroline Nevejan (left) and Mario Tokoro (right) discussing the role of Internet for supporting learner-centered learning. (mw)

with this. It proves that even with children who don't have the possibility to go to school, there is an enormous potential. There is a whole new and different way of learning possible that wasn't possible before. And a lot of it has to do with moving images.

Chapter 2

Integrated Learning Environments

by Caroline Nevejan

Caroline Nevejan graduated in social sciences from the University of Amsterdam. She has been active in web related media, founding a media laboratory in Amsterdam and co-organising the Doors of Perception conference. At the moment she is a chief advisor for educational renewal through computing and web technology at the Hogeschool van Amsterdam, developing novel learning environments and practices with a broad involvement of teachers. Nevejan also researches learning and new uses of media at the Performing Arts Labs (UK).

The rise of the information society due to the launching of the World Wide Web, the increase of personal computers at home, the enormous growth of wireless telecommunication,etc., is also changing the space in which learning processes take place. The physical learning space is extended with a virtual one. In the physical education space, a balance needs to be found, for example, between workshops and selfstudy in the library. The same goes for the virtual space. We have to keep a well-balanced equilibrium between, for example, an assessment through video conferencing and additional communications afterwards by e-mail. We need to find out which kind of learning processes produce the best results in each medium and in each type of space. And how they can be integrated. This is a true challenge because we are dealing with media of which hardly anybody had heard about 10 years ago. In some cases, like the World Wide Web, the medium did not even exist yet. Today nobody has a clue about how these media could be optimally used for education, nor how the learning environments exploiting the new media should be developed.

Nevertheless, the virtual environment can become a very important instrument in enhancing the mutual bond between students, teachers and the college as *alma mater*, as a community of professional people. It could not only grow into a richer and more effective learning environment, but also into a space in which training will finally become a service used by graduated professionals, an expertise center - or portal - for the outside world. A virtual environment changes many practical day-to-day worries as well. For example, if students have wireless access to network services and databases with their laptops, the remark "Oh, you don't have that book here?" will soon belong to the past. Only to make place for another one: "Oh, the network is down!"

This paper introduces some concepts we have found useful while integrating information technology into higher education. It also suggests some guidelines on how this integration can be achieved best. But we are only at the beginning of this process and much of it, if not all, remains to be invented. The text is intermixed with some representative examples of integrated learning environments briefly discussed by Marleen Wynants.

2.1 The Changing Spaces of Education

Information and communication technologies introduce a distinction between physical and virtual spaces. But there is another important dimension, namely time. We can distinguish synchronous versus asynchronous learning processes.

- Synchronous learning processes assume that the learners involved share the same time, for example everybody sits together at a certain time in a certain physical space for a class or a workshop. Chatting (IRC) and video conferencing are in their turn examples of synchronous processes in the virtual space. Several people are connected at the same time, through the same medium.

- Other learning processes are asynchronous, for example, studying in the library, or reading email messages. In this case, everybody is connected through the same medium (library, mailbox), but not at the same time. Visiting websites or consulting online databases are other examples of asynchronous learning processes.

Traditionally, communication in the school environment had to take place either physically and synchronously, by way of classes and meetings, or physically and asynchronously, by way of literature, workbooks and such. With the advent of digital technology, the virtual space can extend the physical space. The traditional sequential communication inside a learning process can thus be enhanced with virtual synchronous and asynchronous communication possibilities. There need no longer be instant direct feedback to the learner, but feedback can be delayed in time and still be personal.

Obviously an optimal conformity of physical - virtual and synchronous - asynchronous activities is necessary. We constantly need to reflect upon: what can you do, where and when? Can you take tests in a chatroom or through video conferencing or is this impractical? What is the possible added value of this way of testing? Is the basic condition for an assessment a physical meeting in a physical space, or does an online IRC session provide certain advantages? And what if a student, instead of handing in a printed paper, e-mails a website? Which are the quality criteria you dispose of to evaluate that? Which activities impose physical presence and which activities allow digital interaction? Which activities need direct feedback and what are the situations in which it is possible to react later?

The experience of international cooperation reveals that the more people work together virtually, the more eminent the quality of the physical meetings becomes. Last but not least, we will have to guarantee a continuity and coherence between the various media and instruments operating in the virtual and physical learning spaces.

DEMI DUBBEL

Demi Dubbels Time Machine is an online project that can be explored by an interaction between the internet and the physical classroom. During the project, two schools go online at the same time. Both get a different part of the Demi Dubbel narrative and have to consult each other to proceed through the adventure and bring everything to a good end. The Demi Dubbel Time Machine is a mixed media cultural adventure that takes one week. The main mission is that children have to prevent that professor Demi Dubbel succeeds in her ambition to take the place of the main characters on painted pictures from various cultures by using all kinds of media. In the mean time, children that have Dutch as their second language, will be able to improve on their Dutch.

The challenge was to build a framework that contains enough complexity for it to be interesting, that is open enough for a variety of contributions, structured enough to capture the attention and deal with a preset curriculum, but still flexible enough to meet with different school rhythms. The narrative is constructed in such a way that the children have to communicate with children from other schools to solve certain problems. Without knowing the kind of solutions the children would come up with, a narrative for 9 times 3 hours had to be designed.

Imagine Demi Dubbel pictured instead of the Mona Lisa or one of Picassos ladies. It would really change books on art and publications radically. What would the panic be in the museums all over the world if Demi Dubbel cannot be stopped? When the children log in on the custom built internet world, they meet children from the other school and they get all kinds of assignments, some of them are to be done online, others in the physical world. The project ends with a collective play on Friday afternoon during which the children all meet in real live.

The Demi Dubbel Time Machine allows children to explore their role as media producers, and not only one medium but various ones: from painting with pencils to a theatre play and constructing cultural meanings, verbally and digitally. Teachers will get an insight in how children can learn by producing their own learning materials and how these materials become part of a collective digital cultural heritage and are a result of learning as a social process. *MW*

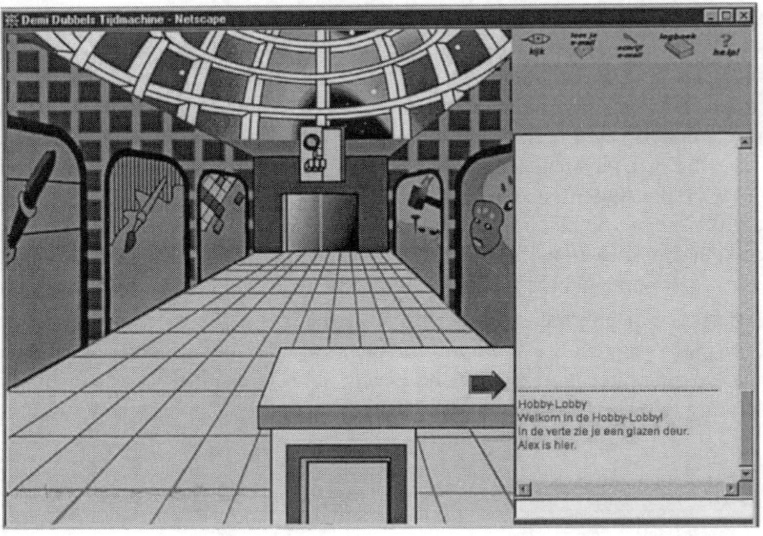

Figure 2.1: Opening scene of Demi Dubbel Time Machine. Children travel back in time to meet painters from the past and thus learn about art history

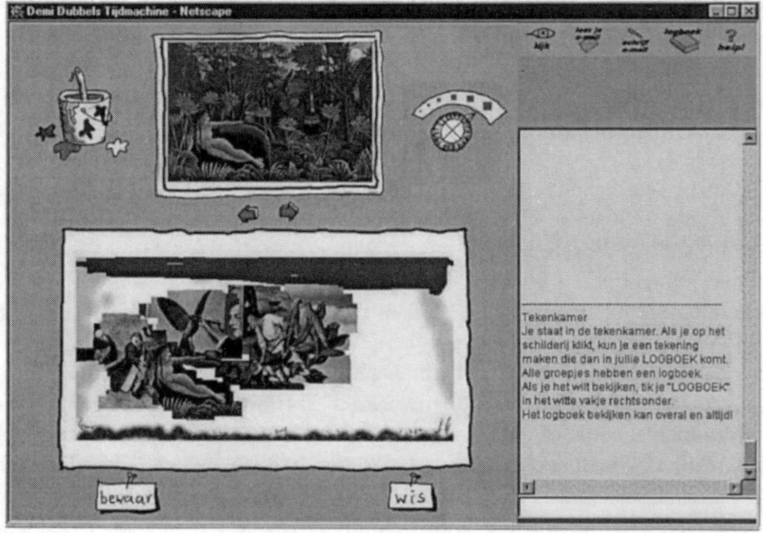

Figure 2.2: The learning environment includes interactive tools to construct drawings with the computer.

Figure 2.3: Children not only interact through cyberspace. They also meet in real life and explore what they have learned about art history through their own visual creations.

2.2 Integrated learning environments

To investigate the use of information and communication technologies in educational practice, the Hogeschool van Amsterdam (HvA) tries to develop integrated learning environments. The Hogeschool van Amsterdam is a very big educational institution (20,000 students) covering a wide range of professional domains, from economics to medicine, from art design to engineering. The Hogeschool is merging with the University of Amsterdam so as to exploit better the interactions between professional and academic teaching and to increase the program options for students. Although it is very difficult to accomplish innovations and changes in such a huge institution, flexibility remains a fundamental asset for institutional education not to fall behind in fulfilling its societal role.

An integrated learning environment consists of different elements from the physical as well as the virtual space. The environment tries to facilitate different learning processes at different times in different places: classes, project groups, intranets, simulations, teleconferencing, online courses, games, portfolio tests, exams, training for skill, assessment, etc. We always search for an optimal mixture of virtual and physical learning environments for each type of training. A training where ICT is a core element of the envisioned profession, will be quite different from one where it is only a means amongst others to accomplish certain tasks. Depending on their optimal effectiveness, certain parts of the program will be oriented towards the virtual or the physical space. In the long run, students should have the opportunity to choose a learning environment according to their learning style, rhythm and capabilities.

Integrated Learning Environments

Integrated learning environments (also called electronical learning environments or digital learning environments) contain tools based on communication and information technology. The way in which they support the learning process is dependent both on the facilities and functionalities of the used hardware and software as well as on the way in which the "meetings" are organized.

Working together in an integrated work and learning environment implies some new information competences and networking. The learning environment and the design of learning processes in this environment will use all kinds of communications spaces in a complementary manner. That is why the emphasis goes to the development of information and network competences. Let's think about a discussion during a workshop where people will be able to listen in with their mobile phone or the publication of a report of the discussion on the web. We could also e-mail some of the core issues to a range of people. A lot of new protocols and editorial formats will have to be developed.

Here are some examples of elements we typically introduce in our integrated learning environments:

- **Intranets** for the organisation of the educational process. An intranet is a protected environment to which only a selected group has access. It is an information and communication environment, personified or not, within which students and teachers can exchange information, communicate, and work together.

- **Web-based (internet) learning environments** are educational tools accessible through the web. The teachers and the students exchange material and give feedback to each other. Examples can be found at the following websites: www.docent.nl, www.blackboard.co www.ecollege.com, www.webct.com.

- **Digital portfolios** are information systems through which students and teachers as well as co-workers and possibly alumni document their own learning process and competence development and visualize it for themselves and others. Sometimes the portfolio is used as an instrument for assessing the students. The portfolio is also a means for the students to demonstrate their skills and accomplishments to future professional colleagues.

- **Simulations and games.** Here the software reacts immediately to the input of the players, through the Internet or directly by a computerprogram. Because of the direct feedback, the learning curve is generally very high. A well known example is SIMCITY, a game that teaches the building of cities. Another example is the flight simulator that is being used in pilot training. Yet another example are the many different virtual business cases circulating on the Internet.

Physical learning environment

Adding integrated learning environment to the educational setting involves a change in the use of space. The physical learning environment and the integrated learning and communication environment should be experienced by the students as two complementary parts of one entity. A interaction between both should be established by means of an alternation in usage, a continuation on the level of content and by references to one another. The integrated learning environment does not make physical encounters superfluous, but puts higher demands on the quality of the encounter. When people meet each other physically, the exchange and mutual impression should allow them later on to work together online in a reassured and clear context. Because a part of the learning process takes place outside the school building, also the visual impact and relevance of the physical buildings becomes more evident. The school is where socialising happens, where the students are recognized by others and acknowledged. The student will not only come to the building for group sessions or discussions, but also to work individually and person-to-person meetings. A pleasent atmosphere and ditto rooms or spaces in the school complex will most likely motivate and inspire students and co-workers. The school should be an attractive environment, a meeting place where people love to come together, where facilities are tuned to the needs of the users, whether they work in group or individually.

Students are becoming diversified, particularly by an increasing in-flow due to life-long learning. It is therefore of main importance that the facilities in the physical learning environment are of a high-quality and guarantee efficiency and comfort. Students may have some tools at home, but the school will always have to facilitate specific tools like simulation tools, skill-labs and other technologies. Archives will be mainly digital and there should be multimedia centers in the school to visualise information on different platforms. Pictures, projection materials, personal digital assistents, facilitycards etc. are all information carriers that are part of the information architecture.

The access to networks within the school buildings is crucial. Also access from other locations outside the school building is a precondition for a good communication process.

2.3 Learning to Learn

Considering the fast changes in the information society and the professional world, education can no longer restrict itself to preparing students for an existing practice. Students need to be taught to shape the changes or ongoing evolution themselves. This is the basic principle of the concept "Learning to learn": The students themselves become responsible for the shaping of their own learning process and they should learn by doing. Information and communication technology can play an important role in the various phases of this kind of continuous learning. Students must learn to find out what they need to know and how they can find their own place within a professional area. The development of such a metaskill is characteristic for 'Learning to Learn'. Learning becomes more and more integrated in work and conversely, working becomes more and more a part of learning. Work gets the notion of "education permanente". Practising your profession means to keep up continuously with new developments and to engage in a continuous learning process.

An example is the training for Informatics and Electrotechnics Engineers at the HvA, where there is a continuous assessment of the learning process via a digital portfoliosystem in which teachers and students cooperate on a day to day basis. Real life meeting moments remain crucial though for the success of the student. And we should not forget that the alternation between virtual and physical spaces requires extra efforts to prevent quality loss. In this context Stephen Heppell of Ultralab (UK) makes a distinction between 'quality control' and 'quality assurance'. Quality control is directed mainly to the monitoring of the quality of the end product. Quality assurance is intended to ensure quality during the *whole* process.

To ensure quality and to enable permanent evaluation, information technology can be used in every phase of the learning process and new roles are defined for students and teachers. Teachers will be given different names according to their functions: the navigator, the assessor, the instructor, the trainer and the consultant. The navigator guides the students and

The Courtyard

Welcome to the Courtyard of Lingua MOO. Signs mark the links to an archi/TEXTural community where language, image, and people are woven together like fine lace...where writing IS the landscape.

Figure 2.4: Lingua Moo starts from a courtyard from which many educational resources are accessible, including a library, a kiosk, ways to collaborate, etc.

makes intensive use of the intranet as a communication medium. The assessor, who assesses the students, wants a conversation with the student and uses the intranet where the products of the students are accessible as source of information for assessment. The instructor and the consultant, who support the student with respect to the content, will heavily use communication facilities and will also have access to tools for knowledge management (from search engines to refined databases, from agents to statistic monitors). Finally the trainers, they operate mainly in the physical learning environment.

LINGUA MOO

Lingua MOO is an academic virtual community for teachers, educators and researchers, based on the MUD Multi User Dungeon - multi user games. It is the foundation for a broader educational MOO open source project called enCore. Educators may obtain the enCore educational MOO database and server software FREE from the enCore website enabling them to set up their own educational MOO customized to meet the specific purpose of their institution or department. At the moment there are more than several hundred enCore MOOs around the world serving the teaching of such subjects as writing, rhetoric, foreign languages, English as a second language, astronomy, library reference and instruction, children's therapy, among others. System requirements for users are minimal because the MOO uses a web browser as the client, so there's no need on their part to download software. Educational MOOs are excellent supplements to traditional classroom instruction, but may also serve as the sole means of delivery for distance learning courses.

Visitors start from a intriguing courtyard drawn by the artist Franois Schuiten. From there on, they can explore this environment and go to the library, the lingua house, the help kiosk, the tower of babble, join in the ComMOOnity, the Communication Center or the Teaching Online in Higher Education Conference Center called TOHE. There is a Role Play Chamber, a Humanistic Informatics Lab and Seminar Rooms. The Agora is a classroom complex where classes meet and group discussions take place in various rooms. There are several entrances leading to the classrooms and a lobby area where students meet for digital coffee or to study.

Ligua MOO was created in 1995 by Cynthia Haynes (University of Texas, Dallas) and Jan Rune Holmevik (University of Bergen, Norway) and functions as both, a learning environment for students and a broader community for research and collaboration on projects situated at the intersection of Arts and Humanities and electronic media. Users may log in as guests or may apply for an account which allows them to create their own virtual room(s) and use the educational tools available or create their own. Primarily the purpose was to serve the Rhetoric and Writing program and the Humanistic Informatics Department of the universities involved, but since its creation other disciplines have been explored in this integrated learning environment. The entry of Lingua MOO in the field of educational MOOs has marked a new direction for electronic composition classroom activities by the addition of synchronous (MOO) and asynchronous (WWW interface) capabilities. The design of the space and the presented features help writing teachers facilitate a learning reality that surpasses the existing ones and positions them for still newer educational realities in the years to come. *MW*

Productive learning

'Productive learning' is a way to learn how to learn. It is actually an old idea, captured in the Latin phrase: *faber fabricandus* or 'practice makes perfect'. Being able to show what you can, your ability to reflect on that and learning from it. The boundaries between educational and work situations fade away. You learn what a business plan is by making one, not only theoretically, but especially in practice, maybe even in front of a real customer.

Productive learning means that you are always aware of your position in your own learning process - even after your official training is supposedly finished. In a society in which people work more and more from a distance, it is also crucial that you constantly communicate what you are doing. Preferable in such a way that others can think and work together with you and can carry on a project in your place if necessary. Your colleague may be somewhere else physically most of the time; so you have to be able to clarify your work through a virtual medium and not only by brainstorming above the legendary beermat.

Productive learning is thus a precondition for an effective information society: Nobody knows what professions will look like in the future. And because of the fast development of the information society everybody needs to learn how to shape it. Hence the accent on the development and evolution of your own learning process: when do I have to learn what and how?

The energy that students put into the learning process is an important indicator of how succesful they will be in their professional practice. Periods of enquiry, production, and evaluation succeed each other. To communicate about their individual learning process, students will produce different outputs in every stage of the learning process. On the basis of an evaluation by the students themselves, by other students, by teachers and external representatives of the professional field and business, new questions will arise leading to new investigations. Students thus become "prosumers", producers as well as consumers. Traditionally teachers have two tasks: They facilitate the learning process by designing learning forms, organising educational activities and guiding students. Secondly, they are the judges of the learning process so that they can steer in turn the behavior of the students.

In the modern educational organisation, the student is also teacher and the teacher is also student. Students are thus producers of their own learning process; the college facilitates it. In the words of Douwe Wielenga, teacher at the Educatieve Faculteit Amsterdam and one of the initiators of their portfolio project: "We use an image of a town where people, that is students and teachers, construct learning practices, but underneath the surface, we find a sewage system, electronic facilities, cable facilities, agreements, a destination plan." And he continues: "Not the delivery of knowledge but the reorganisation of knowledge itself is central. The main value of learning lies in the possibility to participate in the creation of new knowledge."

2.4 How Information Technology Helps

As a result, at the Hogeschool van Amsterdam, we have organized our learning practice on 6 fundamental principles to implement 'learning to learn'. Information and communication technologies affect all of these.

Increasing Self-Steering

Students must be prepared for lifelong learning. This means that students must be allowed to steer their own learning processes during their studies. The integrated learning environment can support this self-steering by optimal organization of information (knowledgemanagement), and through efficient communications applications, so students can study regardless of time and place. Up-to-date information can easily be made available - through the Web and wireless technologies - so students can choose for themselves how they prefer to obtain it.

Teachers facilitate learning processes

The role of the teachers is to facilitate learning processes of individual students and groups of students, as designer and editor of learning environments, as coach, trainer, consultant and/or assessor. In the first stage, when ICT is being integrated, it also demands a lot of time and good will from the teachers. Their efforst are intensily appreciated by the students though.

Core questions

The core questions of a professional practice remain the starting point of institutional learning. The curriculum should therefore focus on core activities, core questions and core problems of the profession. Direct contact with professional practice should be stimulated as much as possible in the form of assignments, teaching practices and work periods. Teachers should be regarded as experts. The virtual space facilitates making and maintaining contacts with the professional field. An exchange of information about companies and organisations is also made easy by using the internet.

Meta skills

Metaskills are skills you need to go through the learning process itself. This is not about the subject matter, but about planning, collaboration, documentation, evaluation, measuring, applying researchmethodologies, reflection, managing, social skills etc. Metaskills are integrated in the curriculum. The students must develop insight in their own learning styles and their own way of working and thus preparing themselves for lifelong working and learning. Students must be capable of determining themselves which knowledge and skills are necessary, whether they possess them, and if that is not the case, how they can obtain them. The necessary information and network competences can be considered as a further elaboration of the meta skills that have evolved because of the integration of ICT in the primary stage of the learning process.

Testing

If we switch the accent from quality control to quality assurance, some questions will immediately emerge: How shall we work together in the virtual space? How shall we organise the feedback between students? Between teacher and students? Between teachers? Are we going to check logfiles to make sure students have logged in, or not? What is the amount of email that will circulate? What status does it have? When the software gives feedback because it monitors the student's input - like a flightsimulator does - can that be considered as a test too? And if an assessment takes place through a virtual medium, will the role of testing exams change? How can we guarantee depth and insight? How can we fix the reliability of digital information (with regard to plagiarism etc..) and how can the privacy of students and teachers be guaranteed in e-mail and other forms of open communication? Much more research is needed on how people behave in virtual environments and some ethical and legal issues need to be adressed.

TERC AND RIVERDEEP

Riverdeep Interactive Learning is a young company, founded in 1995 and jointly headquartered in Cambridge, Massachusetts and Dublin, Ireland. Its web-based and CD-ROM solutions can be found in more than 45.000 schools in over 20 countries worldwide. Their flagship product is Destination Math, a carefully sequenced and comprehensive curriculum that demonstrates how mathematical issues arise out of real-life situations. Some of the programs are only available on CD-ROM, others as an online subscription.

Riverdeep has associated itself with other companies, focusing either on online learning environments and design or with educational partners that develop online courseware for students and teachers, cross-curricular software and services for teacher training and school improvement. The main aim is to integrate all the partners into a rich, online learning experience that includes math, science, language arts, critical thinking, social studies, early learning and special needs.

Demos of different disciplines and themes can be found on the websites mentioned at the end of this article. Most of the gateways include units that use interactive computer simulations and virtual labs to teach science principles.

Riverdeep recently launched a project with TERC to reseach ways to integrate visualization tools with simulation tools. The next challenge is to develop assessment and evaluation

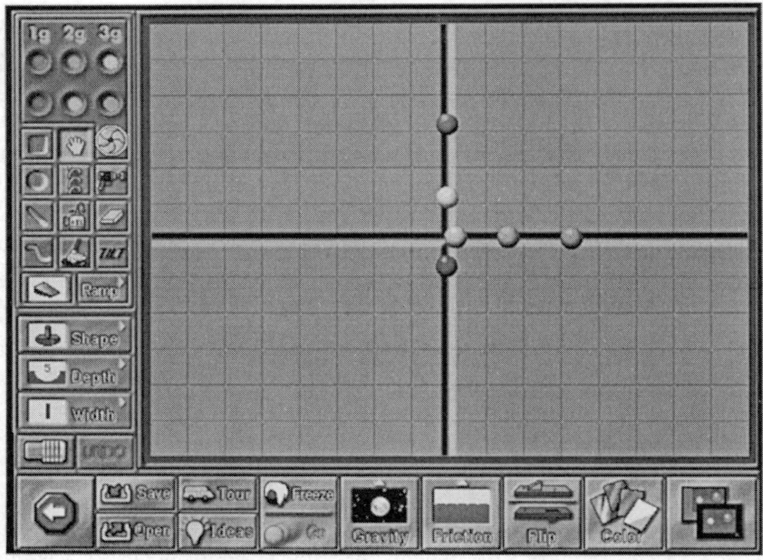

Figure 2.5: Interface to a Riverdeep microworld for exploring kinetics. Users can choose a layout and launch balls of different mass to learn about gravity, friction, inertia and other fundamental physics concepts.

methods to capture the ways these innovative environments influence and contribute to learning. TERC is one of the true icons of American education research and development and was founded in Cambridge, in 1965 as a not-for-profit organization. Their credo was "Lets imagine a future in which learners from diverse communities engage in creative, rigorous, and reflective inquiry as an integral part of their lives." TERC aimed at creating innovative instructional programs and materials and develops, evaluates, promotes, and supports implementation of exemplary, inquiry-based mathematics and science curricula. TERC also maintains and develops online integrated learning environments or websites as they still prefer to call it.

The physicist Robert Tinker directed TERC towards mathematics and science. Tinker concentrated on applying technology to improving education, particularly through improved instrumentation and the use of telecommunications. In the 1980s he became well-known for supporting student investigations by using sensors interfaced to inexpensive microcomputers for real-time measurements and controla technique named microcomputer-based labs. One of his project-oriented education concepts was the National Geographics KidsNet: a new, innovative way to bring inquiry-based learning to elementary school children. These students perform experiments on such topics as acid rain and water quality. They gather data; analyse trends and patterns on topics of current scientific, social and geographic interest; and communicate with each other and with practicing scientists using electronic mail. They send the results of their local experiments to be combined with national and international results.

There were several significant instances in which the children tests led to the discovery that school drinking water and air pollution standards were not being met. KidsNet units

Figure 2.6: Interface to a microworld for learning about letters and their pronounciation. Users can type a letter and hear the sound. A story is illustrated which uses the letters and sounds.

were used in more than 6,000 classrooms in 72 countries and more than 90% of teachers using KidsNet reported that it significantly increased the interest of students in science, and that their classes spent almost twice the amount of time on science than they otherwise did. In the mean time, Tinker left TERC to start The Concord Consortium - where he concentrates on applications of technology in education.

MW

2.5 Design

So far we have not yet invented the new editorial formats we need for learning in these new spaces. We are all familiar with lectures, we know how to take notes or how to look up some texts and references. Some of us know how to set up a workshop, how to give introductions and to write papers. Others know how to communicate the attained knowlegde and insights to a larger, interested public. Publishers have developed certain formats for books, magazines and business models in order to participate in a profitable way in the learning industry.

But we still face a huge lack of design time and investments that enable to explore future learning designs. Until now most progress has been made in the artworld. What follows are three examples of recent explorations of new learning environments with the emergence of new learning goals that can be met with.

The first one is Demi Dubbel, an internet curriculumgame for children about 10 years old (see insert) We developed this at the Waag, a Society for Old and new Media, with theatremakers, softwarepeople, visual artists, writers and with the cooperation of several teachers. It was a complex process because the main goal was to trigger the imagination of children from a variety of backgrounds of whom many do not have Dutch as their mothertongue. The result was an interface that consists for two/thirds of graphics, but the action is in the text, since one of the major aims is learning Dutch. The narrative is contructed in such a way that the children have to communicate with children form another school to solve certain problems. Without knowing the kind of solutions the children would come up with, we had to design a narrative for 9 times three hours. The challenge was to build a framework that contains enough complexity for it to be interesting, that is open enough for a variety of contributions, structured enough to capture the attention and deal with a preset curriculum, but still flexible enough to meet with different school rhythms.

The second and the third example are developed at the Performing Arts Labs in England. This foundation organizes 10 times a year working labs on specific disciplines and invites talented artists to explore new boundaries. In 2001 the Learning Labs were initiated in which artists collaborate with teachers to explore new models, formats and ideas for new learning designs. In spring 2002 PAL started exploring new interfaces for broadband. Broadband sounds very promising and interesting but how shall we tackle it? How do we build visual databases? How will we be able to explore a database like that? So far two demo's resulted that started off from different points of view. The One World team came up with a very simple format to catagorize their filmmaterial by questions raised from the images itself. Users can keep on adding questions to certain images and hence a whole tapestry of images, linked by questions evolves. The other group, from Cambridge, wanted to make the history of the Himalaya's available, not only in the west, but in the first place in the Himalay's itself. Cambridge (UK) has some amazing archives of anthropologists. They came up with an astonishing simple databaseformat and carry-on tool for distribution. While using the database, people can also add their own stories.

The production of demos like this by artists and scientists provides an insight in future possibilities. Very few places do research like this at the moment. Because the technology is a crucial factor in integrated learning environments, it needs constant attention and updating. It is wrong however to assume that the design of new frameworks, of interactive narrative and new editorial formats will just emerge and evolve naturally. Especially for the structured learning process, we will have to concentrate our know-how and efforts if we want these media to deliver added values to our learning processes and to our quality of life. Since popular culture and school culture are merging more and more, finding this culture and its interfaces back in the learning program, will be appreciated by students. Moreover because they are often more familiar with them than most of the teachers are. Hence the participation of artists and graphical and software designers in this research is indispensible for the conceptualization, the design of the perception and the interaction of the environments.

But how to implement or apply this kind of research on the design of learning processes in integrated learning environments? At the Hogeschool van Amsterdam I have defined 6 elements that are part of the information and network competences that we need. Skills and competences to be able to work and learn in a network society and that we are all familiar with: editorial skills, orchestrational skills, reflection, feedback, intercultural communication and presence in networks. However these skills will have to be transformed and redesigned and we will need both, the expertise of people working in 'old media' (crucial for the development of values, ethics and esthetics in the new learning environments) and the expertise of the 'native informants' (children, youngsters) of the information society. So what we are talking about are complex design trajectories, time consuming, but very worthwhile.

2.6 Conclusions

Our experiences have shown that integrated learning environments can give an enormous boost to the assets and effectiveness of learning. But even more important is the fact that they can improve and support processes that educate students in 'learning to learn'. Although we have been heavily experimenting at the HvA with such environments, a lot still needs to be learned by all actors involved: the students, the teachers, and professional practitioners. Already now, an overwhelming set of new instruments for information diffusion and interaction exists. But it is only by taking the plunge, by concretely trying out new practices, that we can hope to use the new technologies in order to cope with the current crisis in education.

```
Websites:
  www.scholastic.com/magicschoolbus
  lingua.utdallas.edu
  www.riverdeep.net
  www.terc.edu
  www.digitalhimalaya.com/index.html
  www.oro.hva.nl
  www.teacherslab.hva.nl
  www.pallabs.org
  www.waag.org/demidubbel
```

This contribution is translated and adapted from chapter 2 in: Nevejan, C. (2001) Synchroon/Asynchroon; Fysiek/Virtueel. Onderwijsvernieuwing en informatiesamenleving. Een verkenning van Caroline Nevejan met Veronica Bruijns onder de redactie van Max Bruinsma, met foto's van Hans Singels. Uitgave Hogeschool van Amsterdam, Amsterdam.

Group Discussion 2
Virtual Learning Environments

The New Role of Teachers

Steels: You organised a big event in Amsterdam in 2000 (ORO-ORO), a Teachers' Lab, where you turned the whole university upside-down and brought people intensely into contact with information technology. What was your motivation for this?

Nevejan: In designing new tools, new methodologies or new designs or doing research, it is very important to have the so-called "end users" present. You cannot design educational environments in closed laboratories and then look how teachers might participate in this. "Why did I organise a Teachers' lab?" Because I need these thousands of teachers to develop the technology with me! So first I have to educate them and then they can be my partner. And I need not only the teachers, but also the children and the students. They are co-designers, co-developers, co-researchers. This is not just a nice label. They are as good as we are! We cannot do it without them, although sometimes it looks like we can.

Tokoro: In the US, some scholars say that students and researchers with access to Internet can learn all by themselves. They become more knowledgeable than their teachers.

Nevejan: But that is only true to a certain extent and it depends a lot on the subject matter.

Hedegaard: And there are equally many examples where computers have had no positive impact at all in the classroom.

Tokoro: Well, we have to make a distinction between computers and the Internet, although the Internet is run by computers and telecommunication. And broadband is yet another thing. Each should be discussed separately. A computer can run a program, like a game that gives training for simple mathematics: It asks 2 plus 3 and if you type 5, the computer says: You got it! Yeah!! For children, fun plays an important role, so this kind of feedback needs to be there. Also learning new words in a foreign language can be done like this. It can be made to resemble playing games. Some people criticize that this is not really learning, maybe it is not, but at least it is equivalent to playing games and one step further than just playing. In addition, computers have a lot of power that can give different types of creativity to children, like for writing, drawing, making music. That is the first level of support for education.

When it comes to Internet, we get to something else. Now children can go anywhere they want to go. If they only go to school, their training or learning is scheduled or planned so that if they want to go beyond the scheduled curriculum, they have to wait another year or so. But by using Internet you can go anywhere at any level. You can even send e-mail to real professionals. Children could e-mail Mark Johnson to find out how people can remember something. How does that work? And maybe he would answer. This is, of course, a very different environment, it is open to children from when they are 10 years old or so. And from 15 they can be like adults. Internet gives tremendous opportunities to those who really want to learn more if they know how to use it. In my talk I argued that broadband is the next thing. It allows shared situations and common grounding, so this may add additional profit to just browsing the Internet. It is more, much more than we can get from Internet right now.

Mogi: Recently I introduced fast speed Internet (through ADSL) into my house and discovered that BBC4 radio is online. They are broadcasting in real time. This was a tremendous experience for me. It is easier to create an ambient environment with audio rather than audio-visual. People talk about broadband and tend to think about audio-visual. But I think it will start with audio transmissions. The idea of people in the UK listening to these programs and me doing the same thing at the same time in Tokyo is wonderful. With audio broadband we can transmit what we are discussing here all over the world. If you are listening to that in your household, you really get the ambient feeling that people are around you. For visual stimulants you need to focus, otherwise you don't get any relevant information. But with audio information you don't need to focus your attention so much. I think there are tremendous possibilities here. As Mario Tokoro said, the educational materials we can get at the moment in schools are limited, but we will have more powerful communication sooner or later, also in our households.

Nevejan : But here you are talking about being a grown-up and using the technology to nurse your intellectual development which is something different from children between 6 months and 6 years learning about the world.

Tokoro : That is quite different, yes.

Mogi: But you can argue about the environment. For very young children it is very important to interact with their immediate environment but you can augment it by connecting to distant areas in the world. We can connect to Reggio Emilio from Tokyo. It doesn't have to stop with what we have available now and here. We can talk about the possibilities. Our brain is just not ready yet to explore all the possibilities of this new communication tool because it is not available. Yet, I think broadband is not just another medium through which you feed people with channels of information. It's a whole new communication medium.

Wynants: This discussion reminds me a lot of teaching experiments by Celestin Freinet in the first part of the 20th century. He launched more than 20 kinds of technologies in his schools, from painting and filming to printing. All with an eye to free expression and a natural, active and complete learning environment. A printing press was brought into the school, not simply as a technology for physical labour, but as an instrument for what he called "free expression". It is not enough to say to children "You can do what you want but you'll have to do it in writing". No, he looked for something children to really express themselves, not only saying what they were doing, but also what they were feeling, what their expectancies were, how they wanted things to evolve, etc. New technologies are fine, but you need the time to explore them, and the necessary technical support and only then will it become possible to construct meaning in relation to different technological environments. There are some social and cultural barriers we have to overcome. But even more important is that boys and girls, teachers and students, artists and scientists, researchers and end-users can exchange design preferences, design possibilities and hence contribute to the creation of contexts in which everybody can play, learn or interact together.

Everybody Can Broadcast

Nevejan: That's why we have to be careful in our speculations about the new technologies, especially about the ones that are not there yet. We talk about the possibilities of broadband, but at the moment, broadband is presented as a broadcast medium, not in a bi-directional way so that people can upload things themselves.

Mogi: It's going to be in two directions.

Nevejan: But it may take another twenty years.

Mogi: Not really, and even so, we should still explore it now. Let's try to imagine what will become possible.

Tokoro: What is very interesting is that everybody can start broadcasting in a sense. That's maybe a starting point of bi-directionality.

Nevejan: But the way the power structure is organised makes this unlikely. Satellites have already had the same possibilities but it didn't happen.

Steels: If you take the Internet, a lot of the services like e-mail were already there in 1975. Some people realised the potential, but not the mass. In 1976, 1977 researchers like myself were already downloading documents and so. The real breakthrough however came with the World Wide Web as an easy to use hyperlink medium in 1992. So maybe for broadband it will be similar. We need the infrastructure but we also need time to develop the right kind of interfaces. And then there is still the problem of how it can be spread on a massive scale, although looking at mobile telephones and Internet, technology sometimes spreads much faster over the globe now than it used to.

Tokoro: There is often an advantage for latecomers. They use the latest technology, so they can immediately use broadband or the web or movies on the web. It's changing fast. But I'm very happy that Learner-centered Learning was launched here as a most important concept. I'm even more happy that Caroline Nevejan has already started using broadband, networking and computers to help people enjoy learning following their own desire, so this is very important. I think that the structure of the educational system will eventually change, I don't know when, but it is changing due to efforts like Reggio Emilia or the Teachers' lab. The process of teaching, the process of learning will change. And Internet, computers, broadband will help to make that happen, I'm sure. But of course we all have to work together to realise this. Today is just the beginning.

Broadband for University Education

Coenen: There is a problem, I think, with simply putting lectures from universities on-line on the Internet. Often in a class if you don't understand a particular point, you can ask the teacher and have immediate feedback. That really makes a difference. If there's only a one-way direction, very little gets learned. So we'll have to make sure that enough feedback is given, which is, by the way, also essential from the point of view of motivation and interest.

Steels: I am skeptical whether professional people will be willing - and even more so - have the time, to provide this kind of feedback to anyone who asks for it. I occasionally get very lengthy mails from students or people who ask questions or reflect on ideas that I have published. I have a lot of sympathy with them, but do not have the resources to respond. In fact, I don't even have the time to respond to all the mails that my students send me.

Mogi: Still, if the lectures continue to be transmitted, they might improve. It is wrong to think only about what broadband can do for us based on today's technologies. Broadband is just beginning and it will get popular by 2006 or so. By then the technology will have matured and people will change and develop ideas of using broadband as a kind of new medium. I appreciate your concern about the need for live human feedback, but we really need to hear suggestions from people in the educational world about what kind of technologies should be developed in the coming 10 years or so.

The concept of computing is changing very rapidly. As an adult, you can now go anywhere and buy any books that you want. As a child, your educational environment is pretty limited. But with the advent of broadband, the sky is the limit. We should start thinking what kind of educational resources could be provided in the broadband area now, otherwise we will be dinosaurs.

Nevejan: Many universities have rushed to the Internet by putting lectures on the net so that students can find information whenever they want to. But that did not automatically yield the desired increase in knowledge transfer. They realize now that they haven't spent any time on the educational methodologies that would work in this new setting. They know very well how to put information on the web, but they don't have a clue as to how this information can become knowledge.

Theme II

The Well-Functioning Classroom

Jumping animals. Ezra, age 6

Children are always disturbing our adult order, our adult rationality. Its good to be on the borderline of chaos and rationality, to always reconsider existing principles; not to try and destroy them but to test them.

Bernard Allien

Chapter 3

The Joys of Preschool Learning

by Carla Rinaldi

Carla Rinaldi graduated from the University of Bologna with a degree in Pedagogy. She developed into the main spokesperson for the fascinating experimental network in Reggio Emilia for pre-school children. She is Director of the Municipal Infant-toddler Centers and Preschools system in Reggio Emilia and Executive Consultant for Reggio Children in Italy.

In 1945, right after the second world war, Italy was in ruins and the school system destroyed. Parents in the town of Reggio Emilia (Northern Italy) decided to create their own schools, and found an inspiring teacher: Loris Malaguzzi, who developed a unique approach to pre-school learning within the tradition of Freynet, Montessori, and Piaget. The people from Reggio are known for a strong sense of community. The school was therefore their project - as opposed to a state controlled or church-governed institution. They built themselves the first school buildings and participated heavily in the organisation and design of curricula. Out of this grew a tremendously exciting new approach to education which continues to flourish today and is seen world-wide as an example, particularly for infant-toddler centers and pre-primary schools. The Reggio pre-school system has now been institutionalised and, faithful to the tradition of documentation and reflection, a lot of time is spent to present the educational approach through exhibitions (such as the 'Hundred Languages of Children'), books [2]), and workshops.

In this paper[1] I will try to identify some of the main principles behind this successful educational project: Our view of the developing and learning child, the quality of our school environments, the community participation in the school project, the way we plan educational activities through a process we call 'progettazione', our continuous efforts for reflection and documentation on the developing process for each child and of our own educational processes, and finally the pedagogy of listening.

New technologies like computers or broadband networking can find a place, particularly for older children, but without a strong educational project such as that of the Reggio schools, such technologies will remain ineffective.

3.1 Our Image of the Child

I believe that the first key ingredient for the success of the Reggio approach lies in our view of the developing child. This has been inspired from the beginning by the constructivist approach pioneered by Piaget [3], but with an additional strongly cultural and social dimension, as argued for by Vygotsky [5], and more recently by Jerome Bruner [1], who has been a frequent visitor to our schools. As Malaguzzi has put it:

> "We believe that the brain is not closed into a cage of genes, that thinking is modifiable because it is in a position to interact with the environment, and that intelligence results from the synergetic cooperation of different parts of the brain. We believe that all the languages in the life of children are born with them. It gives them the ability to organise information and sensations and to seek exchanges with others. Children possess the art of the semiologist and the detective, the art of making hypotheses and reconstructing missing facts."
> (from the catalog of the exhibition "The Hundred Languages of Children")

We view the child as rich in resources, strong, and competent. The children are seen as unique individuals, with rights rather than simply needs. They have potential, plasticity, openness, the desire to grow, curiosity, a sense of wonder, and the desire to relate to other people and to communicate. Their need and desire to communicate and interact with others emerge at birth and are essential elements for survival and identification with the species.

This probably explains why children are so eager to express themselves within the context of the plurality of symbolic languages, and why children are also very open to exchanges and

[1] Some of the material in this text is based on an interview with Gandini and published in [2]

reciprocity as deeds and acts of love that they not only want to receive but also want to offer. These form the basis of their ability to experience authentic growth, dependent on the elements just listed, as well as on conflict and error. Children are curious about the meaning of things and of life. They are competent in formulating questions (the "whys") in searching for answers, constructing answers, interpreting hypotheses and theories, viewed as satisfactory explanations, though provisional, about the surrounding world. Children - all children - are intelligent. They are all trying to explain and find explanations for themselves about the world and their existence in it.

An example of what I mean can be seen in the episode of Laura and the watch (see figure 3.1). It illustrates well the process in which children learn to link up different parts of reality through different sensory modalities. Laura is looking at pictures with the teachers and recognises pictures of watches. Although this child has no symbolic language yet, it is communicating her interest in this object by pointing and eye contact. The teacher reciprocates and shows the watch on her arm - thus making a bridge from the image to the real world. This way the image becomes grounded in reality. The teacher now lets Laura listen to the watch. Laura hears the ticking and she makes the connection back to the image. She listens whether the 'image watch' is also ticking! This remarkable episode shows the child as an active seeker of connections, as performing some sort of thinking although it can surely not be equated yet with abstract logical thinking. But it is undeniable that the child is making progress here in her cognitive construction of reality.

It would be wrong however to just focus on the child as an individual. The child's potentials are expressed and achieved first and foremost within a group learning context. This fact has pushed us in a continuous search for an educational approach that breaks rank with the traditional education "of the individual". We embrace an approach based on adults listening rather than speaking, where doubt and amazement are welcome factors along with scientific inquiry and the deductive method of the detective. It is an approach in which the importance of the unexpected and the possible are recognized, an approach in which there's no such thing as wasted time, but in which teachers know how to give children all the time they need. It is an approach that protects originality, subjectivity, and differences without creating isolation of the individual. It offers to children the possibility of confronting stimulating situations and problems as members of small peer groups. This approach requires that adults - both teachers and parents - offer themselves as a resource to whom the children can (and want to) turn. The task of this human resource is not simply to satisfy needs or answer questions, but instead to help children discover their own answers and, more importantly still, to help them ask good questions.

So the emphasis of our educational approach is placed not so much on the child in an abstract sense, but on each child in relation to other children, teachers, parents, his or her own history, and the societal and cultural surroundings. Relationships, communications, and interactions sustain our educational approach in its complexity; they are powerful terms characterized by two important elements: action and group socialization. We consider them to be fundamental structuring elements toward the construction of each child's identity.

It is our belief that all knowledge emerges in the process of self and social construction. Therefore, the teacher must establish a personal relationship with each child and ground this relationship in the social system of the school. Children, in turn, do not just passively endure their experience, but also become active agents in ther own socialization and knowledge building with peers. Their action can be understood as more than responses to the social environments; they can also be considered as mental constructions developed by the child through social interaction. Obviously, there is a strong cause and effect relationship between social and cognitive development, a sort of spiral that is sustained by cognitive conflict that

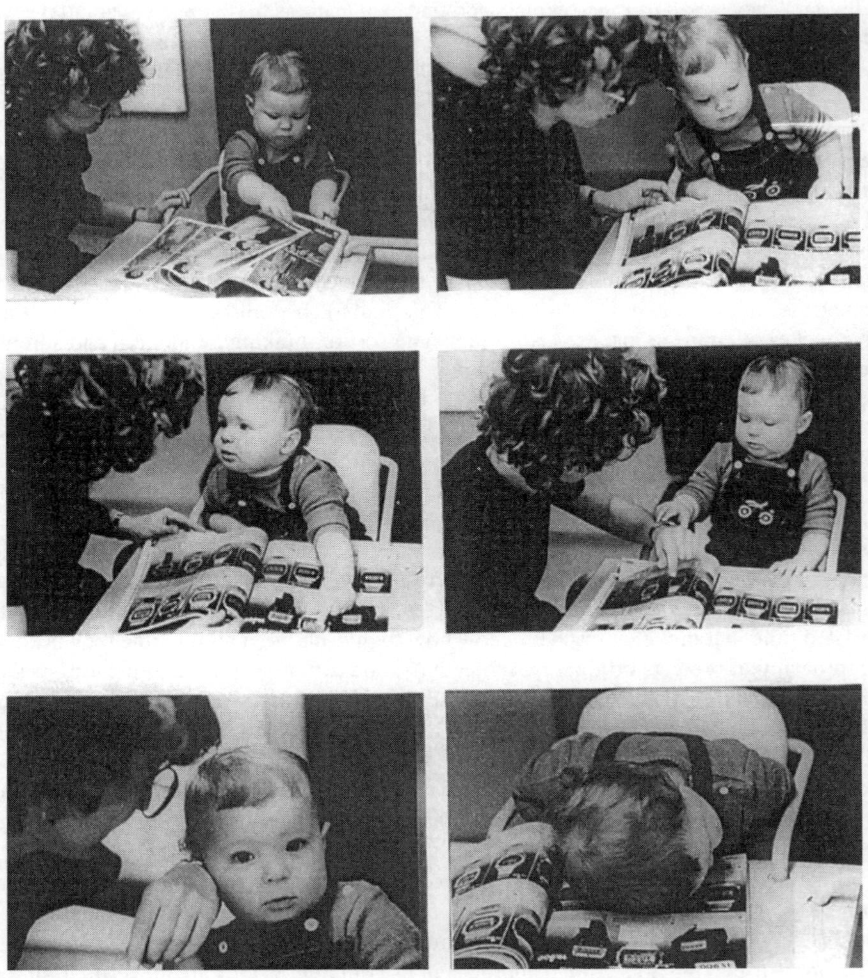

Figure 3.1: Laura learning to connect different manifestations and representations of a watch.

modifies both the cognitive and the social system.

Conflicts and the recognition of differences are essential, in our view. Conflict transforms the relationships a child has with peers - opposition, negotiation, listening to the other's point of view, deciding whether or not to adopt it, and reformulating an initial premise. They are part of the Piagetian processes of assimilation and accomodation into the group. The adults' difficulty is to initiate and nurture situations that stimulate this kind of learning process, where conflict and negotiation appear as the driving forces for growth.

3.2 The School Environment

A second key ingredient of our approach lies in the school environment itself (figure 3.2). This environment has to create a sense of well being in the child. A place where it is fun to be. Where there are plenty of resources for play, but also corners where one can hide, places to cook food and eat, a garden for running outside. Education is based on very complex interactions and a lot of them, particularly for toddlers and preschool children, are simply due to the environments in which they live. The school environment has to be a kind of aquarium in which ideas are reflected, but also the morality, the attitudes and the culture of the people that live in it.

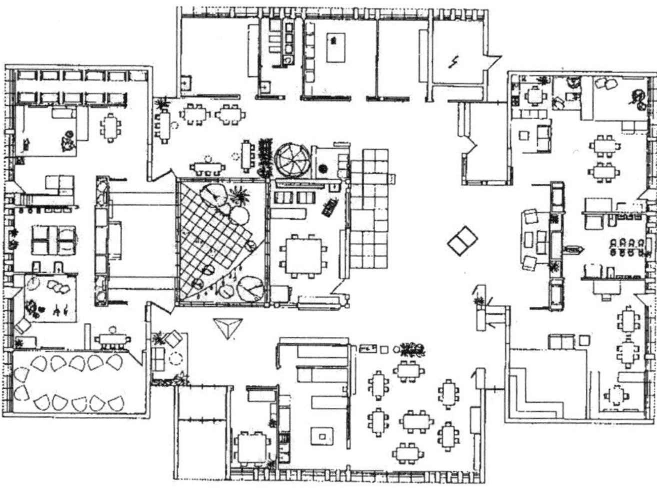

Figure 3.2: Infant-toddler center "Arcobaleno". It is built around a patio and contains plenty of spaces for engaging in a wide variety of activities, from cooking to sleeping.

For the children, the city itself is also part of their environment. They often go to the market, to the church, to other landmarks of the city to make drawings, observe people, see where there parents work and what they do. This extended environment then helps them later to become integrated in the workings of the city. We want to educate our children so that they become members of the community.

3.3 Participation

The next key ingredient of our educational project is the participation of the whole community, not only the children and teachers, but also the families. Fortunately our city is still functioning well and has given a stable environment for the schools to develop. Our schools are not "experimental" schools. They are part of a public system that strives to combine the child's welfare and the social needs of families with the fundamental human rights of the child. This approach links the concept of social services with the concept of eduuation, as we do not see these two as antithetical. In fact, schooling for us is a system of relations and communications embedded in the wider social system.

Certainly one of our basic principles involves participation, in the broadest sense of the word. To feel a sense of belonging, to be part of a larger endeavor, to share meanings - these are the rights of everyone involved in the educationnal process, whether teachers, children, or parents. In our schools, the active participation of the families and collegiality among staff and children working in groups are essential.

The planning of teaching activities is the process of preparation and organization of space, materials, thoughts, situations, and occasions for learning. These involve communication among all three protagonists and interactive partners of the educational process: children, educators, and the families. The educational institution is a system of communication and interaction among these three protagonists, integrated into the larger social system.

To carry out its primary task, then, the school must sustain the children's total welfare, as well as the welfare of parents and teachers. The system of relationships is so highly integrated that the well-being of each of the three protagonists depends on the well-being of the others. There must be mutual awareness of rights, needs, and pleasures and the attention to the quantity and quality of social occasions that create a system of permanent relations. The full participation of families is thus an integral part of the educational experience. Indeed, we consider the family to be a pedagogical unit that cannot be separated from the school.

3.4 Progettazione

Progettazione is our framework for allowing the social constructivist process to develop. It is in strong opposition to the top-down planned educational framework that is now so popular in Western school systems, in wich the objectives of education are defined uniformly in advance and teachers are supposed to optimise the child's activities to achieve these objectives. We believe that the potential of children is stunted when the endpoint of their learning is formulated in advance. Instead, at the initiation of a project, the teachers get together and proceed in terms of 'progettazione'. They discuss all the possible ways that the project could be anticipated to evolve, considering the likely ideas, hypotheses, and choices of children and the directions they may take. By so doing, they prepare themselves for all the subsequent stages of the project, while leaving ample space for changes, for the unexpected, and for moments of stasis and digressions. Because our planning is ongoing, it is impossible to separate what the teacher does beforehand from what actually takes place as the children's work on the project progresses.

The challenge for the teacher is to be present without being intrusive, in order to best sustain cognitive and social dynamics while they are in progress. At times, the adult must foster productive conflict by challenging the responses of one or several children. At other times, the adult must step in to revive a situation where children are losing interest because the cognitive map that is being constructed is either beyond or beneath the child's present capabilities. The teacher always remains an attentive observer, and beyond that, a researcher. The teacher's observations and transcribed tapes are taken to colleagues for group reflection. The documentation stimulates the teacher's self-reflection and produces discussion and debate among the group of colleagues. Such comparisons of ideas among colleagues are as important as those that take place among the children. The group discussions serve to modify, at times radically, the teacher's thoughts and hypotheses about the children and interactions with them.

Schools must sustain the social learning process and help children learn how to learn. Because we believe that the construction of knowledge is a subjective process that proceeds in a spiraling rather than linear stagelike way, 'progettazione' must involve multiple actions, voices, times, and places. Children sometimes work with teachers, and sometimes without them; projects are sometimes short, and sometimes long. The curriculum is at once defined and undefined, structured and unstructured, based more on flexible strategies than rigid plans. There are no preconstituted paths, and consequently no set timetables or tests. Instead, relying on strategies means predicting and activating sequences that are based not only on our initial hypotheses but also on the work as it develops and unfolds. I like to use the metaphor of taking a journey, where one finds the way using a compass rather than taking a train with its fixed routes and schedules.

Teachers work every day in a concrete context with children and parents. If we give credit to the potential of children, we must also give credit to the potential of adults. The search for meaning strongly connects children and teachers, even while their roles and responsabilities are distinct. The traditional relationship of theory and practice, which makes practice the derivative of theory, must be redefined. Theory and practice must become reciprocal and complementary, with practice even allowed some possibility of precedence.

This may seem upsetting and unacceptable to some. We would seem to be renouncing the rule of reason and the ability to determine action on the basis of logic. But we consider that within an organization such as a school, logical reasoning is most needed for inferring connections and causal relations between events that have taken place, not for deducing what is the theoretically correct action to take.

When theory takes over, when it controls and commands what teachers may do and think, then teachers no longer have the duty to reflect, reason, and create for themselves. Excessive emphasis on theory can prevent teachers from being protagonists in the educational process and from exercising their rightful responsabilities. Thus, while we affirm the inseparability of theory and practice, we propose an open theory that is nourished through practice made visible, examined, interpreted, and discussed using the documentation that we produce.

3.5 Documentation

Of great importance is our emphasis on continuing reflection and documentation. Documentation improves the quality of communication and interaction. It is a process of reciprocal learning. Documentation make it possible for teachers to sustain the children's learning while they also learn (to teach) from the children's own learning. It does not mean a final report, a collection of documents in a portfolio that merely helps in terms of memory, evaluation, or creating an archive. It is instead a procedure that is part of 'progettazione', and that sustains the educational process (teaching) in the dialogue with the learning processes of the children.

The work of teachers (or better, the group of teachers working together) involves constant discussion. Hypotheses and predictions are made about the ongoing work with the children. This dynamic activity is closely linked to the other aspects of the teacher's work involving

Figure 3.3: The first foundation for effective learning is interaction. Interaction with objects in the world, interaction between teachers and children, and interaction among the children. (mw)

documentation - namely listening, observing, gathering documents, and interpreting them. We have always maintained that children have their own questions and theories, and that they negotiate their theories with others. Our duty as teachers is to listen to the children, just as we ask them to listen to one another. Listening means giving value to others, being open to them and what they have to say. Listening legitimizes the other person's point of view, thereby enriching both listener and speaker. What teachers are asked to do is to create contexts where such listening can take place.

Listening is thus a general metaphor for all the processes of observation and documentation. Observation involves much more than simply perceiving reality, but also constructing, interpreting, and revisiting it. Because our observations are necessarily partial, it is essential that we leave interpretable traces of them. We use written notes, observation charts, diaries, and other narrative forms, as well as audiotapes, photographs, slides and videotapes. These allow us to make visible the process of children's learning, the ways to construct knowledge, the emotional and relational aspects; in fact, all the facets that contribute to leave traces of a competent observation. However, it is important to note that all these documents provide partial findings and subjective interpretations, and they are biased by the tools employed. In turn, they must be reinterpreted and discussed with others, in particular, with colleagues.

Documentation is a procedure that supports the educational processes and it is supported by the dynamic exchanges related to learning. Documentation is the process of reciprocal learning. Through documentation we leave traces that make it possible to share the ways children learn, and through documentation we can preserve the most interesting and advanced moments of teacher's professional growth. It is a process in which teachers generate hypotheses and interpretation of theories that can modify the initial, more general theories. Documentation makes it possible to create knowledge not only for teachers but also for researchers and scholars.

3.6 The Pedagogy of Listening

Children are researchers. They want to research the meaning of life. In our opinion, learning is the emergence of what was not there before. It is a search of the self as well as the others that surround each individual. Those who participate in an educational process bring their own growth and development into play, and do this on the basis of their own expectation and their own plans.

There is a constant relational reciprocity between those who educate and those who are educated, between those who teach and those who learn. There is participation, passion, compassion, emotion. There must be love. For this reason, the most important verb for us is not "to explain" or "to teach", but the most important verb for school and education is "to listen".

Children, because they want to learn, produce answers to their own questions; they produce theories in the form of explanations that can be satisfying, at least for a while. A theory is something more than an idea or a series of ideas. It must be pleasing and convincing, it must be useful and able to satisfy our intellectual, affective, and aesthetic needs. Theories, or narrations, where possible, must also be pleasing and attractive to others. It needs the listening of others. So any explanation or theorization, from the simplest to the most refined, needs to be communicated, to be listened to, in order to exist.

It is here that we recognize the values and fundamental principles of what we call the pedagogy of listening - listening not only in the physical sense but in the sense of sensitivity to the patterns which connect us to others - with the conviction that our knowledge and our being is a small part of a broader and integrated knowing which holds the universe together. Listening is a metaphor for openness and sensitivity to the act of listening and being listened to. This listening takes place not only with your eyes but with all your senses: sight, touch, taste and smell. We must listen to the hundred, the thousand languages, symbols, and codes that we use to express ourselves and to communicate the languages with which life expresses itself to those who know how to listen to it. Behind an act of listening there is often curiosity, a desire, a doubt, an interest. There is always an emotion

In a metaphorical sense, children are the greatest listeners of all to the reality that surrounds them. They listen to life, in its various shapes and colors. They listen to others (both adults and peers). They quickly perceive that the act of listening (that is, observing, but also touching, smelling, tasting, and searching) is fundamental for communication. Children are biologically predisposed to communicate, to be in relation and live in relations. Children do not need to be taught sociality: they are naturally social beings. Our task is to support their sociality and experience it with them. The methods, the languages (and thus the codes) that our culture has produced are highly attractive to children. And children are highly attracted by other people (both other children and adults). It is a difficult road that requires efforts, energies, hard work, and sometimes pain, but also offers: wonders, surprises, joy, enthusiasm, and passion. Let me now give a concrete example of the pedagogy of listening.

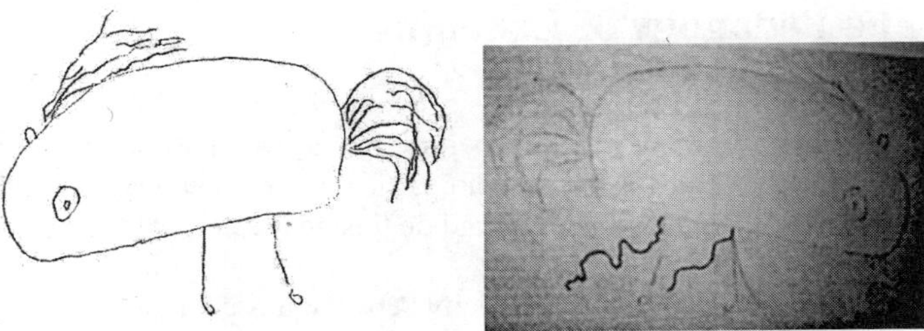

Figure 3.4: Elisa tries to draw a horse. To capture both sides of the horse, she draws two legs on each side of the paper.

Elisa's Running horse

(Author of the example: Federica, 3.5 years, Valeria, 5.3 years and Elisa, 5.6 years. Teachers: Laura Rubizzi and Vea Vecchi)

Federica, three years two months old, is asked if she wants to try drawing a running horse. The elongated bean shape is somewhat approximated, but look how she resolves the problem of the running movement. In order for a horse to run, the legs are indispensable, Elisa must have thought, all four of them. But the legs are on both sides of the horse two on one side and two on the other. (figure 3.4). So she turns the sheet of paper over and draws the legs on the other side. It is an interesting and intelligent cognitive and expressive solution.

We find the same solution used by two 5 years old girls. Drawing a bicycle, both of them, at two different moments, use the back of the sheet of drawing paper. One for drawing a pedal, and the other sets her drawing of a bicycle against the window and traces around the bicycle, commenting aloud: "you see a bicycle from two sides!". The graphic solutions found by these girls highlights a problem that many children encounter in a way that is conflictual: Representing a three-dimensional object and losing parts of it that are there in reality (and children love keeping everything together). But they use a two-dimensional technique such as drawing with great freedom and invention, searching for solutions that can satisfy their cognitive and expressive requirements.

In drawing, then, children autonomously confront complex representational problems, such as the rotation of figures and perspective space. And they resolve them, always autonomously, using different and provisional solutions.

Situations such as these clearly highlight the image of the child, the teacher, and the culture (and listening) that a school may have. I see three possibilities:

- The school is following its own curriculum, and does not even notice drawings like the ones we have just seen, nor considers them important or significant. The school does not listen to them.

- The school notices them, considers them to be erroneous passages and tries, in a more or less correct way, to give quick solutions to the problem, above all by explaining or by demonstrating the solutions of others (such as representations made by draftsmen or painters).

- The school considers the research being conducted autonomously by the children to be intelligent and interesting, and feels that it is important to listen to this research more attentively and support it in various ways. For example, by proposing situations of graphic representation, such as the one in the following example, that can underscore and bring out the problems to be confronted in such a way that the children can focus on them with greater and less dispersion.

Obviously in the Reggio Emilia schools we try the latter approach.

The Crowd

Let me finish with another example of a project that illustrates the key ingredients of our methodology. A project is a sort of adventure. It can start through a suggestion from an adult, a child's idea, or from an event such as a snowfall or something else unexpected. But every project is based on the attention of the educators to what the children say and do, as well as what they do not say and do not do. The adults must allow enough time for the thinking and actions of children to develop. The example I want to discuss is called "The Crowd", a project carried out at the Scuola Diana, documented by Vea Vecchi, and overseen by Loris Malaguzzi.

It began at the end of a school year in a classroom of 4- and 5-year-olds. The teachers, in preparation for the long summer vacation ahead, discussed with the children the idea of saving memories and fragments of their upcoming experiences during the holidays. Although the summer marks an interruption of the school year, our commitment to the children remains in force and we try to find ways to keep their interest in learning alive during the vacation months. So the teachers discuss ideas with children and also propose them to parents. In this case, each family agreed to take along to their vacation sites a box with small compartments in which their child could save treasures, be it a shell from the beach or a tiny rock from the mountains or a leaf of grass. Every fragment and every piece collected would become a memento of an experience imbued with a sense of discovery and emotion.

In the fall, when the children returned to school, the teachers were ready to revive those memories with questions such as: "What did your eyes see?", "What did your ears hear?", and so on. The teachers expected to hear stories about days spent at the beach or hiking, and to learn about the sight of boats, waves, and sunsets, but instead the children brought a very different perspective. Because the children could express themselves vividly, and because the teachers could ask the right questions, an adventure in learning began quite unexpectedly.

What happened was this: A little boy, Gabriele, sharing his experience said, "Sometimes we went to the pier. We walked through a narrow long street, called "the gut", where one store is next to another, and where in the evening it is full of people. There are people who go up, and people who walk down. You cannot see anything, you can only see a crowd of legs, arms and heads." The teachers immediately caught the word crowd, and asked other children what it meant to them. By doing so, they launched an adventure in learning, a project. The word crowd turned out to be fantastically rich, almost explosive, in the meanings it contained for these children. The teachers immediately apprehended an unusual excitement and potential in this word. Here is what some of the children said :

Stefano : " It's a bag full of people all crowded in."
Nicola: "Its a bunch of people all attached and close to one another."
Luca: "There are people who jump on you and push you."
Clara: "It's like a congested place when it is a holiday."
Giorgia: "There are lots of people who are going to see a soccer game who are going to see the game, really they are all boys."
Ivano : "It's a bunch of people all bunched up together just like when they go to pay taxes."

After the group discussion, the teachers asked the children to draw their thoughts and words about the crowd. However, looking at the children's drawings, they observed that the level of representation in their drawings was discrepant from the level of their verbal descriptions. The project was put on hold for a couple of days, during which time the teachers asked themselves what was going on. How could they help the children to integrate their different symbolic languages? How could they make the children become aware of their own process of learning? So the teachers waited for a couple of days and then gave the children a chance to listen to their earlier comments (which had been taped and transcribed, so they could be read aloud, while they looked at the drawings and commented on each others' work).

The teachers now noticed a further growth in the children's vocabulary as they expanded on their stories, and the images prepared in a second set of drawings become more elaborate and detailed. For example, Teresa, thinking back on her memory of the "crowd", said, "It goes left, right, forward, and when they forget something, they go back." But Teresa then confronted a puzzle: She noticed that her statements did not match her drawing, for the figures on her paper were all facing the same way (outward towards the viewer). She seemed uncomfortable, and then before all her friends, came up with a marvelous explanation. She said that in the drawing she had shown only a piece of crowd with people who did not forget anything, and that is why they were all walking forward. Federico also had a problem with his drawing because in it everyone faced forward except the dog, which was in profile. He admitted he was only able to draw dogs this way. Ivano expressed concern about his drawing, saying that if people kept walking forward, as he had drawn them, they would smash against the wall.

At this point, there was an unanimous desire expressed by the children to learn more about how to draw people from rear and profile. The teachers' role was to sustain and support this process. They asked one girl, Elisa, to stand in the middle of the room surrounded by a small group of children placed at different vantage points where they could observe her, describe her body and position, and draw her from four angles: front, back, right, and left. Through this process, the children learned a great deal about the difficult concept of point of view. One child concluded : "We put ourselves in a square, and Elisa has four sides just like us."

The teachers also wanted to take the children outside the school - a typical step in our project work. Children and teacher went to the center of town where they observed and photographed people coming and going in the busy streets. Children mingled with the people, becoming once again, "the crowd". A few days later, the slides of that day were projected on the classroom wall, and the children enjoyed those images, moving through their reflections. Then they made more drawings, and Teresa proudly came up with a picture of herself, her boyfriend, and a dog, all in profile! At this point, the teacher suggested to the children cutting out the figures to add, as in a collage, to their earlier drawings. This evoked many questions : Can we put together in a crowd people undressed for the beach and people dressed up for the promenade?" "Can we put together people of different size?". In this latter instance, children remembered that they had used the photocopy machine to reduce drawings and they decided they should now use it again to make people bigger or smaller so they could look "normal".

The teachers also encouraged the children to use the cutout figures for puppet play, dramatizaton, and shadow play. They also sculpted figures from clay. Finally, the children concluded their exploration with a collective project in which they superimposed many of their figures in a box to create "a crowd" just as Teresa had said, "that goes left, right, forward and when they forget something, they go back."

Looking at this one example of the extraordinary capacity of children, it is clear why it is so important to have the capacity to grow with them. We reinvent and reeducate ourselves along with the children. Not only does our knowledge organize theirs, but also the children's ways of being and dealing with reality likewise influence what we know, feel, and do.

3.7 Conclusion

The first foundation for effective learning, according to me, is interaction. The second is influence from the context and the environment. These are the foundations for awareness and responsibility. The third foundation is assessment. Assessment is not the same as evaluation. Assessment, both self-assessment and group assessment, must be part of the learning process. And that is why documentation and reflection is so important. We must produce traces and documents of the learning process and use them to track and improve them. It is not a portfolio, it is a 'process' folio. Every learning community should construct this to validate what they do, to make it visible. And this will be instructive and challenging also for other communities of learners.

The Reggio experience shows that it is possible to construct rich environments in which children grow up both cognitively and socially. Many tools play a role in this process, a photocopy machine, pencils, a camera, and of course computers and networking could be integrated. But to me it is important that there is a strong educational project first. This project must be based on a high esteem of children and their incredible potential for inventing new languages to deal with reality and each other.

Bibliography

[1] Bruner, J. (1990). Acts of Meaning. Harvard University Press, Cambridge Ma. New York.

[2] Edwards, C. L. Gandini, and G. Forman (eds.) (1993) The Hundred Languages of Children. The Reggio Emilia Approach to Early Childhood Education. Ablex, New Haven.

[3] Piaget, J. (1970). The Science of Education and the Psychology of the Child. Grossman, New York.

[4] Reggio Children (2000) Reggio Tutta. A Guide to the City by the Children. Municipality of Reggio Emilia.

[5] Vygotsky, L.S. (1978). Mind in Society. Cambridge, MA: Harvard University Press.

Group Discussion on Chapter 3: The Joys of Preschool Learning

Assessing Educational Effect

Tokoro: I appreciate very much the learner-centered approach in the Reggio schools, very much. But the most difficult question remains: What is the difference between children raised in that way and children raised in another way? What about the next levels of education? Physical touching and doing research about the world is incredibly important for children from 3 months until 6 years old, but where do we go from there? Maybe at a certain moment something else becomes more important. Or a combination of this approach and another one imposes itself.

Rinaldi: We had a group of colleagues in Sweden and another group in the States, in St Louis. They are trying to develop a new curriculum for older children based on the their own principles and values which are not exactly our values. They work with a cocktail of Piaget, Montessori and similar methods. But the key concepts remain the same: listening comes first. Always start with listening to the kids, in the broadest sense of the word. What are the kids thinking?

When we talk about a bottle, for example, we never start explaining everything straight away but first ask the childrens' own ideas, their own theories. Then you need to collect what they say and use this material, not only as a teacher but as a group of teachers to ask: What is the level of conceptualisation? How can we elaborate on this? The children must not only come up with their own theories but also show these to their friends, so that they can agree or not agree. We have to ask: what is their way of learning in a group? You have to have the courage to take risks and create an environment of support for the whole group as well as the individual. These are the foundations on which our school communities are built. But I admit that it is not easy to maintain this in primary school environments. And it is hard to combine it with other methods or technologies. In that sense the computer is very welcome, as long as the children don't stop using other languages for representation.

Tokoro: There are many important things to learn when children grow up and become 6 or 7. I'm referring to language, to writing, the use of characters. But also computation and mathematics. Can these things be included and done in the Reggio approach or will it have to be in a different way?

Rinaldi: Frankly, I don't know. What we know from our colleagues in the States is that it is absolutely impossible to continue the same method for primary schools. We often use a box of messages in our school. We saw a lot of children of 5 or 6 years old who start to write and to read because they want to communicate with other children. In the States and also in Australia we are collecting traces that allow us to say whether the same phenomenon - to start writing or reading in a spontaneous way - will emerge when children are in schools that can motivate them. The big issue is to invite them to learn. For that we need to set up the right context. A context can be used to solve a problem. For example, children may have to design or help a carpenter build a table for the classroom. That is a great opportunity.

Figure 3.5: Group Discussion. The experiments and experiences of the Reggio approach give great hope for education, but can they be carried over to higher levels? (mw)

The Need for Alternative Education.

Punset: I love the format of the Reggio schools, as something that is inspiring. Learning depends on rich environments. What a rich environment really means, is that there is diversity. There is a very diverse set-up in the Reggio schools. It probably depends on the specific schools, but learning within the constraints of one class, one gender group, one language, one subject, will be less productive than learning in an environment where there is diversity. If we are thinking of the classrooms of the future, then we have to free children from the one classroom concept and send them to science museums or to the streets, to do other things.

Tokoro: Companies in the future may want to hire people that are not educated in an ordinary way. I'm working for Sony, which is a big company. Every year we recruit freshmen. But we recently really started needing people with skills that are very different from the skills that were needed in the past. This is probably a widespread phenomenon. In a few years, companies and societies will not need people who are educated in the former way. We will need creative businessmen. People that can develop and market new fun. How will this fun look I don't know. We need creative developers to concentrate on that. And then try to make it a business. New types of music on demand, of video on demand. Or new types of interactive games. And the students who are trained in the classical way do not necessary fit with the kind of creative people we need. So maybe we will need some who have been playing games all day, or people that go trekking in the mountains for days. People who learned to develop their talents beyond the schooling system. Real personalities. We might recruit them, give them the necessary infrastructure and let them think about creative, innovative ways to do business. So maybe students in high schools should not be that interested in going to MIT or Stanford or the University of Tokyo. Maybe they should just walk around and do their own thing. The current formal teaching system or the current system in which skills and knowledge are evaluated may have no meaning in the future.

Punset: In Catalunya the schools run empty, simply because there are no children anymore. And the consequence is that education is missing out a major target and that is the adults. Institutional education should be revised, re-oriented in order to survive.

Tokoro: In the United States there are already many Charter schools. There is a lot of homeschooling and private schools. Also in Japan private schools are booming. Many parents don't want their children to go to public schools because they are very regulated and discipline-oriented. But private schools have some amount of freedom to teach in a different way. It's a growing tendency.

Steels: I would not abandon the existing school system or the teachers. We have to worry about how the teachers can be freed from educational bureaucracy and unions or whatever restrains them. The power has to go back to the teachers so that they can become responsible and creative again. The idea of 'progettazione' is perhaps something that should become much more common. Also from the viewpoint of the learner, it is essential that they are given much more freedom. Right now, when a student fails according to nationwide criteria, they are shifted to a lower level or to another kind of course. They do not have the right to fail or to do things slower than others. In that sense, everybody: kids, adults, teachers, parents, should become learners and teachers at the same time.

Nevejan: We will need a balance in society. To maintain democracy is not easy. It requires that some people take care of others, it is not always fun. But it gives a good life for the whole community. Public schools may not be cheap and they don't make money but they are important. There are also values that must be addressed through public schools. We will have to do that because otherwise our civilisation will collapse.

Building a Learning Community

Punset: Another good thing about the Reggio approach is the emphasis on forming a learning community. Chimpanzees move around in groups of 25. Humans manage to function very well in groups of 40 or 50. That has been so for years. Of course this kind of community sense gets lost in cities of 3 million people. One of the great things about the Internet is that in this huge planet of six billion you can still be part of a little community, if you can find it. We have to take more care of this feeling of belonging to a community. Since we are more ready to learn as part of a community.

Coenen: Like this workshop. It is a small-scale set-up that is very good for learning. And it's a challenge for education to reach this level of participation and generate this level of motivation and excitement.

Nevejan: You mean conviviality...

Coenen: Yes, it allows one to build up respect for others.

Punset: Has there been any follow up the last ten years on the Reggio children? Are they more clever? Are they happier than others?

Rinaldi: That is a very good question. But I'm afraid I don't have any answers to it. We should have, but we haven't had the courage yet because we don't know what we have to follow up on. Are they engineers because they were in our school? Or are they engineers because of their family background? So for the moment we can only look for answers in the Reggio community itself. In the 30 years in which we have had this kind of school, the community has developed and sustained a culture of childhood, a culture of being a community, of what it means for a community to create a school based on its own values. For us this is a testimony of our success, although not a scientific one. One of our values is learning. Another one is the children. We have managed to create a community of learners.

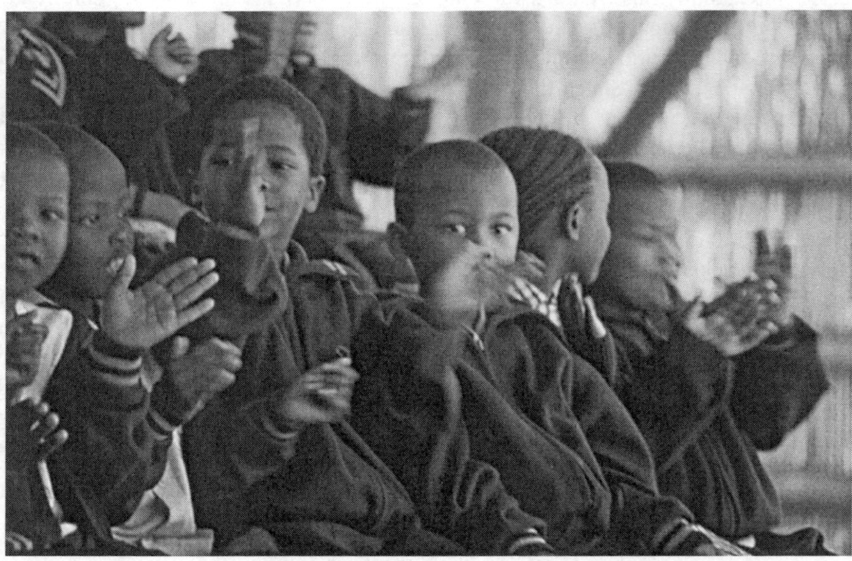

Figure 3.6: We are more ready to learn as part of a community. A challenge of contemporary individual-oriented societies is to create again the feeling of belonging to a group. (am)

Nevejan: The question of follow up is very hard. But one thing is certain: I was a Montessori child and I always recognize Montessori children. I recognize how they think and how they operate. The same way you can recognize people who come from the Steiner schools. So I suppose the children from your school will recognize the other children. Haven't you done any interviews yet?

Rinaldi: We did but we cannot call it a systematic scientific study. But another piece of data we have is that 20 to 38 percent of the children who came to the school come again with their own children, there is a kind of continuity. We also see that there is an increasing demand. Right now only 40 percent of the children of the town can come to the school. There are other public schools but the citizens want their children to come to our school. I believe that it is because of the quality of the culture of education. So now we are experiencing the big challenge between quantity and quality. We could develop more schools or broaden the experiment to primary school level, but the price is very high.

One of the reasons is that public schools are very differently structured from our school. Our school is based on the learning process. The classical Italian school is based on the teaching processes. This is a revolutionary change and a very big political issue. There is also a quite different approach in terms of values. We are talking about choosing one view of human beings in contrast to another one. You can learn on your own, but learning in a group is different. It changes attitudes. For us it is a very important discussion. It is about the quality of the society that we want to build.

Steels: You mean that if the learning process is collective, adults will be more ready later on to participate in democratic processes and feel to be more a part of the community?

Rinaldi: Yes.

Nevejan: In my own work, we're shifting from quality control to quality assurance. The nature of assessment is changing. It's much more about making sure the process happens on a quality level than anything else.

Rinaldi: It's about the why and the how.

Nevejan: The how being more important than the result. If the why and the how are right, the result is of no importance.

Coenen: We want to allow people to explore things. But we also need to offer principles and values as we go along, without being indoctrinating. It's very important allowing people to flourish, but we have to offer them principles by which they can be happy interacting with society.

Chapter 4

Personality and Concept Formation

by Mariane Hedegaard

Mariane Hedegaard is professor of educational psychology at the University of Aarhus, Denmark. She is an expert in an approach to learning emanating from the work of psychologists Vygotsky, Luria, Leontev, et.al., known as activity theory. She focuses on the development of personality and concept formation in schoolchildren and on the integration of immigrant children in new cultural environments. Her recent books include "Learning and Child Development", "Learning in Classrooms: A Cultural-Historic Perspective", and "Learning Activity and Development".

For some time the traditional theory of learning, that the teacher transmits knowledge and the student learns by listening or exact copying, has been abandoned as a model for learning. New topics have come to dominate learning theory, such as participation in social communities and competence. The child is no longer viewed as a recipient but a participant. Learning is no longer exclusively associated with cognitive processes but is a tool-mediated social activity. The aim of this paper is to contribute to this changing perspective. It reports on teaching experiments where each child is seen as an active contributor to the development of the social interplay in a classroom of which the child is an integral part.

Through analyses I will demonstrate that children not only learn through their participation in the social world, but also become involved in a reciprocal process in which their motives and personalities play a part in the interaction with the other people in the classroom the teacher and their classmates, and thereby contribute to their own learning conditions. Motives are related to a person's goals and characterise a person's activities - surpassing the single situation and characterisable only as longer lasting traits.

Expectations of family and community also influence the child's learning. Learning is united with teaching, although in different ways at different phases of development. Learning subject matter content in school is also connected with the children's motives. To demonstrate this, I will use an example from my own research and briefly outline a teaching approach called 'the double move in teaching' that supports developmental learning. Developmental learning is used within the Vygotskian framework as learning within the 'zone of proximal development'.

4.1 What needs to be learned

Vygotsky's theory of psychic development has influenced and inspired recent theories of thinking. Cultural and social aspects have become more common in the conceptualization of thinking over the past 10 years. In general we can distinguish four important approaches:

Approaches to Thinking

The first approach can be called the 'cognitive situated approach' and is exemplified by the work of Resnick [13] and Greeno [6]. Thinking is still seen as an individual function of information manipulation supported by the social context. Collective procedures as a foundation for the development of thinking are not yet introduced.

The second approach can be called the 'cultural daily life approach' with Hutchins [10], Lave and Wenger [11] and Scribner [14] as key people. Thinking is located within the existing practice of daily activities, e.g. manipulating a marine boat, tailoring and milk delivery. This practice can be characterised by procedures for handling daily-life activities. People are socialised into being participants in procedure-guided activities, but they are not seen as modifying or reflecting on these procedures.

The third approach is the 'socio-cultural communicative approach' represented by Wertsch [16] and Billig [1]. Thinking is characterised as a dialog with historical roots. The dialog takes place between imagined different opinions, characteristic of significant in an individual's life. These opinions appear as part of people's internal discourse.

Each of these approaches focuses on aspects which are important to integrate into a cultural-historic understanding of thinking, developed by Vygotsky [15], Elkonin [5], Davydov [3] and myself [8]. In this approach, the social aspect of thinking and its situated and distributed character are formed by everyday practice as well as by the communicative and argumentative character of the thinking process. The integration of these characteristics leads to a characterisation of thinking as a process guided by procedures or social practices, either in daily life or in professional life, with dialog and argumentation as central activities.

There are two other aspects important for qualifying 'thinking'. The first is the content domain of thinking, the second is the motive. By including content in the characteristic of a thinking person, the procedural aspect of thinking becomes related to societal knowledge traditions. The societal forms of knowledge a child meets in their upbringing and education is important for their development of thinking. Education contributes to the child's appropriate knowledge. But knowledge conceived through instruction has to relate to the child's motivated activity to become active personal knowledge.

Personal Knowledge

One of Vygotsky's [15] theses is that although formalised subject matter concepts can be learned at school, they do not become meaningful for the child until they become active in the child's life.

Activities in different fields of life - school, home, and work - with their different forms of practice, result in different forms of concept formation and thinking. The gaps between home, school and work as fields of learning are extended so much that many children have difficulty in combining knowledge of one field with the other. Therefore an issue for school teaching must be to connect the subject matter concepts with everyday concepts in a way that widens and develops children's abilities in these non-school situations.

Vygotsky characterised the differences between pre-school children and schoolchildren's thinking as primarily a difference in systematic methods and amounts of knowldge within the different subject domains. The problem in teaching then is how knowledge conceived at school can be transformed into active knowledge. The aim of teaching must be to teach children concepts and methods that can enrich their understanding and capacity for action in the life they live outside school.

Tool mediation is a central concept for Vygotsky and the cultural-historical approach to psychology and education. In this approach, tools (conceptual and manual) are seen as central in mediating between a person and the world (subject and object) and for developing a person's competencies. It is related to how students appropriate knowledge and skills.

4.2 The Double Move Approach

In a series of teaching experiments based on what I call the double move in teaching, the traditional teaching methods and the methods of cooperation between children changed from learning methods aimed at imprinting the material, to methods of research and cooperation on key problems. The research method dominated in this "experiment". It is characterized by asking a number of questions such as:

- What are we researching?
- What do we know?
- How can we model the relation between the important concepts of our research problem?
- Which methods can we use to find out about what we do not know?

- Does the model need to be revised?

We also worked with methods of narrative knowledge: dialog, argumentation, novel and film interpretation, dramatising and play-acting.

Here is a concrete example, it is from a class where children discuss what is special about being human. The extract is from a research project in experimental teaching with the evolution of animals, the origin of humans and the historical change of society as its theme, in other words an integration of the subjects of biology, history, and geography. We changed the traditional methods of teaching from memorizing facts to exploring problems in cooperation with other children. Instead of transferring empirical knowledge, teaching focused on methods for generating theoretical knowledge [4] and methods for elucidating narrative knowledge [2].

The central goal of this teaching experiment is that children would connect concrete events and situations from the past and present with conceptual categories and be able to through thinking and reflection strategies that they already use in everyday life situations. By building conceptual models, children learn to create a global perspective on the diverse elements of a subject. First we worked with the children to create core models for evolution and later for history. The children had to relate the different matters they worked with in class with their models (see figure 4.1). For example, the children gradually learned to use core models to analyze connections between species and nature, and for humans between tool use and ways of living or between division of work and structure of society.

Classroom protocol

Here is an extract from a class protocol in which children discussed what is special about being human. The protocol is taken from the 14th session of 4th grade. The children have been creating models (see figure 4.1) which schematically illustrate how animals and humans relate to their natural environment and how they are adapted to cope with it. The models hang as posters in the classroom.

Susanne: (comparing within animals) There is more in our model (of humans)

T(eacher): Can you mention some?

Susanne: Work, money, other humans, factories.

Sanne: There is something I cannot understand, because some say that we also come from animals. So there has to be something also from the animals.

T: Are there not some differences?

Cecilie: It is easier for us than for the animals. They have to go hunting to find food, we can just go to the supermarket.

Morten: We use tools.

T.: This you can also find in your models. (He points to the models of human development where they have drawn tools, in contrast to the model of animal development where there are no tools.)

Jrgen: But animals also use tools, when we saw a film about apes, they used tools.

Loke: Some birds at the Galapagos Islands use sticks.

T: (affirms but asks about the difference in animal and human tool use.)

Jrgen: Animals do not write.

Sanne: All humans use tools but not all animals do, what should be in the model should count for all.

T. Do all humans use tools?
Susanne: Yes even primitive people used tools of stone.
Sanne: We also use clothes.
T: Yes, this is also a kind of tool.
Lise: We use tools all the time, now we use it to sit on.
Jarl: The watch is also a tool.

The extract illustrates both the form and the content of children's developmental learning activity. The content is about the importance of artefacts and tools as characteristic of human ways of living (tools are characterised both through activities such as work, buying and writing, and as artefacts, such as money, factories, tools, cloth, watches, chairs). The form of children's activity in 4th grade is a theoretical discussion of the difference between humans and animals. As a foundation for their discussion they point to models they have constructed of the relations between core concepts in the evolution of animals and the origins of humans.

The main characteristics of the developmental teaching approach illustrated here are:

1. Communication and cooperation between the children is guided by the teacher,
2. Procedural research methods are used, inspired by social science research methods,
3. Conceptual models are used as tools for analyzing historical events and periods.

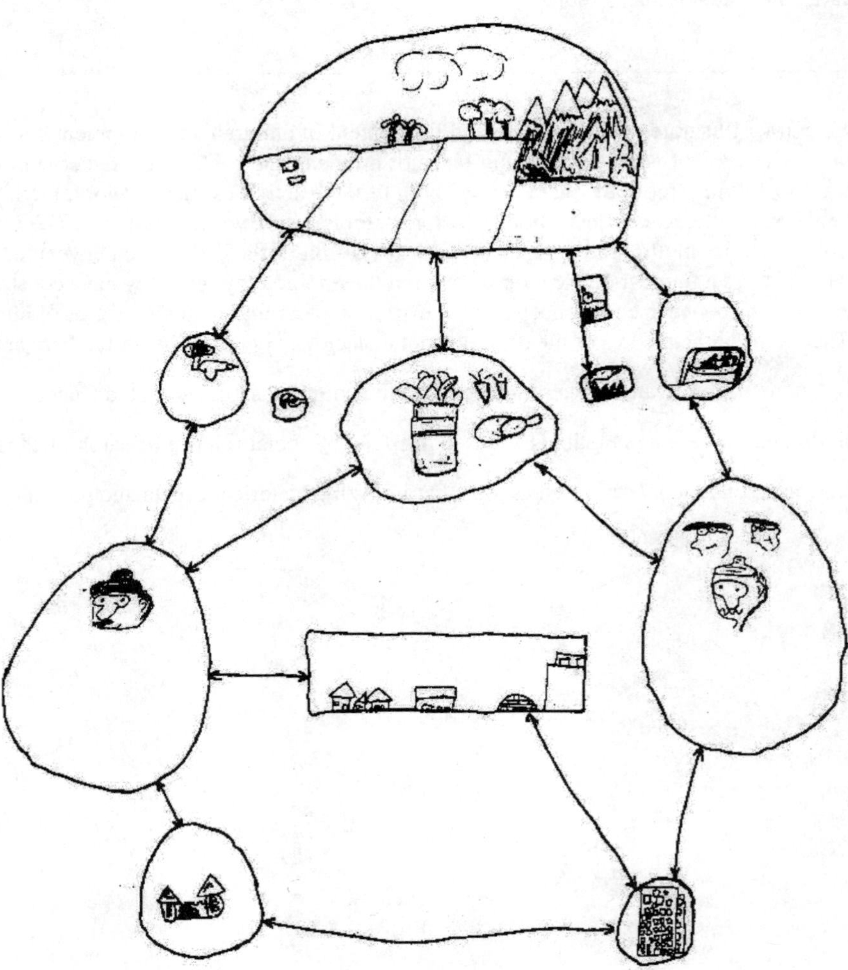

Figure 4.1: Children's models of animals' adaptation to nature, and of the relation of humans to their environment.

4.3 Different Learning Contexts

The Role of the Learning Context

Traditions and practices are important for understanding differences in tool use. This is also true for learning. Learning in school takes place within a specific learning tradition, learning at home is related to another kind of tradition. A tool and its tradition of use exist before a person enters the world and become appropriated by that person through social interaction. The existence of an environment with tools can be seen as both a context and a precondition for the person's development of a relationship with the world.

McDermott [12] demonstrates clearly that children's learning in school is both created and imbued with meaning anchored in school traditions. He shows how a child's learning disability is viewed differently in different institutional contexts. He demonstrates how a child, in the relaxed situation of baking a cake, can read and calculate, but in a test situation does not even try to use his capabilities. The reading skill a child is demonstrating, or the lack of competence diagnosed as a learning disability, is dependent on the context the child is entering. Adam, the child in McDermott's observational study, changes and improves from being in a test situation, to being in the class situation, and finally in an after-school club situation. Adam's reading problem shows the necessity of seeing skills as integrated within specific contexts. His learning problem manifests itself differently in different contexts. The institutional activity and the child's activity are woven together in a given context, so it is neither the child nor the context which creates learning or learning problems but the interaction between the child and a specific practice in a given institution.

We can distinguish between everyday knowledge that children carry with them from their home or community and scientific knowledge or subject matter knowledge that children meet in school. Everyday knowledge is connected to practical activities at home. Examples are cooking, cleaning, and familiar activities. In everyday knowledge, procedures and content have melted together, and can be characterised as "silent" knowledge. In school, knowledge is based on teaching traditions with subject matter knowledge and procedures: language learning with reading and writing procedures, mathematical learning with basic operations for calculating, geography with map reading, history with time lines, etc. The knowledge connected to craftsmanship and professional work dominates workplaces. Content and procedures have developed through work traditions. For the professional, the knowledge has become embodied in procedures and methods, similar to everyday knowledge, with the difference that it can become conscious and reflected upon.

The different practices that one can find in home, school, higher education and the workplace thus create different conditions for concept formation and thinking by children and young adults. For example, Scribner [14] has shown that mathematics is learned and used in different ways in school and in the workplace. She studied American milkmen's delivering practices and found that their way of keeping account of how much milk they had delivered and the payment they received were done in quite a different way than one would expect from the basic arithmetical operations learned in school. Her research showed that mathematical knowledge and skills are not abstract entities which transfer easily but they combine with specific institutional practices.

The goal of schooling is for knowledge and skills to become the person's own tools for the practice they will participate in. Based on the differences between knowledge at home, school and work, we can understand Vygotsky's advice [15] about teaching in different institutions: teaching at home should follow the child's logic, in school it should follow the subject matter logic, and at work it should follow the logic of the professional activity and of the work task.

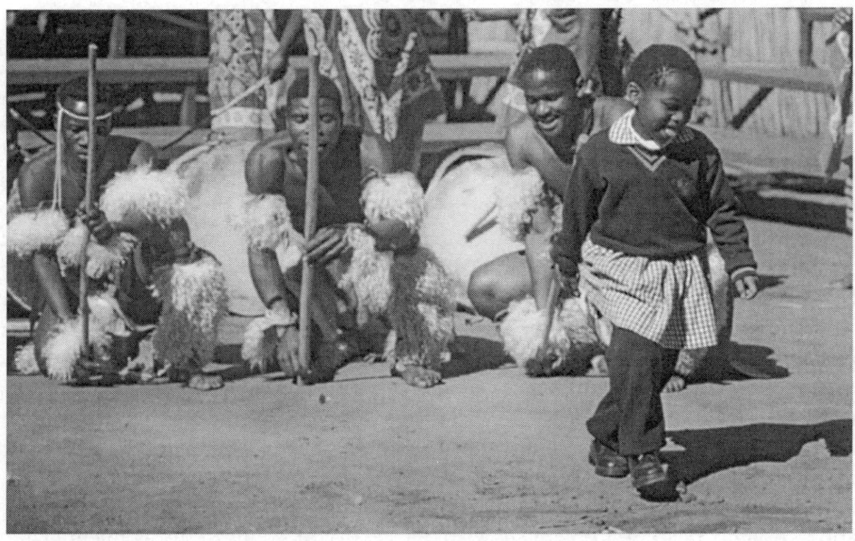

Figure 4.2: The context in which children learn changes. Initially, they participate spontaneously in community or family practices. Later they must adapt to become part of a school institution in which the focus is on learning cognitive skills. (am)

Dynamics of Learning Contexts

The contexts in which children learn are not static entities. Everybody who participates in the social practice of an institution contributes to this practice and leaves his or her mark. A family, a day-care institution, and a school are marked by the children who are involved in the activities. By being in the daily activities in an institution, the children appropriate as well as contribute to the way of being together and the social-historical experiences that are accumulated in these practices; emotionally, motivationally as well as cognitively.

Each child appropriates knowledge and skill to master the demands that they meet, which are always a result of the child's engaged activity in shared practices with other people (e.g., the appropriation of day and night rhythms, reading and writing competencies). But the different activities that characterise the different institutions that children participate in, at different periods of their life, leads to qualitatively different periods in their development. Elkonin [5] has presented this in a theory of developmental periods where the different periods in children's development parallel the different institutions that dominate the child's life. The first period is dependent on practice in home and daycare, and deals with the child's development and direct emotional contact with other human beings. The second period is related to practice in school and deals with the child's development of roles in relation to other human beings. The third period is related to peer group activity and professional education as preparation for work, it deals with close personal relationships and work relationships.

4.4 Motive Development

Stages in motive development

The development of motives for the three periods introduced above is always ahead of the development of cognition in each of the periods. In the early childhood period (the infant and toddler period), children's motives are related to their emotional contact with the key people in their everyday life. This results in the development and mastery of the immediate and close everyday world. This mastery is the foundation for the next period, the middle childhood period, which is the kindergarten and early school age. The children's emotional and motivational world broadens and they develop motives for mastery of the adult world in this period. The learning motive develops and becomes dominant in this middle childhood period. Here, the child's knowledge is characterized by the acquisition of methods and competence that in school are seen as central for entering the adult world. In the third period, the late childhood period, the secondary school age and youth period, the child's motivational development is directed towards engagement and society. The dominating motive is togetherness with school fellows, to be socially accepted and at the same time be oriented towards self-worth. The child's cognitive development can be characterized by mastering methods for reflection on personal relations, work and society relations.

In the school period, the child's learning is directed towards mastering the skills that characterise the adult world. The imaginative motive of play activity is replaced by a real wish to acquire skill. Most children who start school expect to become able to read and write, if they can not already do this when they start. They do not want to play that they are reading, they want to acquire the competence. The dominating motive becomes learning. In this period the child's spontaneous concepts are extended by appropriating subject matter concepts. But it is only when these subject matter concepts become integrated within the child's everyday concepts from home and community life that their everyday concepts rise to a new level, and real cognitive development takes place.

The change of view from seeing the child as a recipient in learning to the child as a participant in learning, and seeing learning as associated exclusively with cognitive processes, to learning as a social activity, should lead to a new way of understanding school-children's learning activity and to new teaching practices. It is this change in view on children's learning and development that I have tried to develop within the context of a classroom. Through my analyses I have attempted to demonstrate that schoolp children not only learn through their participation in the social world, but also become involved in a reciprocal process in which their motives and personalities play a part in the interaction with the other people in the classroom; the teacher and their classmates.

Examples

To illustrate this strong interaction between learning subject matter content in school and the development of children's motives, i.e. personality, I return to the teaching experiment discussed earlier in the paper. The same group is now in the fifth grade. The theme of the teaching experiment in fifth grade was 'the historical change of societies'. The questions which started the activities in the first sessions were: "How can it be that people live differently in different places of the world?", and "How can it be that people have lived differently in different historical periods?"

Figure 4.3: The development of personality plays a very significant role in how children, and even more, young adults, establish relationships and develop motives for learning. Individual personalities need to be taken into account during the teaching process.(mw)

The individuality of the children became apparent in their social interaction with others, which was marked by the motives, interests and intentions each possessed for entering into relationships at various levels with the teacher and the other children in the class. Two students, Morten and Cecilie, had been participating in the teaching experiment. The two children's motives changed considerably through 5th grade, a change that could not only be seen as a result of the class activities.

At the beginning of the school year, Morten's social orientation in conflict situations was to demonstrate his own ability in the subject matter tasks. Morten was interested in both the class activities and his classmates. But he did not like his group partners imitating him when he drew models (in most of the activities the children work in a permanent group of four or five), or when his best friend wanted to look at the books he was reading. He was interested in the different tasks the teacher brought into the class activities, especially drawing models of the historical periods, but he also had a strong motive for being recognized for his work. When he was criticized, he would withdraw into himself and the teacher or his friend had to help him back into the group activity. A change came after he functioned twice in the teacher's role. In the last period in fifth grade, his social orientation changed through the planning and performance of a play. In this activity he took criticism from his group fellows straightaway and solved the conflicts by confronting the matters he did not agree with and asked the ones who proposed these matters to explain more clearly what they had in mind. He was active in formulating the content and instructing his group. Through this activity he arrogated the leader role and functioned as the leader in his group.

In fourth grade, Cecilie had been very concerned about her classmates and the teacher, but in fifth grade the helpful girl became at some point both rebellious and critical in her relation to her classmates and especially in relation to the teacher. She was still primarily the initiator of the activity in her group, as in the previous year, but she never presented herself as a leader of the activities, instead she was very caring. Perhaps her rebelliousness came from the conflict that she wanted to guide and become the leader but did not arrogate this role enough. Her motives in fifth grade were characterized by a constant subject matter interest, but at the same time it became more oriented towards independence and self-determination.

It is as if the content of Morten's and Cecilie's social motives developed in opposite directions. Throughout the year in fifth grade, Morten developed security in the social interaction with his classmates, which he did not have at the beginning of fifth grade. He came to function independently and in a way self-determined. Cecilie on the other hand started out with the care-taking role and gradually rebelled against this role, wishing instead to be recognized as a competent and independent person. She wanted to guide and decide in her group, but she had troubles combining this with the care-taking role that she had brought with her from fourth grade. This brought her into conflicts and rebellious situations in the last part of fifth grade where the self-determination of the activities increased for all children in the class.

To understand the development of motives in children we have to go beyond the activity in the class and integrate the context, i.e. the tradition in which learning and teaching take place. Particularly the expectation of teachers and parents how children should act determines part of their behavior. Different expectations towards girls and boys for example play a very important role in the examples presented.

4.5 Conclusion

Educational psychologists attempt to understand better the processes underlying thinking and concept formation, in order to design more effective learning processes. I have argued that concept learning itself can not be dissociated from motive development, and that learning as well as the application of what has been learned strongly depend on the context.

The paper developed three themes:

1. Learning is seen as a change in the relation between a person and the world through change in their capacity for tool use and interpretation of artefacts.

2. Learning takes place within a context: state, social field, institutional practice tradition, and situated activity.

3. Both context and tool/artefact objectify human needs and intentions already invested with cognitive and affective content.

Bibliography

[1] Billig, M (1978) Banal nationalism. Sage, London.

[2] Bruner, J.S. (1986) Actual minds possible worlds. Harvard University Press, Cambridge, Mass.

[3] Davydov, Y. V. (1977) Arten der Verallgemeinerung im Unterricht. [Types of generalization in Instruction.] Volk und Wissen, Berlin.

[4] Davydov, V.V. (1982) Ausbildung der LerntŁtigkeit [Development of Learning Activity]. In: V.V. Davydov, J. Lompscher, and A.K. Markova (Eds), Ausbildung der LerntŁtigkeit bei Schlern. Volk und Wissen, Berlin.

[5] Elkonin, D.B. (1971) Towards the problem of stages in the mental development of the child. Soviet Psychology, 10, 538-653.

[6] Greeno, J. (1989) A Perspective on Thinking. American Psychologist, 44, 134-141.

[7] Hedegaard, M. (1995) The qualitative analyses of the development of a child's theoretical knowledge and thinking. In: L. Martin, K. Nelson and E. Tobach (Eds) Sociocultural psychology. Theory and practice of doing and knowing. Cambridge University Press, Cambridge.

[8] Hedegaard, M. (1999) The influence on societal knowledge traditions on children's thinking and conceptual development. In M. Hedegaard, and J. Lompscher (Eds.), Learning activity and development. Aarhus University Press, Aarhus.

[9] Hedegaard, M. (2001) Learning and child development. Aarhus University Press, Aarhus.

Hedegaard, M. (1999) The Influence of Societal Knowledge Traditions. In: Lompscher, J. and M. Hedegaard (eds.) (1999) Learning activity and development. Aarhus University Press, Aarhus.

[10] Hutchins, E. (1991) The social organization of distributed cognition. In: Resnick, L.B., J.M. levine and S.D. Teasley (eds.) (1991) Perspectives on socially shared cognition. American Psychological Association, Washington.

[11] Lave, J. and E. Wenger (1991) Situated learning: Legitimate peripheral participation. Cambridge University Press, Cambridge.

[12] McDermott, R. (1993) The acquisition of a child with a learning disability. In S. Chaiklin and J. Lave (Eds.) (1993). Understanding practice. Perspectives on activity and context. Cambridge University Press, Cambridge.

[13] Resnick, L. (1987) Education and learning to think. National Academy Press, Washington, D.C.

[14] Scribner, S. (1990) A socio-cultural approach to the study of mind. In: G. Greenberg and E. Tobach (Eds.), Theories of the evolution of knowing. Lawrence Erlbaum, Hillsdale, N.J..

[15] Vygotsky, L.S. m.fl. (1982) Om barnets psykiske udvikling. [On the child's psychic development] Nyt Nordisk Forlag, Copenhagen.

[16] Wertsch, J. (1991) Voices of the mind: A sociocultural approach to mediated action. Harvard Univ. Press, Cambridge Ma.

Group Discussion 4
Personality and Concept Formation

The Double Move Approach

Steels: You mentioned this concept of the double move approach, what exactly do you mean by that?

Hedegaard: What we call the double move approach is that on the one hand you have to ask: what are the children interested in? And on the other hand: what are the concepts that you want to use? How do you create motivation in the child? How do you use the child's experiences? It's a double move between the child's experiences and the interest and subject material. It's all about a central question: what is the general motivation you want to develop? The general motivation you want to develop for children in schools, is the motivation for learning about different subject-matters.

Tokoro: Is it about bi-directional stimuli or motivation?

Hedegaard: Development is related to prominent activities in different institutions. So motivation is not something that comes from within the individual but something you learn when taking part in communities. So the idea is that in the first period of your life, during the early years, motivation and development take place in direct emotional contact. This leads to methods for manipulating objects. The child can focus or orient himself or herself within the immediate surroundings and towards object-manipulation. This in turn leads to many more capacities and eventually to possibilities for role-playing.

Dautenhahn: This direct object manipulation is indeed very important. Even if you have fantastic educational programs on television and a child is sitting in front of it for five years, it will not work on a learning level! Yes, the child will learn something or will be inspired in a way, but we cannot neglect that the child must play an active role. Information is not just an open channel, you need to digest the information, you need to use it. An active role of the learner is a fundamental condition in the learning process.

Rinaldi: When children are observed, even very young ones, they appear to be thinking while manipulating very concrete objects. We have seen a very nice example with Laura and the watch. But is this abstract thinking? We cannot really talk about phases but have to talk about thinking about concrete things, thinking that comes from reality and that enables you to reflect on what you are doing. I think that an abstract way of thinking is present in the child starting from the first phase where they start to work with images and produce new realities. Then there is a period in which we can see that children seem to become aware of what they are thinking about. Abstract thinking becomes visible to themselves. This happens when they are about four or five years old and that is the moment when they start to say "I think that", "In my opinion", etc. They start to use this kind of language and they also start to produce more metaphors. These are for us indicators that development is going well. I have observed that the children that live in our school are much more able to use symbolic and visual symbols and a sort of abstract image of reality than in the past, because they spend a lot of time watching television and reading the images of this medium. They seem to be able to use or to produce abstract concepts earlier than in the past and to code and to decode reality with these abstractions.

Nevejan: Is that because of mediatisation?

Rinaldi: Yes, definitely. Reggio where the preschool child centers where I work are located, is a town in which the economy is good and many families have a computer at home and when children are four years old, they have the possibility of playing with the computer, or being close to the parents when they work with this tool. Also television is a daily life tool. They like movies a lot. Hence they can produce symbolisation very early on in life. Whether this is good or bad, it depends. If you observe the way in which they play, it is clearly related to what they have seen on television. One problem is that children who have the opportunity to watch often control play situations, where others are left out. There are many other influences of the media. For example in the use of colours. They are much more attracted these days to fluorescent colors and they are also very much influenced by the messages that come from television.

Hedegaard: I think the relation between grounded experience and abstract reflection is very important. I wouldn't call it abstract thinking, but it is when children can use a general concept and use it to analyse the concrete situation they are in, so this move between the experience and the general is very important. Children should have experiences but if they only have experiences, and reflection is not supported in schools, you get confused children. In the Danish tradition and also in Germany there was a kind of "experience pedagogy". Children were supposed to experience as much as possible. They had to bring experiences from home and talk about them but the problem is that they never get the central concepts, so it is just experiences and the move between the concrete and the general is never established. So that's why I think that Carla Rinaldi's comment about reflection is so important and the possibility that computers could be a tool for integrating things, for enabling abstraction from concrete experiences is very exciting.

The Important Role of Teachers

Hedegaard: I believe that part of the failure of new educational technologies comes from giving students not enough guidance. I have been involved in a project in East Harlem, New York, where 17 computers where donated and we did a teaching experiment with 15 children from poor areas. We learned from this experiment that children should first of all go out and do research in their communities, instead of staying in front of the computer screen all the time. They used computers for writing out the results of their investigations, for planning the interviews, for making models. Children who hated writing, actually wrote on the computers. They made nice models and drawings and they loved doing it. Same thing in Denmark. All schools have bought computers and nobody uses them. There are a lot of so called educational games, but they are boring! The children don't want to use them because there is no creativity involved. If we reflect on computers in education we have to do it in a way that children can be active, doing guided research, and reflecting upon it.

Hedegaard: I strongly believe that we should not leave children unguided. When thinking about new technologies, we should think about children and adults together. It is dangerous to make the assumption that you can simply put computers in schools, leave the children alone with the technology, and then they will be alright. They will not be alright! The whole idea of a school is that our everyday life is too complex for children to handle, so we need institutional education and teachers to provide the protected environments and scaffolding that is needed to learn cope with complexity. Otherwise, why do we need schools? If children sit in front of the television or computer screen, there is no need for schools anymore.

Nevejan: You contradict yourself there, on the one hand you say that computers are stifling creativity because their programs are rigid, but on the other hand you argue for the need of simplified protected environments...

Hedegaard: I didn't say that. Children can use computers to reflect upon the research they are doing for example. But they still need guidance.

Nevejan: But there is an area where teachers will have to let go. It is really hard for schools and teachers to figure out when and where they have to do that, but we have to let go in order to let kids find things out for themselves that were not foreseen.

Coenen: I think it depends on the personality. Some kids just start to explore and find all kinds of stuff. And there are others that need guided, well-organised education.

Tokoro: In any case, it is not the problem of the computer. It's a problem of the teachers using the computer.

Punset: To remove the resistance of students and teachers, we should make it fun!

Steels: The time needed to develop good content is often highly underestimated. Perhaps teachers should be allowed to work in teams for this, and be given sufficient time. Moreover curricula are now very full and over-organised, giving very little time to students to do open-ended exploration.

Nevejan: The problem is not the technology, it is the editorial format. The teachers cannot keep up with technological and societal change, with the constant flux between the physical and the virtual, unless they are involved in the development stages. They do not know how to evaluate the work of students. They do not know how to set up collaborations among students. So the teachers are often very right not to use these new technologies. They do not know how to map all the basic educational processes that are forced on them onto the new technologies. Their input is not taken seriously and the industry doesn't work for education because education doesn't give profits.

Theme III

The Developing Brain

Cat. Ezra, age 9

'Constructivism' opposes both the speculation that child development is merely the implementation of a genetic blueprint, and the notion that the infant's brain is a passive slate upon which experience writes. Instead, this point of view argues that genes and environment interact in a constructive manner at multiple levels. The activity or behaviour of cells or the organism at one point in development determines the next step. In other words, the brain selects the appropriate input for its own further development.
Mark Johnson

Chapter 5

The Infant Brain

by Mark Johnson

Mark Johnson is professor of Psychology and director of the Centre for Brain and Cognitive Development at Birbeck College, University of London. He researches developmental cognitive neuroscience, focusing in particular on visual orienting and attention and face recognition. His publications include "Developmental Cognitive Neuroscience, An Introduction" and as co-author of "Rethinking Innateness".

The first two years of human life involve enormous and rapid changes in the size, strength, and relative proportions of the body and the nervous system. These developments coincide with dramatic strides in infants' perceptual, motor, cognitive, emotional, and communicative capacities. Understanding the early postnatal development of the brain, and how this relates to the changing perceptual and cognitive abilities of infants is not only of interest for basic science, but is also likely to be of importance for educational and clinical policies in the future. For example, is it a valuable investment in the future to provide "enriched" environments for young infants? Is it worthwhile attempting to treat some developmental disorders during early infancy, or are such interventions better left until later in development?

The mental capacities of young infants have long been a focus for the nature versus nurture debate. Roughly speaking, it was reasoned that if newborns show evidence of some ability then it is likely to be "innate". If not, it must be learned. These days, most researchers have moved beyond this simple dichotomy. Recently, an alternative viewpoint, sometimes termed "constructivism", has been advanced. This opposes both the view that development is merely the implementing of a genetic blueprint, and the notion that the infant's brain is a passive slate upon which experience writes. Instead, it argues that genes and environment interact at multiple levels in a constructive manner. The activity or behaviour of cells or the organism at one point in development determines the next step. In other words, the brain selects the appropriate input for its own further development.

This paper first explains the main controversies in developmental psychology: the debate between nature and nurture and constructivism as a way to transcend that dichotomy. It then explains how contemporary neuroscience tries to measure brain activity and illustrates with a case study from face recognition what the constructivist point of view really means.

5.1 Nature, Nurture and Constructivism

Nativism and Empiricism

Pre-Darwinian theories of evolution were largely based on preformationism: the idea that a creator, or creative force, "designed" the final forms of species [7]. In contrast, Darwin outlined a specific mechanism through which complex species evolve gradually from simpler, more primitive, varieties. The evolution of species was viewed as the product of an interaction between genetic variation and random mutation on the one hand, and the demands of a particular environment on the other. The process was not directed, but like a "blind watchmaker" [5]. An important point to note is that as a species evolved, its effective environment changed. For example, as sense organs improve, the detail of information that can be extracted from the environment increases, or as wings evolved the effective environment of insects dramatically increases.

There have been theories of cognitive and behavioural development which share the common assumption that the emergence of more complex functions can, and should, be attributed to some pre-existing source of information. The extreme manifestation of these "pre-Darwinian" views of ontogeny are nativism, in which it is believed that information in the genes "codes for" aspects of brain and mental structure (that are merely triggered by aspects of the environment) , and empiricism, in which it is believed that simple but powerful learning mechanisms absorb information about the structure of the environment.

While nativism and empiricism are commonly viewed as two extreme ends of a continuum of theories about development, in fact they both share the underlying assumption that the information necessary for the final state of the organism precedes it, somewhat like an architects plans for a building. Both approaches also attempt to minimise the extent of the transition from simple starting stuff to complex final state. For nativists, the original stuff is more complex than it seems: genes contain complex codes with all the necessary information for building neural circuits dedicated to language or arithmetical computation, and infants are viewed as being born with prespecified dedicated modules for various functions which merely require to be triggered by appropriate environmental input. For empiricists, the end stuff is actually simpler than it seems - the brain may viewed as composed of relatively simple but powerful learning devices. In both cases much of the mystery of development is thankfully eliminated by reference to simple explanatory concepts.

Nativism comes in several varieties, but they all share the common assumption that genes, either directly or indirectly, build brain structures, often argued to be domain-specific, which underlie specific types of computation in the brain. Changes in behaviour during infancy or childhood are thus often attributed to "brain maturation". Gottlieb [7] has characterised this type of viewpoint as "causal epigenesis". Causal epigenesis implies a one way causal relation from gene to brain to behaviour. For nativists of all varieties many (but not all) of the problems of change during ontogeny are essentially reducible to phylogeny. However, this has the paradoxical consequence that developmental biology can be maintained as a separate discipline from psychological development, less germane to the questions of interest than, for example, the cognitive psychology of adults. These tendencies were undoubtedly reinforced by the popular view among cognitive scientists in the 1970's and 80's that the "software" of the mind was best studied without reference to the "hardware" of the brain.

Empiricist accounts of cognitive and behavioural development lost popularity in the past few decades when it became apparent that in several domains infants and children are capable of going beyond the (environmental) information given to them [2], and that the cognitive capacities of young infants had been grossly underestimated. However, rejection of empiricist views is not grounds for rejection of an alternative way of thinking about development, constructivism. Further, most empiricist models involve a static environment that imposes itself on the child's brain. As with evolution, we should aware that the effective environment for the organism is likely to change as it develops.

Constructivism and development

While both nativism and empiricism share the assumption of pre-existing information (be it in the genes or in the environment), constructivist theories of ontogeny, like Darwinist accounts of phylogeny, do not. Constructivism is an orthogonal dimension of development theory to the nature-nurture debate, and is primarily focused on the mechanisms of change and emergence of new structure through interactive processes. It views development as a constructive process through which genes interact with their environments at various different levels, including the environment external to the organism, resulting in organic structures which are more specified or differentiated than those that preceded them. Thus, it puts an emphasis on the activity-dependent nature of development. As we will see, this activity-dependent nature is appropriate at a number of different levels including the cellular and organismal.

Piaget was one of the first to adopt a constructivist approach to psychological development, although the approach has a much longer history in biological development. Indeed, as is well known Piaget based his theories of cognitive change partly on accounts of embryological development. While Piaget's general approach to psychological development may have been sound, the particular theory he advanced clearly looks dated today. Among a number

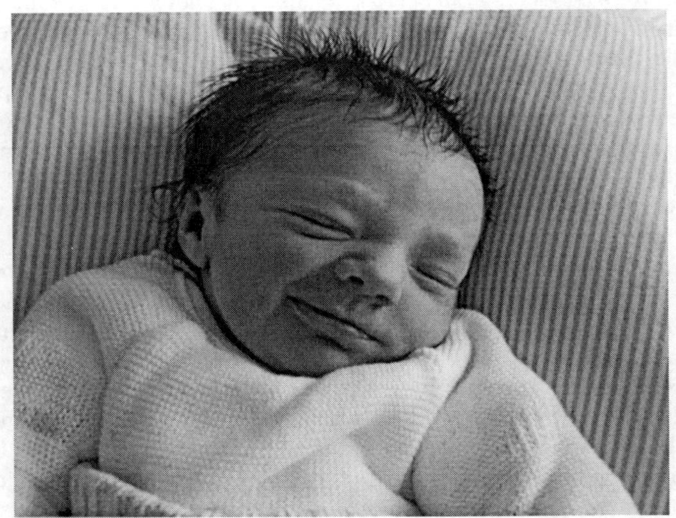

Figure 5.1: Newborn babies are capable very early on to engage in relatively complex behaviors. But this this imply that these behaviors are all innate? (picture with kind permission by Michael Mohnhaupt)

of weaknesses were the rather vague and underspecified mechanisms of change such as "assimilation" and "accommodation", the neglect of the importance of brain development, and his gross underestimation of the abilities of young infants. The latter was no doubt due to the relative lack of procedures for studying infant abilities during the 1950's and early 60's. (It took another biologist, Robert Fantz, to adapt methods from animal behaviour experiments to develop the first infant preference testing procedures). However, while much of Piaget's theory has been correctly rejected by empirical evidence, this does not mean we should reject his general approach, and throw out the baby with the bathwater. Also, there has been a tendency by those of a nativist inclination to conflate constructivism as being the same thing as empiricism, and to use the same arguments against both types of theories. For example, arguments from the poverty of the stimulus in language acquisition are commonly used to support a nativist position, when in fact they only refute an empiricist stance [11]. It is in no way inconsistent with a contructivist approach in which developmental change results in structures that go beyond the information immediately available in either the environment or intrinsic factors.

5.2 Watching the brain develop

Habituation Experiments

There are a number of different ways to study the development of the human brain and mind. First, we can use behavioural experiments. But how do you put questions to a baby who cannot yet speak or even press buttons? The trick is to devise a task centred around

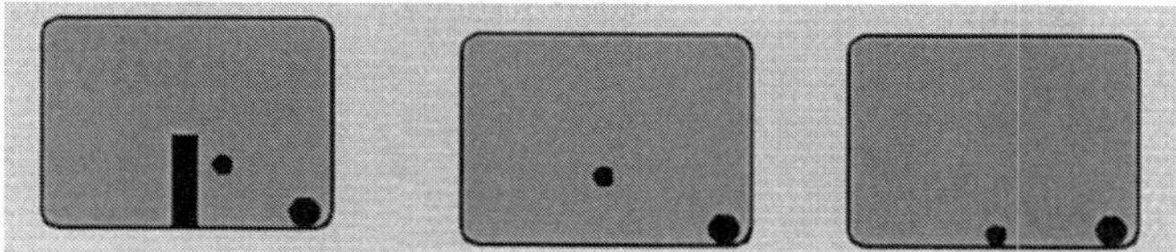

Figure 5.2: Typical example of a habitation experiment. First a scene is shown on the left in which a ball appears to jump over a fence. Next the two scenes on the right are shown. Babies look longer to the scene on the far right, even though in the middle scene the ball follows the same trajectory as in the left scene. This shows that they 'know' about goals and about what is plausible or not. (see [4])

the natural interest babies have in events or pictures they find surprising or novel, and to measure what infants do best: sucking or looking. One such technique is called "habituation" and involves showing an infant the same, or related, pictures or sequences over and over again. At first the baby spends a long time looking at the stimulus, but after several exposures the baby only glances briefly at them. At this point the baby is "bored" with the original image, and the experimenter presents a new one. If the infant categorises the new display as being different, it will return to its original long looking time. On the other hand, if it cannot perceive any difference, or if it regards the test display as the same kind of thing as the training one, it will continue to seem bored and show no return to the original long looking time. Measuring these differences in looking time can tell us about what infants know. Other methods that have proved successful rely on changes in the baby's sucking response on a dummy connected to a computer, or changes in heart rate. These kinds of experiments have taught us that during the first year babies come to know things like that objects are solid, continue to exist even when out of sight, and will fall downwards from table tops.

While such experiments can tell about the state of a baby's mind they cannot give us direct information about developments in the brain. Investigators interested in this question are somewhat more limited in the methods at their disposal. There are several reasons for this. First, while we have learned quite a lot from examining postmortem brain tissue through microscopes, such analyses are difficult and are based on small numbers. Second, children who unfortunately come to autopsy have often suffered from trauma or diseases that make generalisation to normal brain development difficult. Third, some of the methods used for studying the brain at work in adults (such as PET and fMRI) cannot be used with healthy infants. However, at last we have a safe and easy method for directly studying the workings of a baby's brain: so-called "high-density event-related potentials". The advent of this method offers the opportunity to obtain nonverbal "answers" to experimental situations with which we present the baby and promises to revolutionise the study of the baby's brain at work.

This method involves placing a "geodesic net" composed of a large number of passive sensors (electrodes) gently on to the head (see figure 5.3). These sensors pick up the natural electrical changes at the scalp as groups of neurons are activated within the brain. Their combined output generates a map of active regions across the baby's head. A computer can then calculate the likely brain sources that generated the voltages observed on the scalp. The geodesic net is quick to install, safe and comfortable to wear, making it ideal for use with infants. While this method is unlikely to rival the spatial accuracy of adult scanning methods, its resolution over time is much superior, allowing the study of brain events at the speed of

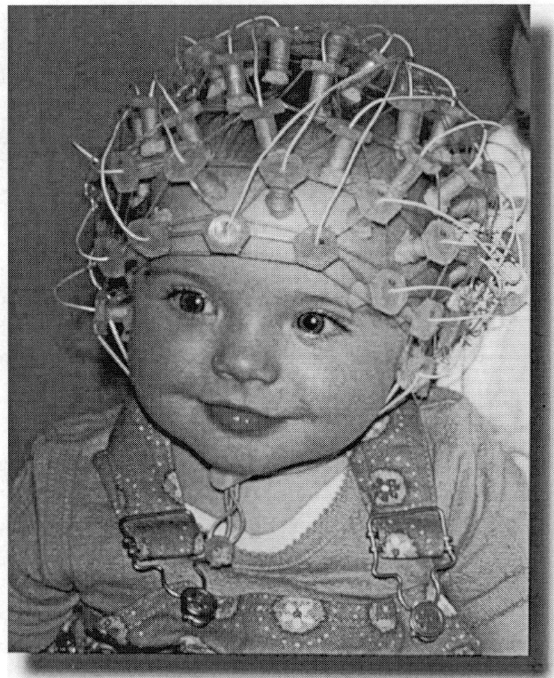

Figure 5.3: Geodesic net composed of passive electrodes put on a baby's head to measure brain events. Picture with permission from CBCD, Birkbeck College, UCL.

thought.

Brain Development

Using these methods a number of important findings have recently converged, which help us to determine whether the brain is a constructivist system or not.

- In a recent review of pre and postnatal brain development, Nelson and Bloom [14] summarise: "An unfortunate misconception of developmental neurobiology is that most aspects of brain development during the pre- and immediate postnatal periods reflects rigidly deterministic, genetic programs that are implemented at different points in time....this view is inappropriate for even the very earliest stages of brain development" (p.979).

- During both pre and postnatal life neural circuits, especially those within the cerebral cortex, are re-modelled in interaction with their input. Recent evidence indicates that during prenatal life much of this input comes from internally generated spontaneous activity (see Katz and Shatz [12] for review). With maturation of sense organs and input from the environment in postnatal life there is a gradual shift to effects of input from the external environment.

- Human brains do not contain any new structures or parts not found in other primates. Rather, our brain development is characterised by (i) greater volume, particularly in the cerebral cortex, and (ii) greatly slowed development, and in particular an extended period of postnatal plasticity (see [9] for review). This relatively delayed sequence of brain development makes our species more open to influence by interactions with the postnatal environment.

Thus, recent reviews of pre- and postnatal brain development have come to the conclusion that brain development is not merely a process of unfolding of a genetic plan, or a passive response to environmental input, but is an activity-dependent process at molecular, cellular, and organismal levels involving probablistic epigenesis (bi-directional relations between genes, brain, and behaviour). In humans this process extends further in to postnatal life than in other primates.

The "rise and fall" of brain development

Since the volume of the brain quadruples between birth and adulthood, it is not surprising that much of brain development involves adding new things. While most of the cells in the brain - neurons - are in place by around birth, during the first months there are dramatic increases in the conducting fibres that emanate from neurons, dendrites and axons, and in the junctions between neurons that pass on signals, i.e. synapses. Furthermore, nerve fibres become covered in a fatty myelin sheath which adds further to the bulk of the brain. Myelin is rather like the plastic covering around houshold electrical wires, and ensures good conductivity along the fibres. Perhaps the most obvious change to be seen through a microscope is the increase in size and complexity of the dendrites of neurons. Often the pattern of connections of a neuron appears to become more specific and specialised. Through more powerful electron microscopes, large increases in the density of synapses can be observed [8]. Such investigations have also revealed something quite unexpected.

Using various different methods, and looking at a number of measures, researchers have reported that later in infancy and childhood there are sometimes regressive or subtractive events during brain development. For example, in most regions of the cerebral cortex studied, the density of synapses increases until it is even greater than in adults (usually around 150Most of the changes in the brain discussed so far concern nerve cells and their patterns of connectivity. However, there are also developmental changes in the surrounding chemical bath, sometimes known as the "soft soak" aspects of the brain. Some of these changes in neurochemistry seem to mirror the rise and fall pattern [1].

How might these neural processes influence behaviour? Some have argued that similar processes of selective loss can be seen in behavioural studies of infants. For example, work on speech (phonemic) discrimination in infants (using a variant of the sucking procedure mentioned earlier) shows that while they initially discriminate a large range of phonemic boundries used in speech (such as "ba" and "da"), including those contrasts not found in their native language (such as "ra" and "la" in Japanese), this ability becomes restricted at around 12 months to those phonemes important for their native language. One explanation of these findings is that there is selective "pruning" of those contrasts which are not engaged by the infant's speech environment. While examples such as this seem convincing at first sight, there is much work to be done before these "selectionist" ideas become widely accepted. For one thing, recent experiments have shown that even as adults we never completely lose our speech discrimination abilities. For another thing, the neuroanatomical measures of synaptic density are but a static measure of a dynamic process. Since there is constant turnover (birth and death) of synapses throughout life, it is unlikely that there will be clearly distinct phases of growth and pruning.

Babies help to build their own brain

Another aspect of infant brain development worth highlighting is that, even while still in the womb, neuronal activity (the electrical firing of cells) is very important. In other words, brain development is not the passive unfolding of a genetic plan, but more of an activity-dependent process. For example, it has recently been discovered that the rhythmical waves of firing of groups of cells in the retina play an important role in helping to structure some of the parts of the brain involved in vision [12]. This activity is not generated by visual input, since the eyes are closed at this stage. Thus, one part of the nervous system appears to be creating a kind of "virtual environment" specifically to aid the development of other, later developing, parts.

Do similar activity-dependent processes occur during postnatal development? An illustrative example comes from research on face processing in infants. Experiments have shown that newborn infants (under an hour old) have a tendency to turn their head and eyes to look at faces more often than to most other complex patterns that have been studied [10]. Evidence suggests that this newborn behaviour is a reflex-like response controlled by some of the older subcortical parts of the brain. I have argued that this bias is sufficient to ensure that, in their natural physical and social environment, newborn infants will look more toward faces than at other objects over the first days and weeks of life. All this staring at faces serves a critical purpose in providing the necessary input for training some of the still developing "higher" parts of its brain within the cerebral cortex.

5.3 The case of face processing

One of the topics in which there has been considerable debate between nativist and empiricist perspectives concerns face recognition abilities in young infants. On the empiricist side of the debate, many studies supported the view that it takes the infant about two or three months to learn about the arrangement of features that compose a face. From this it was assumed that face processing was an acquired skill developed through prolonged exposure to faces.

On the nativist side, two lines of evidence are commonly invoked to support the idea of an "innate cortical module" for face processing. The first is that several studies have shown evidence that newborn human infants preferentially respond to face-like patterns. For example, it has been shown [10] that newborns around 10 minutes old would track, by means of head and eye movements, a face-like pattern further than various 'scrambled' face patterns. The second source of evidence comes from recent functional neuroimaging studies which show that particular regions of the cortex, such as the "fusiform gyrus face area", are specifically activated following the presentation of faces. The assumption is that such specificity within cortex results from genetic and molecular level interaction, and not visual experience.

As discussed in detail by Elman et al. [11] such assumptions can be erroneous. By considering evidence from biology, Morton and Johnson [13] presented an alternative, constructivist, account of the development of face processing in which they argued that there are at least two interacting brain systems in operation. One of these systems, termed Conspec, is present from birth and underlies the tendency for newborn infants to orient toward faces, while the other system was hypothesised to acquire information about faces through exposure to them. Importantly, the first system was argued to bias the input (preferentially toward faces) to the second system, thus ensuring that it specialised for learning about faces.

In developing their theory, Johnson and Morton used two sources of evidence from biology; evidence from the differential development of brain systems, and evidence from conspecific recognition in another species, the domestic chick. The primary source of evidence from other species (ethology) that we used to interpret the human infancy results concerned filial imprinting in the domestic chick, a process by which young precocial birds, such as chicks or ducklings, recognise and develop an attachment for the first conspicuous object that they see after hatching. The results of a series of experiments on the brain basis of imprinting led to the proposal that there are two independent neural systems that underlie filial preference in the chick. The first of these is a specific predisposition for the chick to orient toward objects resembling others of its own species. This system appears to be specifically tuned to the correct spatial arrangement of elements of the head and neck region, and is sufficient to pick out the mother hen from other objects the chick is likely to be exposed to in the first few days after hatching. The neural basis for this predisposition is currently unknown, but the optic tectum, the homologue of the mammalian superior colliculus, is a likely candidate.

The second brain system acquires information about the objects to which the young chick attends and involves a particular part of the chick forebrain called the IMHV (the IMHV is within a part of the chick brain similar to mammalian cortex). A variety of neurophysiological and behavioural manipulations, such as damage to the IMHV, have been shown to dissociate the two systems. In the natural environment, we argued, the first system ensures that the second system acquires information about the particular individual mother hen close by. In other words, the effective environment of the chick is changed such that it is biased more toward conspecifics than it would be otherwise.

The other source of biological data which we used to generate an account of human infant face recognition came from the postnatal development of the human cerebral neocortex. Both neuroanatomical and neurophysiological data indicate that visually guided behaviour in the newborn infant is largely mediated by subcortical structures such as the superior colliculus and pulvinar, and that it is not until 2 or 3 months of age that cortical circuitry comes to dominate subcortical circuits. Consistent with these arguments is the hypothesis that visually-guided behaviour in human infants, like that in domestic chicks, is based on activity in at least two distinct brain systems. Since these systems have distinct developmental time courses, then they may differentially influence behaviour in infants of different ages.

These two sources of biological evidence led Johnson and Morton ([13] to propose the two-process theory outlined above. The first process involves a system accessed via the subcortical visual pathway (but possibly also involving some cortical structures) and which underlies the preferential orienting to faces observed in newborns. However, the influence of this system over behaviour declines (possibly due to inhibition) during the second month of life. This is reflected in the fact that infants no longer preferentially track faces by 2 months [10]. The second process depends upon cortical maturity, and exposure to faces over the first month or so, and begins to influence infants behaviour and responses to faces in a graded manner from 2 to 4 months of age.

However, it remains possible that the "cortical module" for face processing is "pre-wired" by genetic interactions and that it is only activated by visual input or by neurochemical changes at 2 months of age. In order to differentiate between this notion and that of gradual specialisation, my colleagues and I conducted some experiments in which we examined the extent of cortical specialisation for face processing in six month old infants through the use of the geodesic net. This results of this study showed that while some degree of functional specialisation for face processing has taken place by six months of age, it still has not reached the adult level of localisation or specialisation. For example, the infants were less localised in their face processing than adults (e.g. they did not clearly show the right hemisphere localisation seen in adults) and less specialised (e.g. unlike adults they showed the same response to upright monkey faces that they did to upright human faces). This evidence that there are dynamic changes in the cortical processing of faces during the first year of life is more consistent with a process of gradual specialisation/localisation than the activation of a pre-exisiting specialised circuit.

Thus, in this example of human development at least three factors contribute to the specialisation that emerges; first, the primitive tendency of newborns to orient toward face-like patterns, second, the presence of many faces in the normal environment of the young infant, and third, the architecture of cerebral cortical circuits activated when faces are within the visual field. These three factors acting in concert ensure the inevitable outcome of a brain specialised for processing the biologically important stimulus of faces. This specialisation is not "coded for" by genes, or just the result of passive exposure to faces, but it is the result of an active process in which the infants own behaviour selects the appropriate input for its still developing brain.

5.4 Conclusions

The view that babies contribute to the increasing specialisation of their own brains also offers a different perspective on the ways that things can go wrong in development. If a critical part of the newborn's brain is not working correctly, this may have devastating knock-on effects: the initial problem could be compounded through the baby's increasingly abnormal interactions with its environment, resulting in deviant patterns of brain specialisation. But the malleability of the infant brain could also be its salvation. For if the specialisation of regions of the brain can be significantly modified by experience, there is at least some hope for finding ways of ensuring that the brain receives the appropriate inputs when, for whatever reason, the baby is unable to select them.

Bibliography

[1] Benes, F. M. (1994). Development of the corticolimbic system. In G¿ Dawson and K.W. Fischer (eds) Human Behaviour and the Developing Brain pp176-206 Guilford Press, New York.

[2] Bruner, J.S. (1963). Beyond the Information Given: Studies in the Psychology of Knowing. Norton, New York.

[3] Chugani, H. T., Phelps, M. E., and Mazziotta, J. C. (1987). Positron emission tomography study of human brain functional development. Annals of Neurology, 22, 487-497

[4] Csibra, G., Gergely, G., Biro, S., Koos, O., and Brockbank, M. (1999). Goal attribution without agency cues: The perception of 'pure reason' in infancy. Cognition, 72, 237-267.

[5] Dawkins, R. (1987). The Blind Watchmaker. Norton, New York.

[6] Elman, J., Bates, E., Johnson, M.H., Karmiloff-Smith, A., Parisi, D. and Plunkett, K. (1996). Rethinking Innateness: A connectionist perspective on development. Cambridge, MA: MIT Press.

[7] Gottlieb, G. (1992). Individual development and evolution. Oxford University Press, Oxford.

[8] Huttenlocher, P. R. (1994). Synaptogenesis, synapse elimination, and neural plasticity in human cerebral cortex: Threats to optimal development. In C. A. Nelson (Ed.), The Minnesota symposia on child psychology (pp. 35-54). Hillsdale, New Jersey: Lawrence Erlbaum Associates.

[9] Johnson, M.H. (1997). Developmental Cognitive Neuroscience: An Introduction. Blackwell, Oxford.

[10] Johnson, M. H., Dziurawiec, S., Ellis, H. D., and Morton, J. (1991). Newborns' preferential tracking of face-like stimuli and its subsequent decline. Cognition, 40, 1-19.

[11] Johnson, M.H. (1998). Developmental CognitiveNeuroscience: Looking ahead. Early Development and Parenting, 7, 163-169.

[12] Katz, L. C., and Shatz, C. J. (1996). Synaptic activity and the construction of cortical circuits. Science, 274, 1133.

[13] Morton, J., and Johnson, M. H. (1991). CONSPEC and CONLERN: A two-process theory of infant face recognition. Psychological Review, 98(2), 164-181.

[14] Nelson, C.A. and Bloom, F.E. (1997). Child development and neuroscience. Child Development, 68(5), 970-987.

Group Discussion 5
The Infant Brain

Factors in Brain Growth

Steels: Im very happy with this great hope that neuroscientists give us, namely that new cells can generate in the brain, that new connections evolve when the brain is given the right gymnastics, the right stimuli. So the brain is an adaptive system that continues to grow and shape itself like other living organisms.

Nevejan: Still, Im a bit puzzled by the fact that "an infant seeks out the inputs it needs". What about situations in which the children have no input or the wrong input?

Mogi: It can go wrong. But it is very difficult, almost impossible, to observe the infants attention with relation to all the inputs they get.

Johnson: We know that from birth babies will listen for much longer periods of time to speech then to 'scrambled sounds'. One of the methods used to investigate that is sucking. Babies are given things to suck on and they will suck more when they see an image they like or hear sounds, speech in this case, they like. Speech sounds are definitely something they prefer to listen to from birth on. Some even claim that this is due to the fact they heard it inside of the womb. That they develop preferences, thus that even some learning is already going on inside of the womb.

Punset: Some brain activation happens very early in life. But how is the physiological process of learning activated? You can study the birth of brain cells but that is not the most important aspect of learning. The most important thing is to figure out how on earth the learning process works. What happens in the brain? We dont know. We are all teaching, one way or another, and we dont know how the brain works for learning. This is one of the main issues. What happens when this brain is activated? Probably there is a big shock. A global disadjustment. For a brain it must be an incredible experience to face the sun, the street, the noises. So we are confronted with this global disadjustment and maybe education has to do with re-adjusting. Ways of establishing the re-adjustement. It would be very interesting to know more about how we learn. Not only when we are able to learn.

The Importance of Images

Punset: The other main thing is the importance of images. The brain works beautifully with images. Somebody once said that if Martians or other ET beings came to the earth, they would be astonished at the limitless memory capacities of the brain. If I would show you about 60.000 photographs throughout a day, the next day you will be able to perfectly recall a particular one. That is incredible! The same happens with our power of association. That is limitless. Since this is possible, the Martians will really wonder how come that these people do write and communicate in grey lines, some from left to right, from top to bottom, others from bottom up, from right to left. Very boring actually whereas we can manipulate masses of images with the brain. Maybe thats another aspect in learning that should be looked into.

Tokoro: Im not an expert, but with regard to the first part of your comment, I think learning is indeed a kind of adjustment. But it is the internal desire to act towards outside what it is about. It is not the negative side of adjustment, it is about learning what the outside world is, a positive or active desire to be a part of the world. This may not sound very scientific as an explanation, but still. With regard to your second comment, I agree that the memory for images is limitless. A certain image is not memorised in a certain spot, but in a wide area of memory, so it is very robust. Whereas logic or information are a very much abstract type of knowledge and very fragile because of the abstractness. Maybe a word that you havent used for a long time, will be forgotten. When I tell you that this is "kami", the Japanese word for paper, and Ill ask you tomorrow whether you remember what kami means, you probably wont know.

Nevejan: Maybe I will, because you just told me you will ask me about it tomorrow.

Tokoro: Yes, maybe because we share this moment, this situation, the same ground. And maybe you will remember tomorrow. But it is a very vulnerable kind of memory. But maybe the brain scientists around the table can say more about this.

Johnson: Skill learning shouldnt be pushed too far during the first years. You can even say that the visual input of the first months has effects for the rest of your life. They are quite subtle. You really have to look hard for them.

Punset: Is there any trace that the processing of visual images goes slower than the processing of sound for example?

Johnson: We know that babies brains work more slowly. They take longer to process any visual stimuli the first eight months or so. Nobody has yet done any direct comparison between sound and vision. There is some suggestion that young babies mix up their own senses. They dont know whether a source is vision or sound. So it seems like the senses are intermixed.

Tokoro: Is there any conflict between the findings of the existence of critical periods and your statement that the human brain develops itself gradually.

Johnson: The periods in the development of the human brain may be more stretched out in time. There are studies on infants that were blind in the first months of their lives. They could see after 3 or 6 months, but still then 10 years later, there were still subtle effects of this early blindness.

Coenen: Recently people who study the brain started to realise that there is a lot of implicit knowledge available to the mind but there is no direct easy conscious access to it. This explains for example why fire fighters sometimes run into a building and immediately send everybody out, while the building collapses a few seconds later. They cannot process all the data consciously but the data is there, the brain uses it. There is a lot of evidence now that people that have blind vision, i.e. cant see but can nevertheless point to certain things, are bypassing the conscious level.

Figure 5.4: Group discussion. There are individual differences between brains and minds. This needs to be taken into account by educators systems. From left to right Kerstin Dautenhahn, Mark Johnson, Olivier Coenen.

Individual Differences

Coenen: Different people have different brains. There are people whom you can show 100 images and they wont remember a single one. But if you give them a speech of an hour or two they will remember every word. There are people that associate certain sensations like vision with an odour or colours with number and shapes. Most of the time persons never know how the brain of the other person works. But in technology and if youre interacting with computers, then you can fine tune the teaching/learning experience and one person will be able to make more use of these analogies and thus will remember things a lot faster, they will interconnect things more easily.

Tokoro: Would this be a new technique for memorizing?

Coenen: It is about memorizing, but it is even more about understanding the differences between individual brains. For some people, the association of a colour and a number is totally void, for others it is a natural thing to do. It is about establishing your own language. Someone may be more artistic. She would prefer images to make clear what you go through. There are experiments with kittens who have been paralysed during the critical period of vision. They can see things but cannot move around. Later, when their visual critical period is over and the paralysis removed, the kitten will act as a blind kitten. Vision works while you are moving in the world. Your vision changes with your movements. So if you show a child a bottle of water, and it has never been able to touch water, its probably never going to understand the image of water. Just like when the so-called primitive people for the first time saw pictures, they didnt understand what they were. With technology we can have this complete virtual reality where you can also have touching and moving, it doesnt have to be completely artificial either, it could be a real environment but where you add images and objects because then you allow the person to learn from so many different domains and you are not restricted to purely physical environments.

Nevejan: Are you suggesting that learning happens because something changes, something moves?

Coenen: A person will react to a certain input when she can relate it to another one. So in the case of vision, if vision never had a purpose or utility than the brain would not properly store it.

Coenen: Our brains are very complex but we can still understand little bits and pieces, just like we can understand genes and what they do. And then there are all the interactions which makes the whole system even more complex, but still we can do things. We apparently have 3r0.9 00 up to 100.000 genes depending on estimates and we have this incredible diversity across all humans. The complexity comes from the interactions between proteins. Like very simple bacteria have only interactions of two or more proteins whether humans have multiple. So there is some hope to try to understand in little bits and pieces what is happening in the brain and then put that together, despite the enormous diversity in human brains.

Chapter 6

Onceness

by Ken Mogi

Ken Mogi is a physicist and neurobiologist working at the Sony Computer Science Laboratory in Tokyo, which he joined after researching at the University of Cambridge. He focuses on neural correlates of the conscious experience of visual phenomena (qualia).

Figure 6.1: The Philosophers Walk. Kyoto, Japan.

The Philosophers Walk

There is a small path in the east of Kyoto known as the Philosophers Walk (figure 6.1). Kitaro Nishida (1870-1945), a famous philosophy professor at University of Kyoto, used to frequent this path. Legend has it that Nishida had many inspirations (most of them presumably philosophical) while walking along this path. Even by the standards of this tradition rich ancient capital, this small path is almost too perfect to be true. It meanders alongside a small brook, and there are dozens of ancient temples and shrines on the way, including the exquisite Silver Pavilion.

Given the awesome myth surrounding the Philosophers Walk, it is no wonder that many people visit there to seek a source for inspiration. I was no exception. I made the pilgrimage several times, expecting to have some wonderful insight. To my disappointment, I usually failed to have any extraordinary inspiration while on the path. Sure, you come across some small thoughts, but thats it. The Philosophers Walk, as an incubator for wonderful inspirations, falls very short of the expectations you would have from the legends of Kitaro Nishida.

You may point out that only a special thinker like Nishida can have deep inspirations, no matter how stimulating the Philosophers Walk may be. That may indeed be the case. Meanwhile, while contemplating the Philosophers Walk as a stimulant for inspirations, I noticed something. When I do have an inspiration while walking, no matter how humble, typically the environment is something familiar and commonplace. For example, while I am walking from my Tokyo home to the nearest subway station, I do sometimes stumble on a new idea. It appears, in my case at least, that a commonplace, familiar path is a good stimulant for inspirations, much better than the wonderful Philosophers Walk in Kyoto.

How could this be? How could a series of mediocre streets in the Tokyo suburb be superior to the Philosophers Walk in Kyoto in nurturing inspirations? I began to think about this phenomenon, and I soon came to a hypothesis.

It appears that the lack of interesting stimulus in the surrounding, rather than an abundance of it, is a necessary condition for nurturing creative thoughts. Why dont I have any inspirations while walking along the Philosophers Walk? It is because the path is too interesting for me. My brain is so busy taking in and analyzing the interesting scenery along the path, that resources are scarcely left in the brain to generate new ideas. For the philosopher Nishida, on the other hand, everything on the path was familiar. He took the walk almost every day. His brain did not have to analyze the scenery "online". You can even venture to say that he must have been bored. This particular path in Kyoto was a Philosophers Walk for Nishida, not because it had any special merit, but because it happened to be the path that this philosopher walked along every day. Nishida was bored into creativity, so to speak.

In a similar sense, the path that I take every day to go to work is a Philosophers Walk for me. For every person, his or her Philosophers Walk is the path that they frequent in their daily life. You dont have to travel all the way to Kyoto to have an inspiration. Some time ago, I talked about my interpretation of the secret of the Philosophers Walk in a conference. After my talk, an American professor living in the Prairies came up to me. He said the road from his home to the University to his house was his Philosophers Walk. It is not a walk, to be precise. He rides the bicycle to go to work.

Cramming and laissez faire.

Needless to say, we cannot create something from nothing. The brain must take in many materials from the environment to initiate a creative process. "If I have seen further it is by standing upon the shoulders of giants." This statement of Isaac Newton illustrates the importance of learning the achievements of the past, even for the most creative minds among humans. Absorbing stimulating materials from the rich cultural traditions is a necessary condition to create. But then finally, somehow, the magic formula for creativeness seems to be an absence of stimulants, rather than an abundance of it. The brain must somehow be left to its self, freed from the need of online information processing, to kick start the creative process.

This gives us something to think about educating a child. It seems that we need to strike a delicate balance between exposing the child to a rich cultural tradition and "laissez faire." The lesson from Philosophers Walk is that we should not "overdo it" in education. If a child is just pressed to cram, then his or her brain cannot have a space of freedom it needs to nurture a creative idea. The child must be given an adequate input of cultural heritage (that is what we usually call education), and then be left to pursue his or her creative impulse. It is the "laissez faire" part that most educators and parents find difficult.

The Aha! Experience

At present, we do not know exactly what is happening in the brain when somebody has an inspiration, ranging from the humble inspiration on what to eat for lunch, to finding a new solution to Einsteins equation of gravity.

By the very nature of creative insights, it is difficult to study it scientifically. Science is about repeatability. Creativity is not about repeatability. When you come across an idea, something irreversible occurs in your brain. Your brain is in a different state than before. You cannot request the brain to go back to the "before" state and measure the creative process over

Figure 6.2: There is a hidden figure which suddenly becomes clear in this very famous picture.

again. "Onceness" characterizes a creative process, and it is difficult to study it scientifically, though not impossible in principle.

Cognitive scientists approach the problem of creativity by focusing on the more daily occurrence of the so-called "aha!" experiences. When you see figure 6.2, it is very probable that you immediately see a dalmatian in it.

The brain somehow interprets the pattern of blacks and whites as a meaningful scene. The figure is often quoted as an illustration of the fact that the brain does not take in visual information in a passive manner, but rather actively tries to incorporate it into the internal world model.

Figure 6.3 illustrates the brains active way of seeing something in a more dramatic way. If you already know what is in it, you "see" it immediately when presented with the figure. If, however, you do not know what is in the figure, you may find it very difficult to see "it". Actually, when you realize for the first time what is in it, you are likely to experience a strong feeling. You will probably have that enigmatic "aha!" experience the moment you realize what is in the picture.

As an ambiguous figure is relatively easy to produce, and as the experiments can be repeated, the perception of ambiguous figures have been one of the active subjects of cognitive science. What is happening in the brain when you realize that something is in the picture?

Francisco Varela and his colleagues reported a nice study of what happens in your brain when you realize that something meaningful is in an ambiguous figure. They presented the subjects with the so-called "Mooney" faces. These figures are easy to recognize as faces when presented in upright orientation, but more difficult to recognize when presented upside down. Varelas group studied the electroencephalogram (EEG) of the brain as the subjects viewed the Mooney faces either upright or upside down. In a landmark paper, they reported that long range synchronization of neural activities occurred only when the subjects recognized a face.

Namely, it appears that when we realize that something meaningful is in the picture, when

Figure 6.3: Can you see what is in this figure?

we have that "aha" experience, neurons in a wide range of regions in the brain fire at the same time, resulting somehow in the perception of something hitherto unperceived. Although we do not know the exact mechanism yet, neural synchronization is possibly the hallmark of the perception of ambiguous figures.

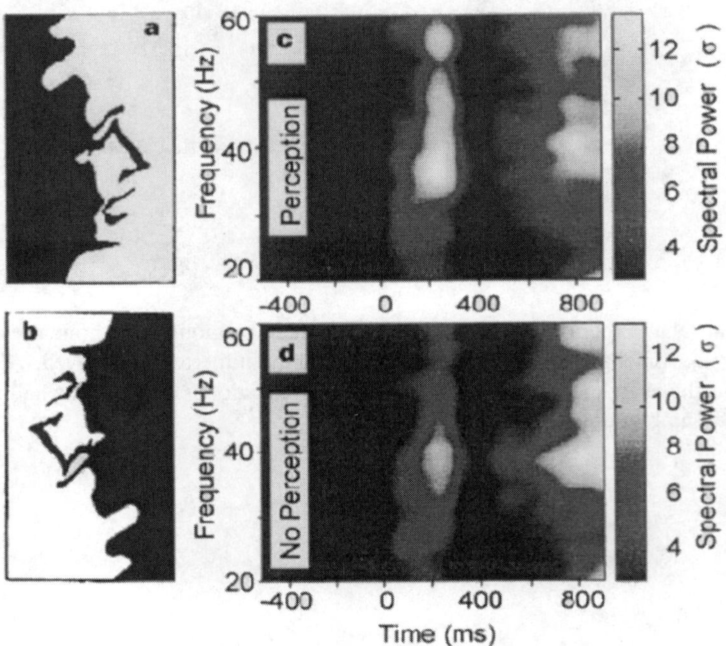

Figure 6.4: Neural synchronization (top right) only happens when a coherent image is experienced (top left). When the same image is seen upside down (bottom left) no synchronisation is observed (bottom right). (With permission from Nature 397, p.431 (1999))

Aha! Sentences.

Now it is time to let the truth out, for those who remained uneasy. Heres the give away. Figure 6.3 is called "Dallenbachs cow". Well, so there is a cow in it. Can you now see it? Even with this knowledge, some people find it difficult to see the cow in the picture. It actually took me a few minutes the first time I saw it. But once you realize that theres a cows face on the left side of the picture, with a fence behind it, and the cows body on the right side, it is difficult to perceive the picture otherwise. "Dallenbachs cow" is a beautiful example of what a difference an active intrepretation process can make in the perception of an ambiguous figure, and how an "aha!" experience changes the perception once and for all.

The so-called "aha sentences" invented by Soraci and others are tools to explore the "aha" experience in a more cognitive domainlanguage. Aha sentences are such sentences that are difficult to understand by itself, but easily interpretable when given an additional cue. For example, the following sentence does not make any sense by itself. "The haystack was important because the cloth ripped." However, when the solution clue "parachute" is given, suddenly everything becomes clear. Similarly, this sentence does not make sense: "The girl spilled her popcorn because the lock broke." With the clue "lion cage", everything becomes clear again.

Soraci and his colleagues originally found that when a sentence is presented as a "aha sentence", it is more likely to be remembered than an ordinary sentence. Recently, they reported that this memory effect probably correlates with a characteristic signal element of the EEG, the so-called N100 (a negative-going peak at 100 msec after stimulus presentation). It is possible that this signal is also related to a large scale synchronization of neural activities in the brain, the kind of activity change that Varela and his colleagues reported.

The Enigma of creativity

Based on these and other evidence, we may surmise that when we have an aha experience, neurons fire together in synchrony all over the brain.

Can we go further and assume that something similar is happening in a creative process? Sure, neural synchrony might be one of the key properties of the creative process. Needless to say, however, we still have to go a long way from the cow or an "aha! sentence" to really come to grips with the enigma of human creativity. After all, creative minds produced such scientific wonders as Newtons laws of motion, Einsteins theory of relativity. We can just sigh at the master works of artistic genius like Vermeer. Cynics may laugh when somebody like Roger Penrose claim that creativity is an access to the Platonic world. But they must also secretly believe that there is something to creativity than meets the eye.

In a more practical vein, as we learned from the Philosophers walk, creative process thrives in the absence of stimulus, rather than in the presence of it. To understand what happens in the brain in the absence of stimulus is a difficult task for cognitive science. Cognitive science has progressed in the past by describing how the brain processes a particular stimulus. If a process (the creative process in this case) occurs only in the absence of stimuli, it becomes difficult to study it, as it is difficult to control the experiment.

The conclusion of this short essay on creativity is that it is likely that when you have a creative idea, neurons in your brain are somehow firing all together. And you are likely to go into that state when your brain is released from analyzing your environment online. So I hope you would relax and take a walk in your familiar environment.

Group Discussion 6
The AHA Experience

Limits of the Reductionist Method

Nevejan: As we have seen also in the contribution of Coenen, a driving force for learning is that you have to feel good yourself. Ken Mogi is right to focus on the 'aha'-erlebnis. It is amazing that you can actually see in the brain whether you are feeling good. It is a crucial thing, this moment that you suddenly see it. That you see something you didnt realise or saw before. And its wonderful that you can actually prove there is such a thing with images from hard core research.

In the mean time, its what I fear the most. Like with mood-tracking or emotional intelligence. Sometimes I think, OK, thats enough! There is more complexity to human beings than everything you can measure or automate. Luc Steels and Kerstin Dautenhahn are building machines to teach me something about cognition and then I think: hold on a minute! I feel like I have to defend a certain sacredness of being a human, of life itself. I prefer a more complex psychology then. I want to fight on the barricades for this. Because one of the awful things that can happen is that we regard people as too simple, too scalable. Its no solution to create 1 million Aha-erlebnissen in the brain for 100.000 people. That cannot be the idea. So I think that it is very important to keep the complexity and the richness of our own being, which is why we act well in a rich environment in the first place. Its not only because of the environment, its because our own complexity needs that.

Steels: You are very right. Science dissects small aspects of a phenomenon and tries to understand that. As pointed out earlier by Mario Tokoro, science, particularly in the past, has been very reductionist. That is when it works best. One advantage with robotic models is that we can study complete agents in full interaction with a complex world. We can study complex systems because we can make a model of many parts: the vision system, speech processing, associative memory, etc. and see what happens when it is all put together. But still, I agree very much that human beings are holistic organisms where everything is connected to everything else. If something is measured in the brain it is not clear whether we are measuring a side effect or a causative process. Things can become dangerous if we let too much depend on one-sided measurements. It is too reductionistic.

Values in Education

Nevejan: It also ignores values. Values should be the starting point. For example, the 'ideal' well-functioning family is disappearing. In Holland they say schools not only have to educate, they have to raise the children. The parents are at work and there is no social environment. When we think of broadband, when there is all the audio and visual material we can imagine and when we can do everything live, there is still the question where the quality feedback on their and our values will come from. Values are culture-specific. So I dont know whether they can become global and I dont know whether we want them to become global. And I dont know whether if we ignore this issue, we will have a completely worthless educational space. So the solution that we ourselves take while developing broadband is that we consider the virtual and the physical as one space. People can only design or develop stuff for an integrated learning environment, it always has physical and virtual elements. You can

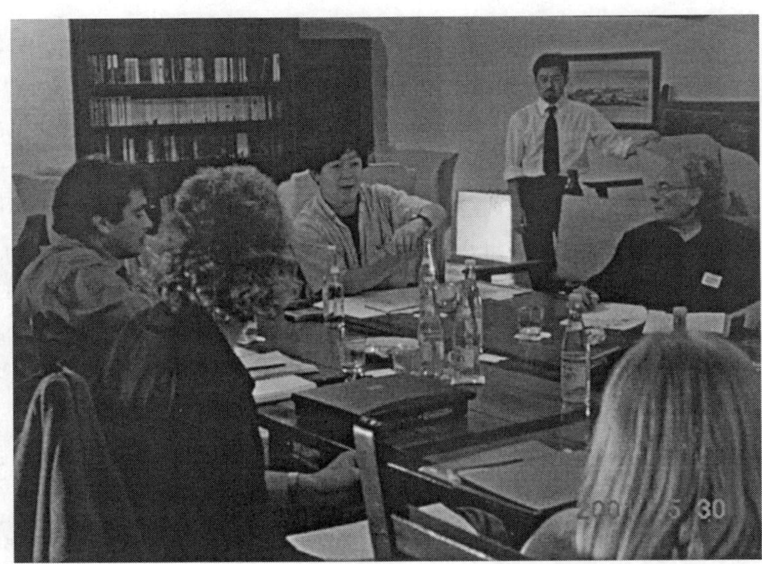

Figure 6.5: Group discussion. Ken Mogi argues that the Aha-experience, which can be measured as a significant event in the brain, might give us crucial insights into what happens during learning.

never design one without the other. I really wonder whether some values can become global or whether we can make neutral environments in which children will be able to learn. The values in Africa are different from those in America. Maybe it will become one world but then we will loose a lot of texture, a lot of richness. We are facing an enormous dilemma.

Allien: We must make sure not to ignore the specificity of each person when he or she is online.

Nevejan: Yes, but maybe you dont want to include this in the computer, you want to keep it out.

Allien: As you said yourself, the computer is not a learning center, its just a tool. Its just a very prosaic tool like the telephone. But not to respect the range of moods the users go through is a mistake I think. So we should try to integrate more complexity in different ways. By the voice of the user, the speed he or she operates the device with, or the way of using the mouse for instance. You can find out a lot about a person this way and use that to adapt the behavior of the computer.

Nevejan: But I vehemently oppose the notion that you can do this by observing a persons behaviour at the keyboard! Psychology has proven that over the last 20, 30 years in moving from the diagnosis of one person to relational family therapy. The diagnosis of one person in an isolated situation, like somebody sitting in front of a keyboard, doesnt give you a clue about what is really going on psychologyically speaking. You have to look at psychology in a much more complex way.

Allien: The context is very important. But if you dont take the interface into account, you rule out a very important element. You have to remain very open to understand the person and the context.

Punset: Probably the history of civilisation is a history of putting into the automation process as many things as possible, so that you have time to think. And then you start using your thoughts, your reasoning capacities, which is the most beautiful thing you have. But I see lots of examples of people suffering today in companies just because they have rationalised and automated various processes that do not need this sort of thing.

Allien : True. We should avoid reductionism. We should not summarize because summarizing in one way or another is always a reduction. And that is very frustrating. In my own life Im very frustrated to be too much into implementation. Im frustrated that I cannot go more into fundamental things. And when I am being fundamental, Im very frustrated too, because I want to implement. Its a permanent feedback.

Punset : What we should try to avoid in the following years is rationally automate too many processes. We dont need this bloody logic. Most things go very well by themselves. Let these automatic and unconscious processes flow because most of what we find comes naturally anyhow.

Gender Differences

Coenen : Different kind of people have different ways of thinking and technology may be a tool that can be a specifically adapted system to do so. There are studies on rats where they stress them by electric shocks and the amazing thing is that the male rats will typically do better afterwards on a learning task whereas the female rats usually do a lot worse. The results remains very consistent and it apparently has to do with the oestrogen hormones. The research that was done on the flight attendants, was on female flight attendants. So it might not apply to male attendants. Over the years of evolution it is possible that male and female responses to stress were tuned for different situations. That the females were trying to avoid stressful situations as a way of survival, which is very speculative I admit but Im just reflecting on this. What I want to state is that maybe we should make a difference between the sexes.

Rinaldi: The brain is considered to be neutral. But the question that we need to answer is whether there are gender differences. That is very important for schools. I am not talking about a feminist approach to the problem but about differences that we can notice, also in approaching computers. The computer is changing our epistemology of learning but its use seems to be very much influenced by gender. We should really look into that.

Nevejan: Do you mean by epistemology how we learn or what we learn?

Carla: The learning processes.

Wynants: Children learn a lot from each other. This is sometimes referred to as "the hidden program". But although there is no doubt about the virtues of co-education, research has shown that boy-boy teams or girl-girl teams work better than mixed teams. The quality of collaboration and interaction between the children was much lower for the mixed pairs.

Theme IV

Learning Must Be Social

Play. Ezra, age 9

With a 'MacDonald's culture' all over the world, where do we expect new ideas and creativity to come from? Ideas are not born from scratch, they come from blending inputs from many different sources. I work with robots and I would certainly like to avoid a world in which you have this one robotic toy imposed on everybody. Whether it is for pure entertainment or for education, I would like to see new robots, or any new technology for that matter, contribute to building cultural contexts that give rise to diversity and identity.

Kerstin Dautenhahn

Chapter 7

Social Language Learning

by Luc Steels

Luc Steels is director of the Sony Computer Science Laboratory in Paris and professor of Artificial Intelligence at the University of Brussels (VUB). Steels researches the origins and learning of language through computational and robotic models. He has developed the framework of evolutionary language games as a way to study the acquisition of concepts and language grounded and situated in experience. The framework allows a systematic study of transactional learning and could lead to novel learning environments for language acquisition.

This paper explores a theory of learning which emphasises social interaction and cultural context. The theory contrasts with individualistic theories of learning, where the learner is either seen as passively receiving large sets of examples and performing some sort of induction to arrive at abstract concepts and skills, or as a genetically pre-programmed organism where the role of the environment is restricted to setting some parameters. I focus the discussion on the question how meaning is constructed, in other words how people go from information to knowp ofledge. I am particularly interested how grounded meaning arises, i.e. meaning anchored in sensori-motor experiences. This is the question raised earlier (in Chapter 1) in the discussion on how information turns into knowledge. I am also interested in how shared meanings can be developed through communication and negotiation. The meanings used by a speaker cannot directly be observed by the listener, so how can a listener who does not know the meaning of words ever learn them?

The paper explores social and cultural learning using a novel methodology, namely the construction of artificial systems, i.e. robots, that implement certain theoretical assumptions and hence allow us to examine with great precision how certain learning mechanisms work and what they can achieve or not achieve. Some implications for education are presented towards the end.

7.1 The Origins of Meaning

It has been argued that one of the main objectives for children, particularly in primary school, is learning how to create meaning. This starts from a first magical moment around the agent of 18 months [16], but continues throughout childhood. As pointed out by Loris Malaguzzi (see Chapter 3 by Carla Rinaldi), the child is a semiologist who invents new meanings, and negotiates words to talk about these meanings with friends or parents and teachers. Also later in secondary school and higher education, the acquisition of new meanings and ways to communicate them is a crucial skill. For example, it could be argued that all significant advances in science arise from conceptual breakthroughs. My objective is to understand this creative semiological process in much more detail so that we can help children to acquire crucial semiological skills.

Let me start by summarising the intense debates that have taken place in the cognitive science literature over past decades on this question of the origins of meaning. These debates echo the nature/nurture debate and the discussion of a constructivist synthesis introduced by Johnson in this contribution (see Chapter 5).

Labelling versus Social Grounding

There are basically two main lines of thinking on the question of how language and meaning are bootstrapped: individualistic learning and social learning. In the case of individualistic learning, the child is assumed to have experienced, as input, a large number of example cases where speech is paired with specific situations. They either already mastering the necessary concepts or are able to extract through an inductive learning process what is essential to and recurrent in these situations, in other words to learn the appropriate categories underlying language, and then associate these categories with words. This is known as cross-situational learning [13]. Others have proposed a form of contrastive learning based on the same sort of data, driven by the hypothesis that different words have different meanings [8]. This type of individualistic learning assumes a rather passive role of the language learner and little feedback given by the speaker. It assumes no causal influence of language on concept formation.

Figure 7.1: Children can solve problems through social interactions which none of them can solve individually. Interacting together with the physical world is part of play. It is as necessary and insightful as instructional learning. (mw)

I call it the labelling theory because the language learner is assumed to associate labels with existing categories.

The labelling theory is remarkably widespread among researchers studying the acquisition of communication, and recently various attempts have been made to model it with neural networks or symbolic learning algorithms [4]. It is known that induction by itself is a weak learning method, in the sense that it does not give identical results from the same data and may yield irrelevant clustering compared to human categories. To counter this argument, it is usually proposed that innate constraints help the learner zoom in on the important aspects of the environment.

In the case of social learning, interaction with other human beings is considered crucial ([5], [35], [30]). Learning is not only grounded in reality through a sensori-motor apparatus but also socially grounded through interactions with others. The learning event involves an interaction between at least two individuals in a shared environment. They will henceforth be called the learner and the mediator. The mediator could be a parent and the learner a child, but children (or adults) can and do teach each other just as well. Given the crucial role of the mediator, I also call social learning mediated learning. The goal of the interaction is not really teaching, which is why I use the term mediator as opposed to teacher. The goal is rather something practical in the world, for example, to identify an object or an action. The mediator helps the goal to be achieved and is often the one who wants to see the goal achieved.

The mediator has various roles: They set constraints on the situation to make it more manageable (scaffolding), give encouragement on the way, provide feedback, and act upon the consequences of the learner's actions. Even though language is being learned, the feedback is not directly about language, and is certainly not about the conceptualisations implicitly underlying language. The latter are never visible. The learner cannot telepathically inspect the internal states of the speaker and the mediator cannot know which concepts are already known to the learner. Instead feedback is pragmatic, that means in terms of whether the goal has been realised or not. Consider a situation where the mediator says: "Give me that pen", and the learner picks up a piece of paper instead of the pen. The mediator might say: "No, not the paper, the pen", and point to the pen. This is an example of pragmatic feedback. It is not only relevant to succeed subsequently in the task, but supplies the learner with information relevant for acquiring new knowledge. The learner can grasp the referent from the context and situation, hypothesise a classification of the referent, and store an association between the classification and the word for future use. While doing all this, the learner actively tries to guess the intentions of the mediator of which there are two sorts. The learner must guess what the goal is that the mediator wants to see realised (like 'pick up the pen on the table'), and the learner must guess the way that the mediator has construed the world [20]. Typically the learners use themselves as a model of how the mediator would make a decision and adapts this model when a discrepancy arises.

Social learning enables active learning. The learner can initiate a kind of experiment to test knowledge that is uncertain, or fill in missing holes. The mediator is available to give direct concrete feedback for the specific experiment done by the learner. This obviously speeds up the learning, compared to a passive learning situation where the learner simply has to wait until examples arise that would push the learning forward.

The Relation between Language and Meaning

The debate between individualistic versus social learning is related to the equally hotly debated question as to whether or not there is a causal role for language in concept learning. From the viewpoint of the labelling theory, the acquisition of concepts occurs independently of and prior to language acquisition, either because concepts are innate (nativism) or because they are acquired by an inductive learning process (empiricism) [17]. So there is no causal role of language. Conceptualisation and verbalisation are viewed as operating in independent modules which have no influence on each other [14]. The acquisition of words is seen as a problem of learning labels for already existing concepts.

Concerning then the issue of how the concepts themselves are acquired, two opposing schools of thought can be found: nativism and empiricism. Nativists like Fodor [14] claim that concepts, particularly basic perceptually grounded concepts, are innate and so there is no learning process necessary. They base their arguments on the poverty of the stimulus [6], the fundamental weakness of inductive learning, and the lack of clear categorial or linguistic feedback. Empiricists claim that concepts *are* learned, for example by statistical learning methods implemented as neural networks [10]. Thus a large number of situations in which a red coloured object appears are seen by the learner, and clustered into 'natural categories'. These natural categories then form the basis for learning word meaning. An intermediate position is found with constructivists, who see a steady interplay between genetic constraints and learning processes (see Chapter 5 by Johnson and [11]), but still view the learner very much as individually bootstrapping their knowledge.

The alternative line of thinking, which is often adopted by proponents of social learning, claims that there *is* a causal role for culture in concept acquisition and that this role is particularly (but not exclusively) played through language. This has been argued both by lin-

Figure 7.2: From the viewpoint of a social approach to learning, interaction beween learners and mediators is absolutely crucial, particularly for the acquisition of language. (mw)

guists and philosophers. In linguistics, the position is known as the Sapir-Whorf thesis. It is based on evidence that different languages in the world not only use different word forms and syntactic constructions but that the conceptualisations underlying language are profoundly different as well [34]. Language acquisition therefore is believed to go hand in hand with concept acquisition [3]. Moreover language-specific conceptualisations change over time in a cultural evolution process, which in turn causes grammatical evolution that may induce further conceptual change [18].

This does not mean that there are no similarities between the underlying conceptualisations of different languages. For example, the distinction between objects (things, people) on the one hand and events (actions, state changes) on the other appears universal [37]. Similarly many categorial dimensions like space, time, aspect, countability, kinship relations, etc., are lexicalised in almost all languages of the world, even though there may be differences in how this is done. Thus, some languages lexicalise kinship relations as nouns (like English: father) and others as verbs [12]. But profound conceptual differences in the way different languages conceptualise reality are not hard to find ([34], [3]) and they also show up in other cognitive tasks such as memory tests [9]. For example, the conceptualisation of the position of the car in "the car is behind the tree" is just the opposite in most African languages. The front of the tree is viewed as being in the same direction as the face of the speaker and hence the car is conceptualised as in front of the tree as opposed to behind the tree [18]. These examples suggest that different human cultures invent their own ways to conceptualise reality and propagate it through language, implying a strong causal influence of language on concept formation. Note that a causal influence of language acquisition on concept formation does not imply that all concepts undergo this influence or that there are no concepts prior to the beginning of language acquisition. In fact, there are probably millions of concepts used in sensori-motor control, social interaction, emotion, etc., which are never lexicalised. The main point here is that for those concepts underlying natural language communication, this causal influence not only exists but is necessary, i.e. these concepts necessarily have a cultural dimension.

Ludwig Wittgenstein is the best known philosophical proponent of a causal influence of language on meaning. His position is in a sense even more radical than the Sapir-Whorf thesis. He argued that meanings are an integrated part of the situated context of use. Thus the word "ball" not only includes a particular conceptualisation of reality in order to refer to a certain type of object but is also a move in a language game, indicating that the speaker wants a particular action to be carried out. Moreover the meaning of "ball" is not abstract at all, i.e. something of the sort 'spherical shaped physical object of a uniform colour', but is very context-dependent, particularly in the first stages. This point has also been made by Quine who argued that basic notions such as object-hood only gradually arise. Children do not start with the pre-given clean abstract categories that adults appear to employ.

7.2 How to Study Learning?

There is a long tradition in psychology that studies learning by observing learning behaviour, particularly that of children, or by performing experiments in which human subjects have to learn something and their performance is monitored. More recently, research in Artificial Intelligence has advanced sufficiently or it to become possible to use an alternative approach. It is now possible to take a particular learning method claimed to be effective for a certain task, turn it into an artificial system (typically a computer program), feed it with the data that a human learner is supposed to have, and see whether the learning method is up to the task. Often the learning method or its implementation attempt to be faithful to human behavioral data or compatible with what is known about the brain.

The Methodology of the Artificial

This methodology has also been applied to the question of meaning and language acquisition (see [4]). However, these modelling efforts so far mainly use an individualistic approach with passive, observational learning. Precise models for social learning are lacking. In the absence of such models, it is difficult to compare the different positions in the debate seriously without sliding into rhetoric. The first goal of my work has therefore been to develop concrete models of social learning and compare their behavior to individualistic learning. What is also lacking are experiments to test the cultural influence of language on meaning creation and propagation. And so my second goal has been to develop precise models showing that cultural influence and context-dependent meaning creation are indeed the most plausible and effective way for individuals to bootstrap themselves into a language culture.

Previous work in the computational modelling of language learning has been entirely based on software simulations. Given the enormous complexity of the cognitive processing required for language, even for handling single words, computer simulations are the only way one can test formal models. But if one believes in the importance of embodiment, social interaction, and the necessity of grounding language in the world, we must go one step further and use autonomous mobile robots. We can then try to set up experiments where autonomous robots, in strong interaction with humans and grounded in the world through a physical sensori-motor apparatus, develop language-like communication systems. If the robots manage to do this, then we have discovered a plausible way in which language is bootstrapped. Recent dramatic advances in robotics technology have made this approach feasible, even though of course it requires building very complex systems, and the remainder of this paper is based on experience gained with such experiments.

To many social scientists, the idea of using autonomous robots for testing theories of cognition and communication is very unusual and they are very sceptical that anything could come out of it. But there are important advantages:

1. The experiments force us to make every claim or hypothesis about assumed internal structures and processes very concrete and so it is clear how the theoretical assumptions have been operationalised.

2. We can use real-world situations, i.e. physical objects, human interactions, etc., to get realistic presuppositions and realistic sources of input. This is particularly important when studying social learning, which relies heavily on the intervention of the mediator, grounded in reality.

3. We can extract data about internal states of the learning process, which is not possible with human beings. Internal states of children going through a developmental or learning process cannot be observed at all.

4. We can easily examine alternative hypotheses. For example, we can compare what an individualistic inductive learning process would achieve with the same data as a social learning process.

But there are obviously also important limits to this methodology:

1. We cannot begin to pretend that robotic experiments model children in any realistic way, nor the environments in which they typically operate. But our goal is to compare theories of how language and communication develop, so realism is not an issue.

2. It is an extraordinary challenge to build and maintain physical robots of the required complexity. For practical reasons (limitations of camera resolution, memory and processing power available on board) we cannot always use the best known algorithms available today. This puts limits on what can be technically achieved today and so experiments need to be designed within these limits.

AIBO's first words

Together with a number of collaborators, in particular Frederic Kaplan, I have been using various kinds of robots in experiments that try to reconstruct the very beginning of language and meaning. The experiments discussed further in this paper are based on an enhanced version of the Sony AIBO^{TM}robot (see figure 7.3). This robot is fully autonomous and mobile with more than a thousand behaviors, coordinated through a complex behavior-based motivational system. The AIBO features 4-legged locomotion, a camera for visual input, two microphones, and a wide variety of body sensors, as well as on-board batteries and the necessary computing power. We have chosen this platform because the AIBO is one of the most complex autonomous robots currently in existence but nevertheless reliable enough for systematic experiments due to the industrial standards to which it has been designed and built. Moreover the AIBO is designed to encourage interaction with humans, which is what we need for experiments in social human-robot interaction. It comes with a very wide range

Figure 7.3: Our robot is an enhanced version of the commercially available AIBO. It is linked to an additional computer through a radio connection.

of capabilities which are necessary to establish the conditions for social interaction, such as the ability to look at an object as a way to draw attention of the speaker to the object.

The experiments discussed further in this paper, described in more detail in [31] work on an enhanced version of the AIBO because there is not enough computing power on-board to do them. We decided to keep the original autonomous behavior of the robot and build additional functionality on top of it. Our system thus acts as a cognitive layer which interferes with the already available autonomous behavior, without controlling it completely. A second computer implements speech recognition facilities which enable interactions using spoken words. In order to avoid recognition problems linked with noise, the mediator uses an external microphone to interact with the robot. The computer also implements a protocol for sending and receiving data between the computer and the robot through a radio link. The mediator must take into account the global "mood" of the robot as generated by the autonomous motivational system. For example, it is possible that a session becomes very ineffective because the robot is in a "lethargic" mood.

By using real-world autonomous robots, our experiments differ from other computational experiments in word learning (such as [24]) in which situation-word pairs are prepared in advance by the human experimenter, and even more from more traditional connectionist word learning experiments, where meanings are explicitly given by a human. Here we approach much more closely the conditions of a one year old child who is moving around freely with no preconception of what the meaning of a word might be. In fact, we tackle a situation which is even more difficult than that of a child, because we assume that the robot has not yet acquired any concepts that could potentially be used or adapted for language communication.

7.3 Language Games

In previous work we found that the notion of a game, and more specifically a language game, is a very effective way to frame social and cultural learning [30]. A game is a routinised sequence of interactions between two agents involving a shared situation in the world. Psychological research into the transition from pre-linguistic to linguistic communication has found clear evidence for an important role of game-like interactions, which initially are purely based on gestures, before including vocalisations that then become words [15]. The players in a language game have different roles. There are typically various objects involved and participants need to maintain the relevant representations during the game, e.g., what has been mentioned or implied earlier. The possible steps in a game are called moves. Each move is appropriate in circumstances determined by motivations and long term objectives and the opportunities in the concrete situation, just like a move in a game of chess. Games are much more all-encompassing than behaviors in the sense of behavior-based robots [32]. They may run for several minutes and invoke many behaviors and cognitive activities on the way. They may be interrupted to be resumed later.

Competences in a language game

Here is an example of a game played with a child while showing pictures of animals:

```
Father: What does the cow say? [points to cow] Moooo.
Child: [just observes]
Father: What does the dog say? [points to dog] Woof.
Child: [observes]
Father: What does the cow say?
   [points to cow again and then waits ... ]
Child: Mooh
Father: Yeah!
```

The learner learns to reproduce and recognise the sounds of the various animals and to associate a certain sound with a particular image and a particular word. The example is very typical, in the sense that (1) it involves many sensory modalities and abilities (sound, image, language), (2) it contains a routinised set of interactions which is well entrenched after a while, so that it is clear what is expected, (3) the learner plays along and guesses what the mediator wants and the mediator sets up the context, constrains the difficulties, and gives feedback on success or failure. (4) The meaning of words like ‘cow’ and ‘dog’ or ‘mooo’ and ‘woof’ involves both a conceptual aspect (classification of the animals and imitations of the sound they make) and a game aspect (moves at the right moment). Every parent plays thousands of such games with their children and, equally important, after a while children play such games among themselves, particularly symbolic games.

Games like the one above are typical for children around the age of two. This example focuses exclusively on language learning. Normally games try to achieve a specific cooperative goal through communication, where language plays an auxiliary role, such as:

- Get the listener to perform a physical action, for example move an object.
- Draw the attention of the listener to an element in the context, for example, an object that she wants to see moved.
- Restrict the context, which is helpful for drawing attention to an element in it.

Figure 7.4: Language games rest on a rich substrate of competences concerned with turn-taking, face identification, and sharing attention. These are acquired through play in the first years of life. (Picture by Jan Belgrado)

- Transmit information about one's internal state, for example to signal the degree of willingness to cooperate.
- Transmit information about the state of the world, for example as relevant for future action.

For all these games there must be a number of prerequisites for social interaction like the following:

1. Become aware that there is a person in the environment, by recognising that there is a human voice or a human bodily shape.
2. Recognise the person by face recognition or speaker identification.
3. Try to figure out what object the speaker is focusing attention on, independently of language, by gaze following and eye tracking.
4. Use the present situation to restrict the context, predict possible actions, and predict possible goals of the speaker.
5. Give feedback at all times on which object you are focusing, for example by touching the object or looking at it intently.
6. Indicate that you are attending to the speaker, by looking up at the speaker.

These various activities are often associated with having a 'theory of mind' [1]. It is clear that these prerequisites as well as those specifically required for the language aspects of a game require many cognitive capabilities: vision, gesturing, pattern recognition, speech analysis and synthesis, conceptualisation, verbalisation, interpretation, behavioral recognition, action, etc. This paper will not go into any technical detail how these capabilities have been achieved in our robots (in most cases by adopting state-of-the-art AI techniques) nor how they are integrated. It suffices to know that we have a large library of components and a scripting language that handles the integration and scheduling in real-time of behaviors to implement interactive dialogs. We do not pretend that any of these components achieves human level performance, far from it. But they are enough to carry out experiments addressing the issues raised in this paper and observers are usually stunned by the level of performance already achieved.

The Classification Game

We have been experimenting with various kinds of language games, most notably a guessing game [29], in which the listener must guess an object in a particular context through a verbal description that expresses a property of the object which is not true for any of the other objects in the context. Another game we have studied intensely is the classification game, and that game will be used as a source of illustration in the rest of the paper. The classification game is similar to the guessing game, except that there is only a single object in the visual image to be classified.

Figure 7.5 gives an idea of the difficulties involved in playing a classification game and they dramatically illustrate the difficulties that children must encounter when constructing their first meanings. All these images have been captured with AIBO's camera. Different ambient lighting conditions may completely change the colour reflection of an object. An object is almost never seen in its entirety. It can have a complex structure so that different sides

Figure 7.5: Different views of a red ball as captured by the robot's camera.

are totally different. Consequently segmentation and subsequent classification is extremely difficult. For example, the red ball may sometimes have a light patch which looks like a second object or fuse so much with the background that it is hardly recognisable. We feel that it is extremely important to start from realistic images taken during a real-world interaction with the robot and a human. By taking artificial images (for example pre-segmented images under identical lighting conditions) many of the real-world problems that must be solved in bootstrapping communication would disappear, diminishing the strength of the conclusions that can be drawn.

Learning Classes

Obviously the classification game must rely on a cognitive subsystem that is able to classify objects. There are many possible ways to implement such a system and many techniques are known in Artificial Intelligence literature as to how to learn the required classes. I believe that it is not so important which learning technique is used, rather how the method is integrated within the total behavior of the learner.

The first question to be addressed in building a classificatory system is how to segment objects. Twenty years of research in computer vision have shown that object segmentation is notoriously difficult. It is even believed to be impossible, unless there is already a relatively clear template of the object available. Edge detection, 3-d segmentation, colour segmentation, segmentation based on change from one image to the next, etc., all yield possible segments but none is foolproof. So the learner is confronted with a chicken and egg problem. There is no way to know what counts as an object, but without this knowledge it is virtually impossible to perform segmentation. By not relying on prior segmentation we resolve this paradox. It implies however that initially concepts for objects will be highly context-sensitive, as opposed to clear Platonist abstractions. This situated, context-sensitive nature of object knowledge is in line with Wittgenstein's point of view and has also been argued on empirical grounds.

The second question concerns the method itself. We have used an instance-based method of classification ([2]), which means that many different 'views' are stored of an object situated in a particular context, and classification takes place by a nearest neighbor algorithm: the view with the shortest distance in pair-wise comparison to the input image is considered to be the 'winning' view. We cannnot really say that the memory "represents" objects, because the robot has no notion yet of what an object is, and its memory always stores an object within a certain context.

Instance-based learning was used for two reasons: (1) It supports incremental learning. There is no strict separation between a learning phase and a usage phase. (2) It exhibits very quick acquisition (one instance learning), which is also observed in children. Acquisition can of course be followed by performance degradation when new situations arise that require the storage of new views. Once these views have been stored as well, performance quickly goes up again. This type of learning behavior is very different from that of inductive learning algorithms (such as the clustering algorithm discussed later) which show random performance for a long time until the right classes have been found.

Word learning

To play the classification game, the robot must also have a cognitive subsystem for storing and retrieving the relation between object views and words. Each association has an associated score, which represents past success in using that association as speaker or listener. When speaking, the robot always chooses the association with the highest score so that there is a positive feedback loop between the success of a word and its subsequent use. Word learning takes place by reinforcement learning [33]: when the classification conforms to that expected by the human mediator, there is positive feedback, and the score of the association that was used goes up. At the same time, there is lateral inhibition of alternative hypotheses. When there is a negative outcome of the game, there is negative feedback. The score of the association that was used is decreased. If there is a correction from the mediator, the robot stores a new association between the view and the correcting word, but only if the association did not already exist.

Scripts

The robot has a script, implemented as a collection of loosely connected schemas, for playing the classification game. Here is a typical dialog based on this script, starting when the robot sits down.

```
1. Human: Stand.
2. Human: Stand up.
```

The robot has already acquired names of actions. It remains under the influence of its autonomous behavior controller. Forcing the robot to stand up is a way to make it concentrate on the language game. Because speech signals have been heard, the robot knows that there is someone in the environment talking to it. The human now shows the ball to the robot (figure 7.6 a).

```
3. Human: Look
```

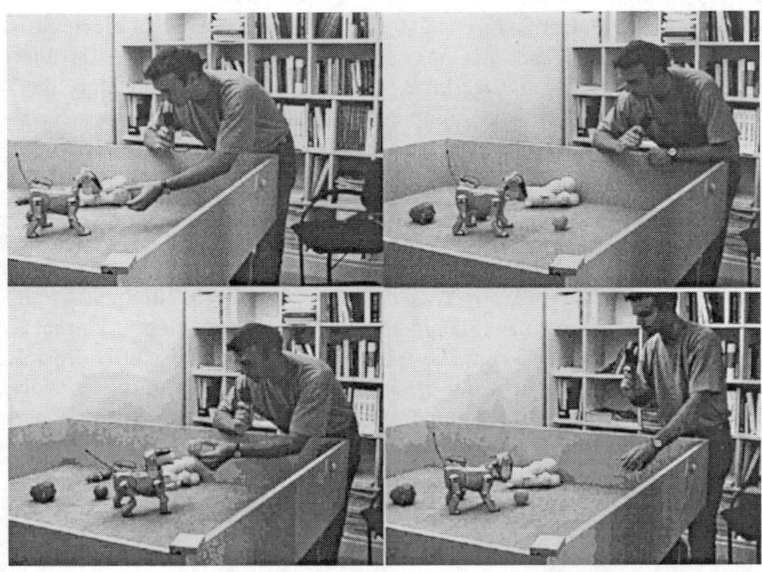

Figure 7.6: Different steps in a language game.

The word "look" helps to focus attention and signals the beginning of a language game. The robot now concentrates on the ball, starts tracking it, and signals focus by looking at the ball (figure 7.6 a) and trying to touch it (figure 7.6 b). It further signals attention by looking first at the speaker (figure 7.6 c) and then back at the ball (figure 7.6 d). In fact, these are all emergent behaviors of the object tracker. The other autonomous behaviors interact with the schemas steering the language game.

```
4. Human: ball
```

The robot does not yet know a word for this object, so a learning activity starts. The robot first asks for feedback of the word to make sure that the word has been heard correctly.

```
5. Aibo: Ball?
6. Human: Yes
```

Ball is the correct word and it is associated with a view of the object seen.

Note that several things could go gone wrong in this episode and the human mediator would typically spontaneously provide additional feedback. For example, the wrong word might be heard due to problems with speech recognition, the robot might not be paying attention to the ball but, because of its autonomous behaviors, might have started to look elsewhere, etc. By maintaining a tightly coupled interaction, the mediator can help the learner and this is the essence of social learning: constraining context, scaffolding (the human says "ball" not "this is the ball" which would be much more difficult), and pragmatic feedback.

Figure 7.7: Evolution of the classification success for four different training sessions.

7.4 Experimental Results

We have implemented all the necessary components to have the robot play classification games of the sort shown in these examples and experimented for several months in human-robot interactions. The objects we used were an AIBO imitation called Poo-Chi, a yellow object, Smiley, a red ball, etc. The experiments were performed on successive days, under very different lighting conditions, and against different backgrounds in order to obtain realistic data. These experiments have shown that the framework of language games is effective to enable the learning of 'the first words' and the classificatory concepts that go with it.

Successful Learning of 'the first words'

Figure 7.7 presents the evolution of the average success for four sessions, each starting from zero knowledge (no words and no concepts). The success of a game is recorded by the mediator, based on the answer of the robot. We see that for all the runs the success climbs regularly to successful communication. It is interesting to note that from the very first games the classification performance is very high. It only takes a few examples to be able to discriminate successfully the three objects in a given environment. But as the environment changes, confusion may arise and new learning takes place, pushing up performance again. This is a property of the instance-based learning algorithm.

	Exp1	Exp2	Exp3	Exp4
Average success	0.81	0.85	0.81	0.80

Table 7.1: Average success during the training sessions

If we average the classification success over the whole training session, we obtain an average performance between 0.80 and 0.85 (table 1), which means that on average the robot uses an appropriate name 8 times out of 10. This includes the period of training, so the learning is extraordinarily fast. A closer look at the errors that the robot makes (table 2), shows that the robot makes fewer classification errors for the red ball than for the other two objects. This is due to the focus of attention mechanism available for tracking red objects. It eases the process of sharing attention on the topic of the game and as a consequence provides the robot with data of better quality. The lack of this capability for the other objects does however not cause a failure to learn them.

word/meaning	Poo-chi	Red Ball	Smiley	Classif. success
Poo-chi	34	8	9	0.66
Red Ball	0	52	4	0.92
Smiley	6	2	49	0.86

Table 7.2: This table shows the word/meaning success rate for one of the sessions.

It is obviously possible to make the perception and categorisation in these experiments more complex. Instead we have adopted the simplest possible solutions in order to make the experiments - which involve real-time interaction with humans - possible. If more complex methods had been adopted they would not fit on the available hardware and the dialog would no longer have a real-time character.

Comparison with non-social learning

Two counter-arguments have been advanced against the need for strong social interaction on first word learning: (1) unsupervised learning has been claimed to generate natural categories which can then simply be labelled with the words heard when the same situation occurs (the labelling theory), and (2) some researchers have proposed that innate constraints guide the learner to the acquisition of the appropriate concepts.

To examine the first counter-argument Frédéric Kaplan has done an experiment using a database of images recorded from 164 interactions between a human and a robot drawn from the same dialogs as those used in social learning. The experiment consisted of using one of the best available unsupervised clustering method (the EM method) in order to see whether any natural categories are hidden in the data. The EM algorithm does not assume that the learner knows in advance the number of categories that are hidden in the data, because this would indeed be an unrealistic bias which the learner cannot know. Unsupervised neural networks such as the Kohonen map would give the same, or worse, results than the EM algorithm.

As the results in table 3 show, the algorithm indeed finds a set of clusters in the data; eight to be precise. But the clusters that are found are unrelated to the classification needed for learning the words in the language. The objects are viewed under many different lighting conditions and background situations, and the clustering reflects these different conditions more than the specific objects themselves.

Clusters	C0	C1	C2	C3	C4	C5	C6	C7
Poo-chi	9	0	2	11	6	20	0	3
Red Ball	6	2	13	6	0	24	3	2
Smiley	5	2	5	2	12	25	3	3

Table 7.3: Objects and their clusters, obtained from unsupervised learning.

If we had to assign a name to a single cluster, Poo-Chi would be assigned to C3, the red ball to C2 and Smiley to C5. With this scheme only 30% of the instances are correctly clustered. If we associate each cluster with its best name (as shown in table 4), it would not be much better. Only 47% would be correctly clustered. We suspect that the clustering is more sensitive to contextual dimensions, such as the light conditions or background of the object rather than the object itself.

Cluster	Best name	
C0	(Poo-chi)	9
C1	(Red Ball, Smiley)	2
C2	Red Ball	13
C3	Poo-chi	11
C4	(Smiley)	12
C5	Smiley	25
C6	(Red Ball, Smiley)	3
C7	(Poo-chi, Smiley)	3

Table 7.4: Clusters and names that best correspond with them.

An additional point is that the EM clustering methods, as any other clustering method, arrive at different clusters depending on the initial conditions (random seeds). There is not necessarily a single solution, and the algorithm might get stuck into a local minimum. This implies that different individuals, that all use unsupervised learning to acquire categories are unlikely to end up with the same categories, which makes the establishment of a shared communication system impossible.

The conclusion of this experiment is clear. Without the causal influence of language, a learning algorithm cannot learn the concepts that are required to be successful in language communication. Note that the clustering experiment makes use of very good data (because they were acquired in a social interaction). If an agent is presented with a series of images taken while it is simply roaming around in the world, a clustering algorithm produces even more irrelevant classifications.

I now turn to the second counterargument, namely that innate constraints could guide the learning process. The question here is what these constraints could be. There is nothing in the observed visual data that gives any indication whatsoever that we are dealing with objects. As mentioned earlier, the robot is not even capable of properly segmenting the image (which would require some sort of template and hence already an idea of what the object is). It therefore seems much more plausible that the social interaction helps the learner zoom in on what needs to be learned.

These experiments only give a glimpse of our methodology at work and we, as well as other colleagues in this field, have done much more. What is important is that we can examine the implications of different theoretical assumptions by varying components of the artificial system, feed it different data, put it into another environment, etc. Each time we can carefully monitor the results of the experiments and examine the causal relation between a theoretical assumption and observed behavior. This approach therefore introduces an experimental methodology into the study of learning which is not possible with human subjects.

7.5 Implications

What can we learn from this kind of experiment that is relevant for the future of learning? I believe there are three important take-home lessons.

The Nature of Early Word Learning

First, these experiments tell us something about the nature of learning, more concretely the learning of the very first words and their associated meanings. They show that there is not a single magical mechanism but that the key lies in the integration of many different skills, ranging from sharing attention, turn-taking, vision, and categorisation to word learning. They also show that it is not enough to look at the individual in isolation.

The interaction with a mediator is crucial and games are a good way to structure these interactions. I believe that mediation is important for the following reasons:

1. The language game constrains what needs to be learned. In the specific example developed here, this is knowledge for classifying objects. So, rather than assuming prior innate constraints on the kinds of concepts that should be learned or assuming that unsupervised clustering generates 'natural categories', the social learning hypothesis suggests that constraints are provided by the language games initiated by mediators.

2. The language game guarantees a certain quality of the data available to the learner. It constrains the context, for example with words like "listen" or through pointing gestures. This helps to focus the attention of the learner. Adequate data acquisition is crucial for any learning method and the more mobile and autonomous the learner, the less obvious this becomes.

3. The language game induces a structure for pragmatic feedback. Pragmatic feedback is in terms of success in achieving the goal of the interaction, not in terms of conceptual or linguistic feedback.

4. The language game allows the scaffolding of complexity. The game used in this paper uses a single word like "ball" for identifying the referent. Once single words have been learned, more complex games become feasable. We have already experimented with games for learning names of actions or more complex descriptions of scenes.

5. Social learning enables active learning. The learner does not need to wait until a situation presents itself that provides good learning data but can actively provoke such a situation. We have particularly used this for the acquisition of speech. The robot first asks for the confirmation of a wordform before incorporating a new association in its memory.

Figure 7.8: The emphasis on learner-centered learning and IT-based learning tools used on an individual basis, should not make us forget the important role of interaction as a motor and enhancer of learning processes.

Teaching Practices

Our research results are too recent to have had any impact on educational practice. However I believe that they are potentially far reaching. The child needs to learn to become a semiologist, capable of inventing new meanings for dealing with reality and of externalising meanings through words or other representations, and so better understanding this process can help to enrich or give a theoretical foundation for teaching practices, particularly for first language teaching. The main message of this paper is that our vision of 'meaning creation' processes needs to shift from the traditional nativist or empiricist stance, which assumes a passive learner confronting in isolation reality, towards the view of an active being engaged in meaning construction in a social fashion.

It also becomes obvious why children (and adults) have such great difficulty to acquire a second language within a traditional school environment, whereas they learn it (seemingly) effortlessly in grounded social interaction with others. The 'school' style of learning language differs in three ways from the social learning of language modeled in our robotic experiments

1. Grounding: Traditional language teaching usually takes place in a de-contextualised setting, without any grounding in the real world. This makes it very difficult to form meanings, i.e. to map information to knowledge.

2. Mediation: When there is a single teacher in front of a classroom of 30 or more pupils, it is not possible to have the one-on-one interaction that is necessary for social learning.

3. Active learning: Our research shows that the learner must be able to take the initiative, testing out different hypotheses and filling in missing holes. In a classroom context it is very difficult to achieve this form of active learning.

This is not meant to be a criticism of teachers. It is remarkable what a teacher can achieve given the 'unnatural' circumstances of a classroom.

Learning Tools

The methodology of building artificial systems for investigating issues in the theory of learning has an additional benefit. It can potentially lead to new new educational technologies, through robots or artificial animated agents in virtual environments that are fun to interact with, but at the same time induce moments of social learning. Robots like the AIBO excite children enormously and induce them to various forms of social play (see also the next chapter by Kerstin Dautenhahn). This suggests that robots could potentially be a platform in which grounded, situated learning may be embedded, including activities in meaning construction. Robots could either play the role of mediator for helping to learn certain concepts and the language that goes with them, or the learner could play the role of mediator and thus be forced to reflect on their own concepts or language. Experiments have not yet been done in this direction, and they would in any case require many more advances in modeling learning processes on robots. But the potential seems undeniable.

Acknowledgements

This research was conducted at the Sony Computer Science Laboratory in Paris. The experiments with the AIBO were conducted in a collaboration with Frédéric Kaplan and Angus McIntyre. I am indebted to the members of the Bagnols workshop for much feedback on the issues discussed in this paper.

Bibliography

[1] Baron-Cohen, S. (1995) Mindblindness: An Essay on Autism and Theory of Mind. MIT Press.

[2] Mel, B. (1997) SEEMORE: Combining Color, Shape, and Texture Histogramming in a Neurally-Inspired Approach to Visual Object Recognition Neural Computation, 1997, 9 , 777-804

[3] Bowerman, M. and S. C. Levinson (2001) Language acquisition and conceptual development. Cambridge Univ. Press, Cambridge.

[4] Broeder, P. and J. Murre (2000) Models of Language Acquisition. Inductive and Deductive Approaches. Oxford University Press, Oxford.

[5] Bruner, J.S. (1990) Acts of Meaning. Harvard University Press, Cambridge Ma.

[6] Chomsky, N. (1975) Reflections on Language. Pantheon Books, New York.

[7] Chomsky, N. and H. Lasnik (1993) The Theory of Principles and Parameters. In: J. Jacbos, A. von Stechow, W. Sternefeld and T. Vennemann (eds) Syntax: An International Handbook of Contemporary Research. Walter de Gruyter, Berlin. p. 506-569.

[8] Clark, E.V. (1987) The Principle of Contrast: A constraint on language acquisition. In: MacWhinney, B. (ed.) Mechanisms of Language Acquisition. L. Erlbaum Hillsdale NJ.

[9] Davidoff, J., I. Davies, J. Roberson (1999) Color categories in a stone-age tribe. Nature, vol 398. 230-231.

[10] Elman, J.L. (1993). Learning and development in neural networks: The importance of starting small. Cognition, 48, 71-99.

[11] Elman, J., Bates, E., Johnson, M.H., Karmiloff-Smith, A., Parisi, D. and Plunkett, K. (1996). Rethinking Innateness: A connectionist perspective on development. Cambridge, Ma: MIT Press.

[12] Evans, N. (2000) Kinship verbs. p 103-172. in: In: Vogel, P.M. and B. Comrie (eds.) (2000) Approaches to the Typology of Word Classes. Mouton de Gruyter, Berlin.

[13] Fischer, C., G. Hall, S. Rakowitz, and L. Gleitman (1994) When it is better to receive than to give: syntactic and conceptual constraints on vocabulary growth. Lingua (92) 333-375.

[14] Fodor, J. (1983) The modularity of mind. The MIT Press, Cambridge. Ma.

[15] Golifkoff, R. (1983) (ed.) The Transition from Prelinguistic to Linguistic Communication. Lawrence Erlbaum Ass. Hilssdale NJ.

[16] Halliday, M.A.K. (1984) Learning How to Mean. Cambridge Univ. Press, Cambridge.

[17] Harnad, S. (1990) The Symbol Grounding Problem. Physica D 42: 335-346.

[18] Heine, B. (1997) Cognitive Foundations of Grammar. Oxford University Press, New York.

[19] Labov, W. (1994) Principles of Linguistic Change. Volume 1: Internal Factors. Basil Blackwell, Oxford.

[20] Langacker, R. (1987). Foundations of cognitive grammar, vol.1. Stanford: Stanford University Press.

[21] Lightfoot, D. (1991). How to set parameters. MIT Press, Cambridge Ma.

[22] Lightfoot, D. W. (1998). The Development of Language: Acquisition, Change, and Evolution. Blackwell, Oxford.

[23] Pinker, S. (1994) The Language Instinct. The New Science of Language and Mind. Penguin, Harmondsworth.

[24] Siskind, J. (2000) Visual Event Classification Through Force Dynamics. AAAI Conference 2000. AAAI Press, Anaheim Ca. pp. 159-155.

[25] Smith, L. (2001) How Domain-General Processes may create Domain-Specific Biases. In: Bowerman, M. and S. C. Levinson (2001) Language acquisition and conceptual development. Cambridge Univ. Press, Cambridge. p. 101-131

[26] Steels, L. (1996) Self-Organizing Vocabularies. In: Langton, C. and T. Shimohara (ed) (1997) Proceedings of the Artificial Life V. The MIT Press, Cambridge, Ma. pp. 179-184.

[27] Steels, L. (1997a) The Synthetic Modeling of Language Origins. Evolution of Communication Journal 1(1), 1-35. (1997)

[28] Steels, L. (1997b) Constructing and Sharing Perceptual Distinctions. In: van Someren, M. and G. Widmer (ed.) (1997) Proceedings of the European Conference on Machine Learning, Springer-Verlag, Berlin. pp. 4-13.

[29] Steels, L. (1998) The origins of syntax in visually grounded robotic agents. Artificial Intelligence 103 (1,2) p. 133-156.

[30] Steels, L. (2001) Language Games for Autonomous Robots. IEEE Intelligent systems, September/October 2001, p. 16-22.

[31] Steels, L. and F. Kaplan (2001) AIBO's first words. The social learning of language and meaning. Evolution of Communication 4(1).

[32] Steels, L. and R. Brooks (1995) The Artificial Life Route to Artificial Intelligence. Building Embodied, Situated Agents. Lawrence Erlbaum Ass, New Haven.

[33] Sutton, R. and A. Barto (1998) Reinforcement Learning. The MIT Press, Cambridge, Ma.

[34] Talmy, L. (2000) Toward a Cognitive Semantics: Concept Structuring Systems (Language, Speech, and Communication) The MIT Press, Cambridge, Ma.

[35] Tomasello, M. (1999). The Cultural Origins of Human Cognition. Harvard University Press, Cambridge, Ma.

[36] Traugott, E. and Heine, B. (1991) Approaches to Grammaticalization. Volume I and II. John Benjamins Publishing Company, Amsterdam, 1991.

[37] Wierzbicka, A. (1992) Semantics, Culture and Cognition. Oxford University Press, Oxford.

Group Discussion 7
The Social Learning of Language

The Problem of Grammar

Johnson: You showed us how robots could acquire basic perceptually grounded concepts and the words for them, but what about grammar?

Steels: Well I didn't have time to talk about grammar, but that is another direction in which I am working very intensely. We are setting up experiments in which robots play language games with each other and build up not only concepts and names for these concepts but also grammatical conventions for expressing things like predicate-argument structure, determination, time, aspect, modality, topic-comment structure, etc. I do not believe in the Chomskyan idea that there is a kind of abstract system that exists prior to the first data and in which parameters are then set based on linguistic evidence. Instead I believe that grammar is something that arises gradually, that is constructed by the child. Consider the distinction between nouns and verbs. Even assuming they were given innately, how would you know whether a word like "fiets" (bike) in Dutch was a noun or a verb, unless you already know the language? Moreover the language data is confusing because even though "fiets" is basically a noun, it can also be used as a verb (as in "ik fiets naar huis" (I bike home)). And how would you explain that there are languages such as Mundari, an Austro-Asiatic language, which do not make a distinction between nouns and verbs. Any lexicalised predicate can be used as a verb in the sense that it can be used as predication and takes tense and aspect markers, agreement, voice, etc., *and* as a noun, in which case it takes case markers and is used referentially. Words therefore denote both things and events. For example *lutur* means both ear and listen, and *kumRu* a thief and to steal.

So I believe that grammar, even the basic grammatical notions like nouns and verbs, are constructed by language users and that children have to perform this constructive effort themselves, using their generic cognitive apparatus. They have to use mechanisms like analogy, generalisation, etc. I don't believe there is a strong innate system that specifies that there is something like nouns and verbs in a language. I realise that we have an enormous amount of work ahead of us to actually prove all this through experiments of the sort I have shown you, but this is my plan anyway.

Rinaldi: The development of one language can be influenced by the development of another language, of the interaction between different languages. In the Reggio approach we talk about the hundred languages of children, which are all different representations they use to cope with reality. And we know from our practice that children 'discover' and construct these languages. Are you working on the interaction between different modes of representation?

Steels: This is a very interesting idea but we have not done anything on it. Your point is very well taken because if you look at the many languages of expression and the feedback relationship between them, one could bootstrap the other, and in this way they could all gradually be constructed. This is a fantastic idea to expand our research program.

Rinaldi: We would be very grateful for a deeper understanding of all this in Reggio.

Nature versus Nurture

Ken Mogi: This whole question of nature versus nurture doesn't seem very productive to me. In this particular experiment that you did, the robot is programmed to play the game. This is in some sense genetically determined. Without this kind of determination, there would be no game.

Steels: Yes, of course. This is true. But the claim of nativists is much stronger than that. Consider colour. Psychologists like Sheppard would say that the focal points, the prototypes, for the basic colours like blue, green, red, etc., are innately given. Also for phonetics, they would say that phonetic categories, like whether a consonant is voiced (as /d/) or unvoiced (as /t/), which allow a distinction between different speech sounds, are innately given. The argument is not whether you need a genetic determinate structure of some sort, clearly you do, the argument is about "What are they?", "How language-specific are they? And then you have those taking a strong stance that concepts, grammatical conventions, etc., are innate. And I am saying: they are not.

Mogi: I'm not a linguist. But I see Chomsky and his colleagues as strawmen in research nothwithstanding that strawmen are fun, I think it is fair to say that genes and experience work together.

Steels: Of course. But you must agree that one's theory of learning is going to be very different if you assume that colour categories are innate, that they're fixed and universally shared, what I called the labelling theory, or if you assume that colour concepts are shaped by ecology, culture, and language. As long as we do not go into detail about what is exactly innate, we can argue until we fall asleep.

Mogi: My question is: can you state again what is innate in this system?

Steels: There are a number of generic abilities, e.g. the ability to categorize, to use an associative memory, to visually extract features from the environment, to share attention, etc. What is not innate is which categories there are, what words will be used, which word is linked to which meaning. It is like neural networks. They have the capability to arrive at some generalisation but you don't put in what the generalisation is going to be.

Punset: The most convincing argument of Steven Pinker's theory is that it is impossible for children to learn a language in less than three years, and it has convinced lots of people. Children at that age can only handle very simple calculation problems. But language seems extraordinarily complex and children can do it.

Steels: I believe that children take much more time than three years to learn a language! If you interact with three year olds you have the impression they master a lot of language but if you probe deeper you find they use a lot of canned phrases without really having meanings well established or without mastering the proper generalisations. For example, if you ask a four year old about the colours of their clothes they can answer perfectly because they have been playing games to name these colours. But if you ask colours of unknown objects they can't do it. Colour words, just to take this example, only stabilise around the age of eight or so. For grammar it is much more dramatic. Many children cannot produce well-formed complex sentences (with dependent clauses, etc.) until sixteen years. Many adults cannot properly write out their thoughts. I strongly resist the idea that language learning is finished at three years old. Instead I believe that we learn and invent language all our life

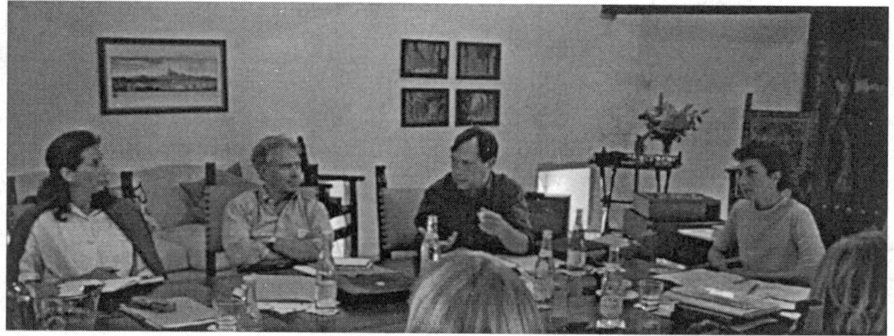

Figure 7.9: Group discussion. How far can we learn anything from building artificial systems for the practice of education? From left to right Caroline Nevejan, Bernard Allien, Luc Steels, and Marleen Wynants.

and consequently that teaching language, writing, etc., must be based on this assumption. We must teach children to be active participants in the language community instead of assuming that all they have to do is set a number of parameters in an innate language acquisition device.

Punset: But would a theory based on learning not take too much time?

Steels: No, we have done many simulations and things go often surprisingly fast. For example, in the domain of speech there are many constraints that naturally limit what behaviors the learner can acquire. For example constraints coming from the articulatory system (tongue, vocal chords, shape of mouth, etc.) restrict the kinds of sounds you can make. These constraints don't have to be innately given in your brain. They don't have to be learned. Some sounds simply cannot be made. There are many other constraints which push learners naturally towards certain types of solutions. The arguments usually given for innateness are arguments from ignorance, we don't understand how children can learn it so it must be innate. But if we work harder at it, I believe that we can understand the learning process.

Hedegaard : In learning language, we find that children have two strategies, one for learning names of objects and another one for learning names for action. Have you done anything on actions?

Steels: Yes, I did not talk about it but we have experiments on this. The basic idea is that the robot comes with a repertoire of behaviors organised in a network and tries different actions to find out which one is to be connected with a certain name.

Hedegaard: I don't mean learning the action. I mean naming the action.

Steels: Yes. But the learning of the action, and the conceptualisation and the naming of it, they all go together. Of course all this is very difficult, but we're trying to do it.

Collective Learning

Nevejan: Can you say more about your experiments in which groups of robots together developed a shared set of words and meanings, without human intervention?

Steels: Yes, this is our way to investigate the impact of culture on meaning creation and language. We created a set-up with a limited number of 'robotic bodies' able to make contact with the world through a pan-tilt camera, and a large open-ended growing set of 'agents', software entities, that could use these bodies to interact with each other about a shared situation in the world. The agents played a guessing game, another kind of language game, in which the speaker had to draw the attention of the hearer to an object before them by using words. In the experiment, the agents did not have any *a priori* concepts or any pre-given lexicon. They constructed new meanings to distinguish the objects in their environment, named these meaning, and above all negotiated shared meanings for the words. There is a lot to say about this experiment, which ran for several months and involved thousands of agents, but the key point is that it showed that language can emerge through a collective self-organising process when each of the participants in the community has the ability to construct their own meanings and words and at the same time adapt their constructions to that used by others.

Wynants: Collective learning, sharing a vision in order to learn and to develop together is fundamental to the development of cognition. Justine Cassell accentuates the importance of self-efficacious storytelling about the self, through collaboration with other children and through the development of real projects. It helps children see their own power and possibility, to establish their belief that they can have an effect on the world around them. Or in the words of psychologist John Dewey: "I think that every kind of learning takes place through the participation of the individual in the social consciousness of humankind."

Chapter 8

Playing and Learning with Robots

by Kerstin Dautenhahn

Kerstin Dautenhahn graduated from the University of Bielefeld (Germany) with degrees in biology and robotics. She is currently professor in the computer science department at the university of Hertfortshire (UK) and leads the adaptive systems group. She researches computational and robotic models of learning, social interaction and emotion. She has been using robots to investigate social and communication breakthroughs with autistic children.

8.1 Introduction

Since the early days of mobile robotics, research people have been interested not only in a single, autonomous robot, but also in how such robots can interact socially with each other or people. For example, the first mobile autonomous robots that could move around without being connected to a computer or power source were built by the neurophysiologist W. Grey Walter in the late 1940s. The robot 'tortoises' were named Elmer and Elsie and could move around each other in a dance-like fashion [28]. Since then many researchers have been investigating robots that behave socially, that can learn from each other [7],[8], and that are able to interact with humans [3]. Due to an increasing interest in everyday service robotics, i.e. robots that can inhabit our offices, homes and public places, robot-human interaction has become a popular area of research. Such research is often greatly inspired by findings on how humans interact with each other, and it is hoped that the same factors are also applicable in robot-human interaction.

A main challenge in this field is to make robots believable and "easy-to-interact-with". In order to achieve this goal, many robots are designed to mimic humans or other social animals. For example, many of these social robots are designed to imitate the appearance and behaviour of human beings ; for instance, they are given a humanoid shape and/or a face that can display different emotional expressions. Many examples of anthropomorphic or zoomorphic robots now exist [5]. Two basic assumptions underlying such projects are that (a) humans are social animals and like to interact with other social animals (including humans), and (b) in order to build believable social robots, it is most effective to "imitate life", namely to make resemble these robots the way humans and other social animals interact with each other in terms of appearance and behaviour. This "life-like agents hypothesis" [7], i.e. that in order to build believable agents interacting with people it is most effective to "imitate life", has proven very successful for commercial, educational and entertainment products. Excellent examples are robotic toys that look like pets, such as the AIBO. Because humans have an enormously rich and complex mental world of imagination and fantasy, if a machine looks like a dog and behaves like a dog, then most humans are able and willing to suspend disbelief and treat this machine as a dog, or even attribute "dogness" to the robot.

However, this natural tendency to anthromorphise and animate the world does not apply to people with autism. Little is known about how to design robot appearance and behaviour that is appealing to people with autism, let alone use a robot in a therapeutic role. This chapter discusses the potential use of robots in autism therapy. In this project we face particular constraints and challenges due to the nature of autism and the play-scenario in which we use the robots.

The structure of this chapter is as follows. Section 2 gives a brief introduction to how autism is characterised and how people with autism perceive and interact with the social world. In section 3 we discuss the background and motivation of the Aurora project which studies the use of robots in autism therapy. Section 4 summarises the trials and results that have been achieved in the Aurora project. Section 5 relates the approach taken in the Aurora project to the general question of how learning is best approached, specifically it compares learning through instruction with learning through play. Section 6 discusses some of the challenges the Aurora project faces, in particular from the perspective of building suitable therapeutic robotic tools. Section 7 contains a few preliminary conclusions.

Figure 8.1: Children have a natural tendency to see robots, such as the AIBO shown here, as life-like entities, and incorporate them as such in their play activities. This is not the case with autistic children.

8.2 Autism

The autistic disorder is defined by specific diagnostic criteria, specified in DSM-IV (Diagnostic and Statistical Manual of Mental Disorders, American Psychiatric Association, 1994). Individuals with autism present a broad spectrum of difficulties and abilities, and vary enormously in their levels of overall intellectual functioning. However, all individuals diagnosed with autism will show impairment in the following three areas: Qualitative impairment in social interaction, qualitative impairments in communication, and restricted repetitive and stereotyped patterns of behaviour, interests, and activities. Depending on what is included in 'autism', rates of occurrence are given which range between 5-15 in 10000, although recent discussions suggest that figures for the incidence of autism might be much higher.

Instead of a physical handicap, which prevents people from physically interacting with the environment, people with autism have great difficulty in making sense of the world, in particular the social world. Autism is accompanied by learning difficulties in approximately 75 percent of cases. At the higher functioning end of the autistic spectrum we find people with Asperger Syndrome. Some of them manage to live independently as adults and to succeed professionally, but only by learning and applying explicit rules in order to overcome the 'social barrier' (as in the case of [14]), thereby demonstrating the benefit of explicitly learnt/taught social knowledge (see the discussion in section 5). Instead of picking up and interpreting social cues 'naturally', autistic children can only learn and memorise rules about what kind of behaviour is socially appropriate during interaction with non-autistic people.

Many theories exist trying to explain and understand the primary causes of autism at the psychological or cognitive level of explanation, ranging from theory-of-mind approaches that focus on the manipulation and representation of mental concepts ([18], [1]) to theories that explain autism in terms of disorders of executive functions that control thought and action [24]. Much attention has recently focused on the significance of early impairments in interaction dynamics [23] and shared attention [1]. Many therapy methods exist for autism [11]. Some therapy methods seem to work better for a particular child with autism than others. But autism therapy is still a very active area of research.

Despite huge differences in abilities of people diagnosed along the autistic spectrum, they generally have particular deficits in social interaction, communication, imagination and fantasy in common [17]. To an autistic person, other people's social behaviour often appears overwhelming, unpredictable, confusing and therefore threatening. On the other hand, many people with autism enjoy using computers or other machines that are predictable and provide a "safe" environment for them, away from the demands of a social environment that they cannot make sense of and that they cannot "properly" respond to. Also, people with autism usually focus on the "literal meaning" and details of things, rather than perceiving the world in aholistic and socially and culturally *interpreted* sense. For example, they might play with a stuffed animal, but not because it looks to them like a bear and so they treat it like a bear, but because the bear's eyes have an interesting colour or shape or texture. Computers and other machines are much closer to this perspective of "literal meaning". Because computers follow simple rules in a predictable way, their behaviour requires less "interpretation" than e.g. a human's facial expressions or linguistic utterances.

8.3 Robots in Autism Therapy

It seems that people with autism enjoy, and can benefit from interacting with computers [4], [21]. A pioneering study in the 1970s at the University of Edinburgh investigated how one autistic child reacted when he could control a remote-controlled 'turtle' robot [29]. Unfortunately the scope of this study was limited: only one child was studied, and it is not known whether the test had any long-term benefit for the child. In contrast, in the Aurora project (Autonomous robotic platform as a remedial tool for children with autism) which I initiated, we take a novel research direction by investigating direct, embodied interactions of autistic children with autonomous interactive robots.

The Aurora Project

The project was founded in 1998 and is based at the Computer Science Department of University of Hertfordshire in Hatfield, United Kingdom. It is a highly interdisciplinary initiative which requires research at the intersection of robotics, psychology and education. The project is strongly therapeutically oriented.

Unlike many autism research projects which focus on identifying how autistic children are different from typically developing children, the Aurora project focuses on what autistic children *can* do, and how these capacities can be used for educational and therapeutic interventions. The main goal of this long-term project is to help children with autism to enjoy social interactions and ultimately to bond with the (social) world (e.g. other adults and children at school or at home). Our specific approach is to use robotic interactive toys that encourage the children to play games with the robot, games that practise skills which are important in human-human interaction. The project explores what kind of interaction skills the children can learn by interacting with the robot. It is hoped that the child will later be able to generalise what he/she learnt during interactions with the robot to interactions with other children or adults. Note, that generalisation is a huge problem in autism therapy.

Since we started the Aurora project in 1998 other researchers took up the challenge of investigating the design space of interactive robots for children with autism [20]. The Aurora project is less engineering-oriented. We take an explicit therapeutic and systematic approach involving repeated trials and the development of evaluation techniques that allow us to compare precisely how the children interact with the robot as opposed to other objects. This work has a strongly exploratory character, but as we will show below we already have encouraging evidence which demonstrates that many children with autism happily accept the robot as an interactive toy that engages them in interaction games.

The Set-up for the Trials

In most of the trials done to date in the Aurora project we have used a small, autonomous, mobile robot with a few sensors that can detect moving or static obstacles as well as human beings. The studies described in sections 8.4 used a Labo-1 robot, an intelligent indoor mobile robot platform, donated by Takashi Gomi, director of the Canadian/Japanese company Applied AI Systems, Inc. Labo-1 has a 4-wheel differential drive in order to navigate indoor environments. Obstacles are avoided with eight active infrared sensors. A heat sensor allows the robot to detect warm objects such as humans. The metal chassis is very robust. The robot's dimensions are 28cm (width), 38cm (length) and 15cm (height). It weighs 6.5 kg and can operate autonomously with on-board batteries for about 3 hours. Using its sensors, the robot is able to avoid obstacles and follow a heat source such as a child. Additionally, the robot is equipped with a speech synthesiser unit that can produce short spoken phrases using a neutral intonation. The robot is heavy enough to be difficult for the children to pick up and is robust enough to survive an average trial, including being pushed around. The robot is programmed to perform basic actions, including behaviour such as avoiding obstacles, following children and producing speech (typically short phrases such as 'can't see you' or 'where are you ?'). The robot tries to approach the child, responds vocally to its presence, and avoids obstacles. All trials are videotaped for later study and evaluation.

The trials described in sections 4.1 and 4.2 were conducted at a room in Radlett Lodge School - the boarding school that the autistic children participating in the trial attend. Trials reported in section 4.3 were conducted at both Radlett Lodge School as well as at Colnbrook School. Both schools are located in Hertfordshire. Conducting trials at the school rather than bringing the children 'to the lab' has many advantages such as familiar surroundings for the children and the availability of teachers who know the children well. Also, the children do not need to travel. Due to this choice it is hoped that trials involve a minimum amount of disruption to lessons and also help the children to adapt to the change in schedule. The rooms in which the children are exposed to the robot are approximately two meters by three meters. They are set aside for us and so do not contain too many extra features or excess furniture.

In each trial autistic children interact with the robot for a particular period of time, e.g. ten to twenty minutes, in a totally unrestricted and playful context, i.e. the children can touch the robot, pick it up, etc. A teacher and an experimenter are also present in the room where the trials take place, so the general set-up is inherently social. Indeed, as I explain in more detail below, due to this specific set up we sometimes observe that a child uses the robot as an object of attention and discourse in order to establish communication with adults who are present during the trials [11].

The experimenters adopt a basically 'passive' role: if the child addresses them then they respond, but the experimenter is not initiating interactions. The role of the teacher during the trials is to bring in the child, monitor interactions, provide a familiar contact person to the child and return the child to class. The teacher also provides feedback to us at a later stage. In the first trials described in section 8.4 with the mobile robot, the teachers adopt a 'passive' role, i.e. they do not initialise interactions with the child during the trials, although encouragement can occur at the beginning of the trial in the form of 'Look, there is a robot you can play with'. Due to the 'game-like' set-up with a humanoid robot doll (described in the last part of section 8.4), teachers showed much more involvement, so that in fact teacher-directed activities often dominated the trials. In all trials, the child is allowed to leave the room and return to class at any time, for instance when he or she gets bored or otherwise seems to want to leave.

The robot is able to play simple interaction games with the children, such as the "chasing game" and the "follow-me game". A key element in both games is turn-taking, a central element that regulates human-human interaction and that is a therapeutically important behaviour. The robot is programmed so that during the "follow-me game" it follows the child around in the room. The child (e.g. when lying on the floor) moves its legs/arms so that the robot approaches her, or the child walks away and waits for the robot to follow. The children often walk around the robot or step aside in order to "test" if the robot can see them and they check to see if it follows. In the "chasing game" the child might discover that the robot moves backward when approached. Eventually child and robot take turns in approach/avoidance games (see figure 8.2). If the child does not react for a while then the robot tries to engage the child by using programmed movements and synthetic speech such as the phrase "Can't see you!". Like most children, children with autism have fun "trapping" the robot, i.e. by making it get stuck in a corner of the room. Generally, many children very much enjoy the interactions with the robot. We typically observe positive expressions such as smiling and laughing.

Evaluation

An important issue in the Aurora project is evaluation. How can we evaluate the interactions of children with a mobile robot? All trials are videotaped from at least one fixed angle, but how should the video data be evaluated? Desriptive narratives are certainly useful and can give first impressions of what kind of interactions happen, but in order to make progress towards learning about how to use robots in autism therapy, a more systematic approach is needed. Since many of our children are non-verbal, questionnaires are not suitable in order to assess the robot's 'success' in terms of engaging the children in interactions. Therefore, many techniques usually used in human-computer or human-robot interface design are not appropriate.

On the other hand, techniques such as CARS (Childhood Autism Rating Scale) used in autism research and therapy are not very suitable for our purposes either, since they require that the child's behaviour and abilities are very well known. Teachers or other people having long-term, repeated contact with the children can use such a scheme, but for experimenters who do not have formal training in autism therapy, and who only see the children during the trials, it seemed inappropriate. Eventually, we chose two different evaluation techniques,

Figure 8.2: A child with autism playing a 'chasing game' with the mobile robot.

discussed in more detail in [6]. A quantitative technique is based on micro-behaviours where the video sequences are classified according to a list of criteria. This technique was inspired by Tardiff [27]. It allows statistical analysis and comparisons (see [30] and section 8.4). The quantitative technique analyses the video data on a second-by-second basis, applying fourteen criteria including eye gaze, contact, operation, handling, touch, approach, moving away, vocalisation, speech, and others. The focus of the actions is also documented. A second technique that we use applies Conversation Analysis (CA) to analyse the communicative competencies of children with autism while interacting with the robot (and possibly other children or adults). CA is a qualitative technique which was developed for a systematic analysis of everyday and institutional 'talk-in-interaction' [16]. The qualitative and the quantitative technique are complimentary, identifying different aspects of the interactions. Ultimately a range of evaluation techniques might prove necessary.

8.4 Trials and Results

Trials I: Comparative Study of Robot versus Toy Truck

In a comparative study we tested how the children behave towards the robot as opposed to a passive toy. Trials were done with seven children with autism who interacted separately with the mobile robot and a non-interactive toy (a toy truck of approximately the same size as the robot) (see figure 8.3).

For each child the trial consists of three phases. In phase one the child interacts with the robot. In the second phase the robot is switched off and both robot and toy are present. In the third phase the robot is removed so that the child is exposed only to the toy. The order of phases one and three are reversed in half of the trials. The length of the phases may vary, although phases one and three are usually 4 minutes long, phase two is usually two

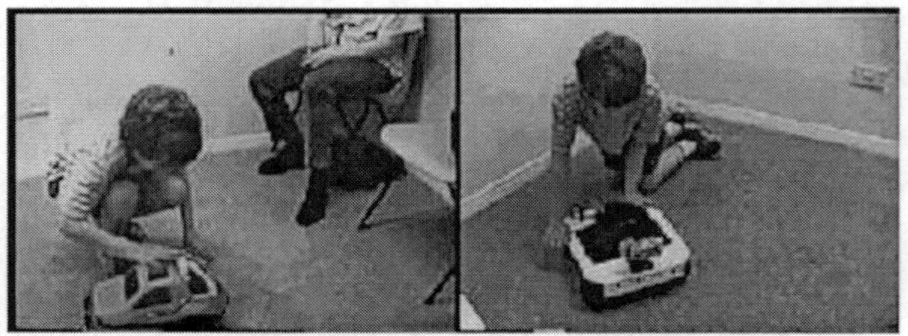

Figure 8.3: An autistic child playing with the toy truck (left) and with the mobile robot (right).

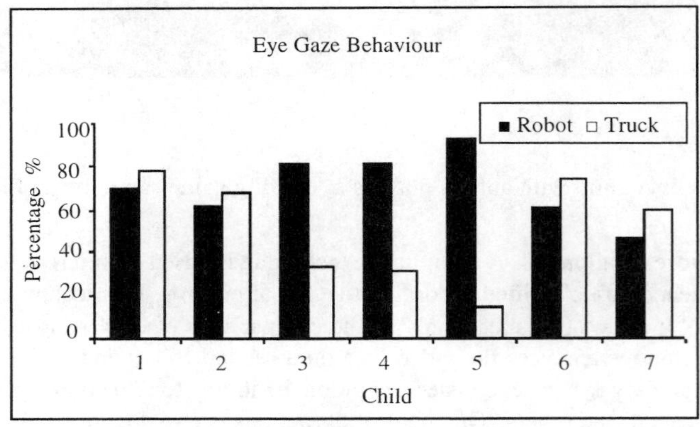

Figure 8.4: The histogram compares the eye gaze behaviour of seven children with autism playing with a robot (dark columns) and separately playing with a toy truck (white columns).

minutes long. When we began the trials we had planned a strict 4+2+4-minute schedule, but depending on how much the children enjoyed the interactions we extended or shortened the phases.

Results of a quantitative evaluation [30],[6] of the videotapes suggest that at least some children pay more attention to the robot and generally show more "interactive" and less repetitive behaviour when playing with the robot. Figure 8.4 compares for example eye gaze behaviour which is an indication of attention. The percentages refer to the duration of this particular behaviour judged against the total length of the time interval that was analysed. The evaluation allows us to compare different children in different contexts. These are important results that provide the foundation for future work.

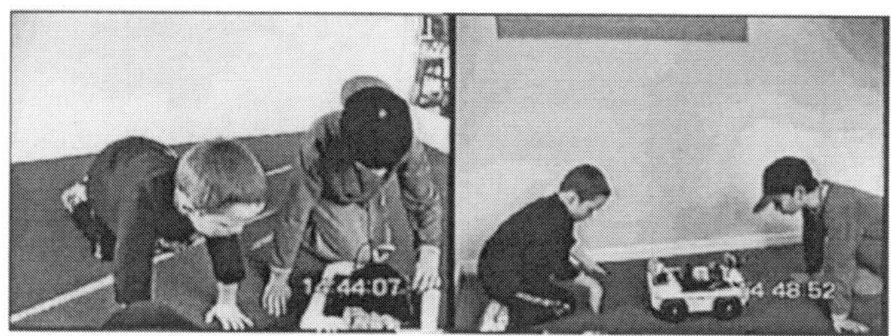

Figure 8.5: Two children playing with the robot in the 'pair trails'.

Trials II: Potential Role of the Robot as a Social Mediator

In another study we investigated the potential role of a robot as a *social mediator*, i.e. a robot that can facilitate contact among autistic children. The teachers paired the children according to their social abilities before they were simultaneously exposed to the robot. We found that a variety of different play styles could be observed, ranging from social play (among autistic children whose social abilities were quite well developed), to non-social or competitive play among the less able children, see table I. These different play-styles matched how the children interact in a social setting without the robot.

Figure 8.5 shows two very able children who during the pair trials used the robot extensively as a focus of attention and object of discussions among themselves and with adults present in the same room (teacher and two experimenters). This initial study shows the potential of a mobile robot to serve as a vehicle, a mediator, or a focus of attention that can help children to make contact with each other, and possibly adults, in a playful context. This is a major problem for autistic children otherwise. For more details of this trial, see [30].

Trials III: Children with Autism Playing with Robota, a Humanoid Doll

Recent trials in November 2001 with a group of 14 autistic children studied how the children interact with a humanoid robotic doll developed by Aude Billard [2]. In 1998 we tested a first prototype of the robot with a few autistic children, but the interactions were not videotaped. This time, all interactions were videotaped so that they can be evaluated. The doll, called "Robota", can sing and dance and imitate children's arm and head movements (see figure 8.6). The basic set-up in this trial was very much 'game-like'. A typical example of interactions (between a child, its teacher and Robota) is as follows:

1. Child and teacher enter the room. Robota is located on a table, sitting next to an experimenter. Teacher and child sit down on chairs at the table. The teacher 'introduces' the child to the robot, e.g. 'Look, this is Robota, you can play with her'.

2. The teacher demonstrates what the robot can do. For example, the teacher lifts her right arm and tries to encourage the child to do as she did. Via a small webcam a program developed by Aude Billard can detect when the child raises his/her arm, or both arms, and this behaviour is then imitated by Robota.

Social Abilities	Interest Level	Play-style	Robot-directed behaviours
Highest	High interest in robot, which is a very strong focus of attention and curiosity during the whole trial, good verbal and communication skills used to interact with adults (robot-centered communication).	Social play: playing and communicating with each other, the robot, and the adults presents. Social learning/teaching: Experimenter instructs one child how to chase robot, the child instructs the other child.	Exploratory and interactive play with robot (touching, operating etc.), interest in chasing, following and robot's speech, questioning experimenters about robot's skills, great interest in "what robot should do" etc.
Medium	Little interest in people, varied interest in robot: one child with high interest in car park visible through the room's window, the other child treating people as "audience".	Non-social play: playing with robot simultaneously, but not playing with each other, "accidental" interaction when both competed for robot's "attention", teacher occasionally had to give guidance /calm children down when children grew bored.	Interest in robot's destructive skills, cornering robot, shouting at robot to get it to move, operating robot.
Lowest	Both children interested in robot.	Non-social play: One child dominates interaction, open competition for robot, using social skills in obstruction of other child e.g. "leave him alone".	Giving vocal commands and directions to robot, operating robot.

Table 8.1 Different play styles observed in the 'pair trials'.

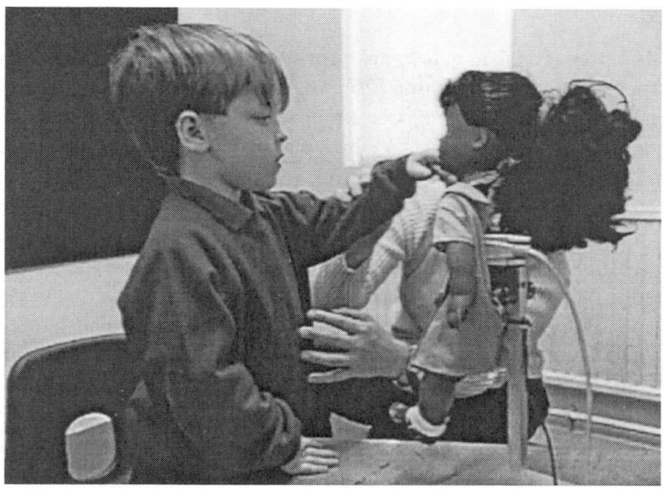

Figure 8.6: A six-year old boy with autism playing with Robota, a humanoid robotic doll designed by Aude Billard.

3. The teacher verbally points out the correspondence 'Look, Robota imitates you'. The teacher then repeats this game using the left arm or raising both arms. The teacher can also initiate a different game where the child moves Robota's arms and head, and where Robota learns this sequence and can replay it (music can possibly accompany this game).

Generally, and very differently from the trials described above where the teacher hardly ever intervened, the children's behaviour in these trials was very much teacher-directed and teacher initiated.

The videotapes are currently being evaluated, so at this stage it is difficult to draw any general conclusions. We clearly observed many instances in which the children played imitation games with the robot. Given that children with autism often show less imitative skills than normally developing children, this is a very interesting avenue for future work, in addition to using the mobile autonomous robot. We also observed clear signs of enjoyment (smiling), or a boy kissing Robota goodbye before he left the room. More information about background of this particular work is described in [10].

In future work with Robota it will be particularly interesting to see how the robot can be used in more 'free-form' play scenarios, without requiring extensive teacher intervention. Note, that sometimes the teacher had to intervene because the child was about to break the robot (e.g. forcefully pulling the arms). We are therefore currently seeking funding in order to develop a more robust version of Robota, more specifically adapted to the needs and abilities of autistic children.

8.5 Instruction or Play

Conceptually, the approach taken in the Aurora project is strongly related to Seymour Papert's *constructivist* approach towards learning [26]. His approach focuses on active exploration of the environment, namely through improvisation, self-directed, 'playful' activities in appropriate learning environments ('contexts') which can be used as 'personal media'. In the mid of 1960s Papert and his colleagues at the MIT AI LAB developed the programming language LOGO which has been widely used in teaching children. A remote controlled device (a robot-turtle) was developed which moved according to a set of LOGO instructions, cf. the LEGO/LOGO Artificial Life Toolkit for children [22]. Interactive toys are increasingly being developed for usr in educational contexts [12]. Such new interactive systems and novel interfaces are also likely to impact on methods of therapy and rehabilitation. 'Persuasive' technology [13], i.e. technology that can influence people's opinions, attitudes and behaviour are likely to change how we can teach social intelligence to humans who have difficulties in understanding and showing social behaviour.

Generally, we got very positive and encouraging feedback to the Aurora project project from parents, educators, teachers and autism researchers. However, occasionally the issue is raised as to whether it might be more beneficial to pursue a more instruction-oriented approach, as is done in many existing autism therapy forms where children with autism go through intensive (often several hours a day for many days a week and continuing for many years), highly structured sessions where particular repetitive (reward-based) tasks are exercised. Indeed, a central question in our project is 'Do we need to *teach* social interaction skills explicitly ?, or 'Can we create situations where the children have the opportunity to *explore playfully* and learn social interaction skills'.

Personally, I am a strong supporter of the latter approach, and therefore this is the approach that we have taken so far in the project. Mainly, this view is based on my understanding of how typically developing children learn about social interactions and develop their social skills. Clearly, human societies and cultures have a huge variety of norms, telling us 'how to behave', 'what is appropriate and what is not, and many of these culturally determined behaviours need to be taught quite explicitly. Such everyday teaching outside the classroom involves fairly strong encouragement to 'Say hello to uncle Charlie', 'Sit still at the table', 'Use your fork and not your fingers', etc. A child might develop such behaviours by observation and imitation, but it usually does not come 'naturally' without any kind of encouragement.

Similarly, a prominent product of human cultures, namely language, involves a great amount of teaching. A child has to learn the writing system of a language, and a child learns one, two or more second languages in school, often involving highly structured sessions with intensive instructional elements. Such teaching sessions are often regarded by children as 'not fun', and it can even lead to a disinterest in foreign languages. However, this is not how a child usually learns its native language (and it is possibly not the best way to learn a second language). Children learn a great amount through play, playing with parents, siblings and peers, 'picking up' meaning and labels by observation, imitation, exploration, testing, and, importantly, by shaping and further developing these skills through the practical application of these skills in social interactions. Children learn a language by being immersed in language-based human culture, exploring and exercising their skills in situations where interaction is 'useful', rewarding and enjoyable. Children do not only learn a native language, they usually seem to enjoy it tremendously, applying newly learnt skills readily and on their own initiative.

Learning by exploration and play in meaningful and pleasurable interactions seems far more powerful than strict instructional teaching sessions. A similar point has been made for language learning in non-human primates, where instructional teaching was much less successful than learning in a social context, 'picking up' what to do and what to 'say' [25]. Humans are social animals, they are born with basic social skills (such as the ability to imitate [19]), and these and further social skills rapidly develop while the child is being immersed in a social environment. Some elements of social skills possibly need to be explictly taught (such as a handshake as part of a greeting used in Germany), but it does not mean that tge experience is enjoyable and 'fun' (from my own experience, many Germans do not like to shake hands, and I have never observed children 'handshaking' in play and for fun). However, in typically developing children most social skills evolue in a social and 'meaningful' (e.g. emotionally rewarding) context.

Temple Grandin gives a good example of a high-functioning person with autism who learnt explicit rules of human interaction and communication, and is therefore able to 'do the right thing'. [14]. However, she is using these skills in the same way as we use a fork and knife at dinner time: it is the 'appropriate' choice of behaviour, but we do not find any enjoyment in it. For this reason Temple Grandin coined the expression that she feels like an anthropologist on Mars, a stranger in a foreign culture. She learnt the 'social language' of this culture, but does not have access to its deeper meanings, possibly since as a child she did not learn this language in the same way typically developing children do.

Similarly, autism therapy can teach social skills explicitly, showing 'what the right answer/behaviour' is in a given context, then exercising the application of this behaviour repeatedly, until the child responds 'correctly' in a given situation. However, for typically developing children, such highly-structured and intensively instructional teaching sessions with the teacher strongly in control are not usually very enjoyable, and one can hypothesise that the same applies to children with autism. On the other hand, playful, constructivist learning in Papert's sense [26] might allow children with autism to discover that social interactions and communication with other people can be very pleasurable, enjoyable and 'meaningful', something they might seek rather than avoid. Thus, it is not unreasonable to assume that playful learning might complement explicit teaching practices in autism therapy. Play is already used in schools for children with autism as an enjoyable experience, with or without explicit learning objectives. In the Aurora project we assume that interactive robotic toys might add another dimension to the scope of learning experiences for children with autism.

8.6 Challenges

Based on our current data in the Aurora project it is not possible to claim that the interactions with the robot have a long-term positive impact on the children. However, we showed that the robot can serve as an enjoyable toy that facilitates interactive games during the trial sessions. While children with autism have great difficulty interacting with people, our data shows that the robot is able to successfully engage children with autism in interactive games, such as imitative turn-taking games which are therapeutically relevant. Also, we reported on data that shows how children with autism use the robot as a vehicle in order to make contact with non-autistic adults who are present during the trials [6]. Future work in the Aurora project will continue to investigate different robotic designs and scenarios, more specifically to address the issue of how imitative interaction skills can be facilitated. Long-term studies are necessary in order to show that the robots have a long-term impact on the children's behaviour. It is not enough to show that the children respond positively towards the robot in a given trial. It is necessary to show that they can generalise to other contexts, i.e. that the interactions with the robot help them in their development of social skills applied to other humans in the classroom or at home.

The project involves a number of challenges. From the perspective of people designing social robots, in particular robots that can interact with people, our application area poses particular constraints.

Robotics Challenges

Firstly, the mobile robot is interacting with children: this means that we cannot generally expect cooperative behaviour, that the interactions are not likely to be of a cautious, tentative nature as may be expected with adults. The children (when interacting with the robot) are essentially free to do as they wish, with no constraints on movements. Children play with the robot in a completely unconstrained fashion (e.g. they touch the robot, push it around, step on it, lift it up and transport it, turn it over, etc.). Furthermore, the trials are conducted in a social context which means that in addition to the robot and one or two children, other people are usually present in the room, providing confusing information to the robot's sensors. At any one time there will be at least one researcher from the Aurora team present in the room, as well as one teacher from the school. This makes the development of reliable perception and control systems for the robot very difficult. In the case of the humanoid doll which identifies arm movements, the child is required to sit at a table, although it would be desirable if the child could move around the room freely. However, in such a case the recognition of body movements or gestures becomes extremely complicated. Simplifications of the problem, e.g. by using coloured batches or caps, are not desirable for autistic children. It is a very difficult application area for interactive robots as this is an unstructured, poorly defined kind of interaction. Technology is advancing quickly but a robot showing robust behaviour in unstructured, highly dynamic and populated environments still poses a challenge today. Simple kinds of games (e.g. chase or imitation games) are far more realistic.

Design Challenges

In autism therapy we cannot rely on well developed tendencies to anthropomorphise the robot, neither can we use the robot in pretend-play scenarios. People with autism usually concentrate on the literal meaning of objects and language. Thus, we cannot assume that by making the robot 'cute' or 'animal-like' it would automatically become more appealing to them. Also, we cannot assume that an anthropo- or zoomorphic robot, such as Kismet [3], will elicit pro-active, social, or even caregiver-like behaviour in autistic children. Our approach to keeping the robot as machine-like as possible (at least for the mobile robot) is quite different from most other projects in the area of social robotics and socially intelligent agents that are designed to interact with humans. For autistic people, life-likeness usually means complexity, unpredictability and confusion. Many people with autism enjoy using a computer as a safe, predictable and controllable environment. For this purpose we use a simple robot with an explicit machine-like shape. The doll robot has a humanoid shape, but a very simple one. Indeed, none of the children we worked with has ever shown strong signs of fear, resentment or confusion during interaction with the robot. Although the appearance of the robot and the simplicity of the robot's sensors and actuators are easily understood and accepted by the autistic children, the robot is being developed as a therapeutic tool and not only as an interesting toy, even though providing a playful and enjoyable environment for children with autism represents a worthwhile research goal in itself. The big challenge for the

Aurora project is therefore to 'get the interaction dynamics right', namely programming the robot so that it can engage the children in therapeutically relevant interactions. This includes basic interactions such as turn-taking, as well as imitation games.

8.7 Conclusion

Talks presented at the first and very successful international workshop on "Robotic and Virtual Interactive Systems in Autism Therapy", held at University of Hertfordshire at the end of September 2001, gave evidence of a growing community of researchers trying to integrate autism therapy and interactive technology. Ultimately, I believe that robotic and other computer technology can empower people with autism by giving them a choice: the choice of either finding a way to relate to the outside, non-autistic social world by becoming a bit more "like us", or to develop their own specific ways of perceiving and interacting with the world, supported by technology. Whatever they decide, the choice should be up to them.

8.8 Acknowledgement

This project is supported by an EPSRC grant (GR/M62648). The robotic platform used is kindly donated by Applied AI Inc, and we are grateful for the continued support of the staff and pupils of Radlett Lodge School and Colnbrook School. Our particular thanks go to Patricia Beevers and Liz Bannister. The trials with the mobile robot and its evaluations that are briefly summarised in this paper are part of Iain Werry's PhD research. Thanks to Penny Stribling, Paul Dickerson, John Rae, Bernard Ogden and William Harwin for discussions on the Aurora project.

Bibliography

[1] Baron-Cohen, S. (1995) Mindblindness: An Essay on Autism and Theory of Mind. MIT Press.

[2] Billard, A. (to appear) Play, Dreams and Imitation in Robota. In Socially Intelligent Agents - Creating relationships with computers and robots. Editors K. Dautenhahn, A. Bond, L. Cañamero, B. Edmonds, Kluwer Academic Publishers, to appear.

[3] Breazeal, C. (2000) Sociable Machines: Expressive Social Exchange Between Humans and Robots. Doctoral Dissertation. Department of Electrical Engineering and Computer Science. MIT AI-Lab.

[4] Colby, K. M. and Smith, D. C. (1971) Computers in the Treatment of Nonspeaking Autistic Children. Current Psychiatric Therapies, 11, pp. 1-17.

[5] D'Aluisio, F. and C. C. Mann, Eds. (2000) Robo sapiens. MIT Press.

[6] Dautenhahn, K, Werry, I., Rae J., Dickerson, P., Stribling, P., Ogden, B. (to appear) Robotic playmates - Analysing interactive competencies of children with autism playing with a mobile robot. To appear in: Socially Intelligent Agents - Creating Relationships with Computer and Robots, Kluwer Academic Publishers.

[7] Dautenhahn, K. (1995) Getting to know each other - artificial social intelligence for autonomous robots. Robotics and Autonomous Systems 16, pp 333-356.

[8] Dautenhahn, K. (1999) Embodiment and Interaction in Socially Intelligent Life-Like Agents. In: C. L. Nehaniv (ed): Computation for Metaphors, Analogy and Agents, Springer Lecture Notes in Artificial Intelligence, Volume 1562, Springer, pp. 102-142.

[9] Dautenhahn, K. (1999) Robots as Social Actors: AURORA and the Case of Autism. Proc. CT99, The Third International Cognitive Technology Conference, August, San Francisco.

[10] Dautenhahn, K. and Billard, A. (to appear) Games Children with Autism Can Play With Robota, a Humanoid Robotic Doll. Proc. 1st Cambridge Workshop on Universal Access and Assistive Technology [CWUAAT], to appear in: Universal Access and Assistive Technology, Springer-Verlag (London).

[11] Dautenhahn, K., Werry, I. (2000) Issues of Robot-Human Interaction Dynamics in the Rehabilitation of Children with Autism. Proc. From Animals to Animats, The Sixth International Conference on the Simulation of Adaptive Behavior (SAB2000), 11 - 15 September 2000, Paris, France, MIT Press, pp. 519-528.

[12] Druin A. and Hendler J., Eds, (2000) Robots for Kids: Exploring New Technologies for Learning. Morgan Kaufmann Publishers.

[13] Fogg, B. J. (1999) Introduction: Persuasive Technologies. Communications of the ACM 42(5): 27-29.

[14] Grandin, T. (1995) Thinking in pictures. Doubleday Publisher, New York.

[15] Grandin, T. and Scariano, M. M. (1996) Emergence: Labeled autistic, Warner Books.

[16] Hutchby, I. and R. Wooffitt (1998) Conversation Analysis: principles, practices and applications, Polity Press, Cambridge.

[17] Jordan, R. (1999) Autistic Spectrum Disorders - An Introductory Handbook for Practitioners. David Fulton Publishers, London.

[18] Leslie, A. M. (1987) Pretence and representation: the origins of 'theory of mind'. Psychological Review 94(4): 412-426.

[19] Meltzoff, A. N. (1988) The Human infant as Homo imitans. In T. R. Zentall and J. B. G. Galef, Eds., Social Learning: Psychological and Biological Perspectives, Erlbaum, Hillsdale.

[20] Michaud, F., Clavet, A., Lachiver, G., and Lucas, M. (2000) Designing toy robots to help autistic children - An open design project for Electrical and Computer Engineering education. Proc. American Society for Engineering Education, June 2000.

[21] Powell, S. (1996) The use of computers in teaching people with autism. In: Autism on the Agenda: Papers from a National Autistic Society Conference. London: NAS, 1996.

[22] Resnick, M. (1988) Lego, Logo and Life. Proc. of an Interdisciplinary Workshop on the Synthesis and Simulation of Living Systems, Los Alamos, New Mexico, September 1987, Ed. C. G. Langton, pp. 397-406.

[23] Rogers S. J., Pennington, B. F. (1991) A theoretical approach to the deficits in infantile autism. Development and Psychopathology 3: 137-162.

[24] Russell, J. (1997) Autism as an Executive Disorder. Oxford University Press.

[25] Savage-Rumbaugh, S. (1994) Kanzi - the ape at the brink of the human mind. John Wiley and Sons.

[26] Seymour Papert, S. (1980) Mindstorms: Children, Computers, and Powerful Ideas. Basic Books, New York.

[27] Tardiff, C., Plumet, M. H., Beaudichon, J., Waller, D., Bouvard, M., Leboyer, M. (1995) Micro-Analysis of Social Interactions Between Autistic Children and Normal Adults in Semi-Structured Play Situations. International Journal of Behavioural Development 18(4): 727-747.

[28] Walter, W. G. (1963) The Living Brain. W. W. Norton, New York.

[29] Weir, S. and Emanuel, R. (1976) Using Logo to catalyse communication in an autistic child. DAI Research Report No. 15, University of Edinburgh.

[30] Werry, I., Dautenhahn, K., Ogden B. and Harwin, W. (2001) Can social interaction skills be taught by a robotic agent? The role of a robotic mediator in autism therapy. In M. Beynon, C. L. Nehaniv, K. Dautenhahn (Eds.) Cognitive Technology - Instruments of Mind. Lecture Notes in Artificial Intelligence 2177, pp. 57-74..

[31] Werry, I., K. Dautenhahn, W. Harwin (2001) Investigating a Robot as a Therapy Partner for Children with Autism , Proc. 6th European Conference for the Advancement of Assistive Technology (AAATE 2001), 3-6 September 2001 in Ljubljana / Slovenia.

Group Discussion 8
Playing and Learning with Robots

Technology and Values

Steels: Can you tell us more how your work is received by the community of people involved in autism therapy?

Dautenhahn: Over the last few years I became very interested in autism therapy. What is different from my previous work as a robotics researcher is that now I have to be very specific about why am I doing what I am doing. Previously when I worked with robots, when I presented my work it was self-evident. I wanted to build intelligent robots and make them more and more complex. People never really asked why, so I never had to justify myself because I was part of a community where everybody developed this technology. Now I talk to autism researchers and teachers and if I mention to them robots, they are not impressed at all. They all know science fiction movies like Terminator where it is a fact that humanoids exist. If I tell them how still difficult it is to realise that, they do not get that. They are not at all impressed by the robot itself, by the technology or when I try to explain how it is programmed. What they are interested in is why and how we want to use the robots.

Nevejan: What was quite shocking to me is that these children were ready or were actually talking to the machines, before talking to the therapists or the grown ups. We really should reflect upon this.

Dautenhahn: They had a very natural approach in talking to the robot, and in talking to us about the robot. Most of the time they were also talking to the teacher, a very familiar person they know. Sometimes, because we were there anyway, they would spontaneously start talking to us.

Nevejan : Technology is always a representation of something else. You can attribute all sorts of values to this representation, which is why I believe you need real people around, to help create values.

Dautenhahn : Children with autism are very much like natural scientists, even more so than non-autistic children who very soon become social scientists. The latter are very interested in their friends, in what their friends are thinking about them. Whereas children with autism sometimes seem in a way purer in a naturalistic sense. They very much want to figure out what is going on in the world. The laws of physics, cause and effect and so on. One of the functions of technology could be to give the opportunity to children to understand these things better.

Steels: I suppose that the robot could be a way for them to make the transition to become more interested in social intelligence. It is less unpredictable than real people but a robot can still be given appearances and behaviors that are life-like, as the AIBO shows.

Dautenhahn: If I drop this pencil for instance. They say, oh, it's falling down! By interacting with robots, children are noticing that there are a lot of sensors involved. What are these sensors doing? What will happen if I put my hand on it? Oh, the robot is moving backwards. Thus, if technology is on a relatively simple level, you can still try to understand it. But as Caroline Nevejan says, there are certain values in technology itself and one of the properties that I like to see in technology is how it works. For mobile phones, you can have certain ideas how they work, but you cannot grasp how it really works. Still you can recognize how to operate them. Within a limited context you can do your own little experiments with them.

Transference

Steels: But isn't technology magic for many people, even less understandable than the real world? Most people have no idea how a computer or a telephone really works.

Dautenhahn: I am sometimes concerned about technology that is surrounding us everywhere and that we cannot recognize. I would like technology to give us a chance and to help usunderstand, to advertise how it works, how it should be used. Other than relying on us by miracle figuring out what it is about. I do not like the 'disappearing computer' metaphor for example. I like computers that I can see and that I can touch. Where I can see what is happening when I push a button. If technology is all around us and we do not even know where it is and what the function is, how should children be able to find out how the world works? Even without technology there are already so many things as a child that you are not in control of, all these pressures and all these external constraints. But they remain very interested in trying to find out what is happening.

Coenen : That makes me think of the VCR where in most households the kids know how to do it, and the parents do not. The thing is that most kids figure this out by trial and error. So I am not so sure that technology needs to explain itself, because kids figure it out differently anyway. And often it is on a complete different level compared to how we are using it.

Rinaldi: We did experiments in introducing computers to our children as well. The first reaction we saw is an extraordinary effort to consider an object not as object but as subject. The concept of animation, to consider everything living. So they immediately started to have a dialogue with the computer. That's how they perceived that reality. We can say that the computer is a tool, but I think it is a very different tool from a pencil or a pen for instance. We are interested to understand better what kind of epistemological change could be brought about by the computer. I don't have an answer.

Dautenhahn: Interaction can be a prime motivation and foundation for learning. But transference or generalization is even a bigger issue. What we are dong with the robots is not about theory of mind, it is about interaction dynamics. It is not about teaching mental states explicitly. I often get asked the question that is crucial in any form of autism therapy, namely: How can you generalise this work to other contexts. First of all it is possible that they will nicely interact with a dog or a dolphin but they cannot transfer these skills to other human beings or any other creatures. For example, during one of our trials, a particular child started explaining to the researcher how the robot it was interacting with had feelings. At the back of the robot there is a small LCD display which shows what program is running on the robot, but for the child this was an indication of the robot's mood. So after the initial interactions with the robot, the child tried to explain the concept of mood in a series of conversations with the researcher. That was very interesting for us and something we want to build further upon. It showed that the child was collaborating with the researcher and forming a concept about the robot's behaviour. So what it was learning went beyond mere interaction.

Theme V

Learning Must Be Fun

Fun. Ezra, age 9

I think we shouldn't underestimate the destroying power of boredom in education. We are living in a knowledge society while half of the planet knows nothing and the other half is bored with education. I think it is terribly important that we start thinking about ways not to bore people.

Eduardo Punset

Chapter 9

The Motivated Brain

by Olivier J.-M. D. Coenen

Olivier J.-M. D. Coenen received a Ph.D. in Physics from the University of California, San Diego. He was a research associate at San Diego Children's Hospital and at the Computational Neurobiology Laboratory of the Salk Institute in San Diego before recently joining the Sony Computer Science Laboratory in Paris. He has been working on models of the cerebellum and the vestibuloocular reflex, on information theoretic approaches to neural coding and plasticity, recurrent neural networks and reinforcement learning.

There is a deep interaction between the functioning and growth of the brain and motivational and environmental factors. In this contribution, a few recent findings from neuroscience related to this issue are presented. The essay is not a rigorous nor exhaustive presentation of the scientific results available, but a promenade among interesting topics that are still a matter of debate. The results presented show in particular a tight relation between stress levels, hormonal functioning, brain plasticity and maintenance, and cognitive functioning. The discussion focuses on the hippocampus but other brain areas are likely subject to this kind of influences.

9.1 The Impact of Stress

In a recent study, Cho [4] studied the effect of jet lag on the brain of flight attendants. The study showed that chronic jet lag caused cognitive deficits and temporal lobe atrophy of the brain that became apparent after flying for five years. The volume of their temporal lobe was estimated by computing the contour area of their temporal lobe on magnetic resonance imaging (MRI) images [4].

Cho studied 20 healthy female flight attendants, age 22 - 28 with at least 5 years experience, that were divided in two groups. The first group, the short-recovery group, had rest intervals of less than 5 days between transmeridian flights across at least seven different time zones. The second group, the long-recovery group, had more than two weeks interval between their transmeridian travels and flew only short flights of less than 3 time zones during these two weeks. The total flight duration was approximately the same in the two groups.

The temporal lobe volumes for the two groups of flight attendants are presented in figure 9.1. The results show that the short recovery crew had a significant decrease in their right temporal lobe volume compared to the long recovery crew.

Cognitive Impairment and Stress

The results of the study also showed that the flight attendants of the short-recovery crew had a longer reaction time to a visual memory classification task than the long-recovery crew. The task was a delayed matching-to-sample task in which four different target locations given by black dots had to be classified after an initial presentation. The flight attendants first had to study four target locations that appeared four times. They then had to classify the location of a series of targets presented. The results showed that the flight attendants of the short-recovery crew had a longer reaction time (823 ± 32 ms) to the visual memory classification task than the long-recovery crew (741 ± 22 ms). The short-recovery crew also made significantly more mistakes ($15 \pm 2\%$) than the long-recovery crew ($6 \pm 5\%$) [4].

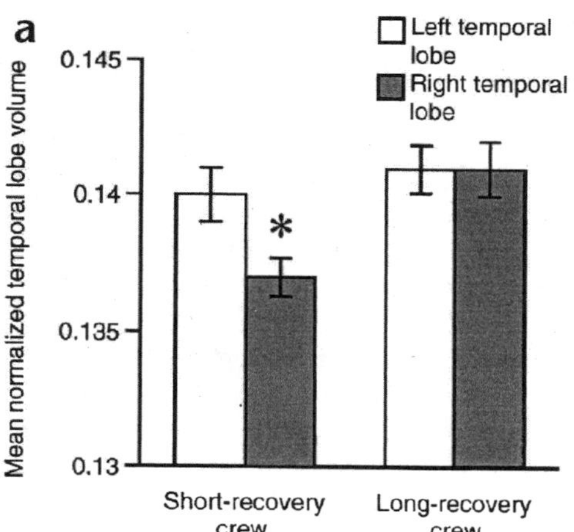

Figure 9.1: Comparison of temporal lobe volume between short and long recovery crew. The short-recovery crew had a significant decrease in their right temporal lobe volume compared to the long recovery crew. The short-recovery crew rested less than 5 days between trans-meridian travel across 7 different time zones, whereas the long-recovery crew rested more than two weeks between such flights. Reproduced with permission from Cho, K., *Nature Neuroscience*, 4:6, 567-8, June 2001.

Cortisol and Stress

What is the cause of such deficit? In an earlier study, Cho and coworkers [3] measured the level of cortisol in the saliva of 62 flight attendants; cortisol is a steroid used as a biochemical marker of stress. They found that the cortisol level was significantly higher in short-recovery crew (18.4 $\pm$ 0.6 nmol/l) than in long-recovery (14.7 $\pm$ 0.3 nmol/l), whereas the latter had the same level as the ground crews working similar schedule (14.4 $\pm$ 0.3 nmol/l).

Normal cortisol level has a diurnal rhythm with a maximal level in the morning and a nadir during the night. Cortisol is released as the response to physical and physiological stresses and is part of the hypothalamic-pituitary-adrenal loop. Brief high levels of cortisol are generally beneficial for the organism to respond correctly to trauma or higher levels of activity, e.g. during intense physical exercise or in escaping response. In a short term crisis, cortisol release provides energy at the expense of long-term processes that are not as important for immediate survival. Conversely, chronic (long-term) exposure to high level of circulating corticosteroids impairs cognitive function in both animals and humans. In particular, it causes damages of the hippocampus and impair hippocampus-dependent learning and memory [17].

9.2 Role of the Hippocampus

The hippocampus is located deep within the temporal lobes just beneath the thalamus, and posterior to the amygdala. In appearance, it resemble the marine organism after which it was named (New Latin, from Greek *hippokampos*: sea horse). The hippocampus is important in spatial learning and short-term memory. Damage to the hippocampus or to the surrounding regions, causes anterograde amnesia, or the inability to form new memories.

The now famous case study of a patient known as H.M. led researchers to focus on the role of the hippocampus in behavior. In 1953, then a young man, H.M. had his hippocampus and surrounding structures (including the amygdala) from both hemispheres removed to alleviate epileptic seizures that had become debilitating and unresponsive to medication. Although H.M.'s epilepsy improved following surgery, he was left with a serious selective memory deficit. His intellect and personality were left unchanged, but he suffered from severe anterograde amnesia, a loss of ability to form new memories. He has memory from events and persons met over 40 years ago, but he has not formed new memories since his surgery. H.M. can store new information briefly, but has difficulty recalling it especially when distracted. Even though H.M has severe difficulties in learning new facts and remembering events (declarative memory), he is able to learn new motor skills although he cannot remember learning them. The hippocampus is, apparently, not the site of long-term memory storage but rather involved in the formation of new memories.

The hippocampus is affected in Alzheimer's disease where neuron loss is unquestioned. It is also in the hippocampus that place cells and direction cells are found in rats. These cells are tuned, for example, to the particular position or orientation of the rat in a maze.

Hippocampus and Stress

In response to acute stress, the pituitary gland releases the ACTH hormone (adrenocorticotroph stimulating hormone) that stimulates the adrenal gland to produce glucocorticoids, primarily the cortisol and the corticosterone hormones. One long standing hypothesis suggests that these stress hormones increase the vulnerability of neurons to age-related damage. Hence, prolonged exposure to these hormones reduces the resistance of neurons, thereby increasing the rate at which neurons are damaged by toxic compounds or ordinary attrition. Since the hippocampus normally inhibits the release of ACTH by the pituitary gland, this means that increased neural loss in the hippocampus due to chronic stress can trigger a positive-feedback loop of continually increasing stress hormones levels and more rapid hippocampal decline (figure 9.2) [23].

Evidence consistent with this hypothesis has been accumulating steadily for 20 years in rodent and a recent paper suggests that it may also hold in humans [16]. Their study shows that aged humans with prolonged elevation of cortisol, the major stress hormone in humans, have hippocampal damage and cognitive deficits in correlation with cortisol level changes (see figure 9.3). A high and increasing level of cortisol over the years correspond to lower hippocampal volumes.

9.3 Brain Plasticity

Hebb published his plasticity postulate in 1949 [12]; the postulate suggested that the connection between two neurons may strengthen whenever the two neurons are coactive, possibly creating a causal relationship. Hubel and Wiesel [35] were one of the first to demonstrate cortical plasticity in visual cortex by patching the eye of a kitten during what was found to be the critical period of the visual system. Many experiments since have clearly demonstrated activity-dependent plasticity in cortex and different models have illustrated potential mechanisms of plasticity, e.g. see [1].

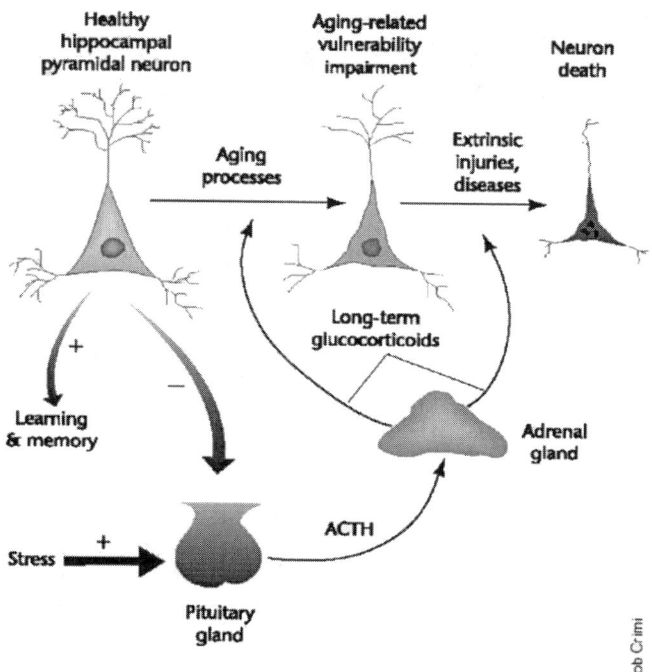

Figure 9.2: Effects of stress on neuronal structures causing cognitive decline. The glucocorticoid hypothesis of cognitive decline in aging says that stress increases pituitary release of ACTH, which causes the adrenal gland to produce more glucocorticoids. Long-term exposure to these stress hormones increases neuronal vulnerability to aging, extrinsic injuries and disease, causing hippocampal deterioration and eventual cognitive decline. Reproduced with permission from Porter, N.M and Landfield, P.W., *Nature Neuroscience*, 1:1,3-4, 1998.

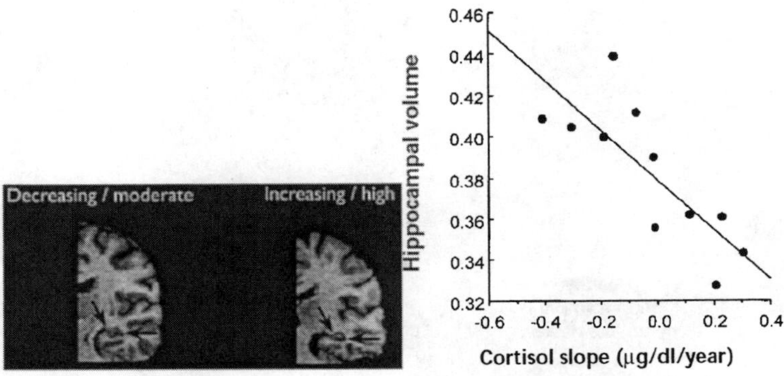

Figure 9.3: Correlation between stress, high cortisol levels, and cognitive deficits. The left panel shows MRI images of human subjects with moderate and decreasing levels of cortisol (left image) and with high and increasing levels of cortisol (right image). The hippocampal volume is greater on the left than on the right. This corresponds to the results shown on the right panel, which presents hippocampal volume as a function of cortisol changes per year. A high and increasing level of cortisol over the years correspond to lower hippocampal volumes. Reproduced with permission from Lupien, S.J. *et al.*, *Nature Neuroscience*, 1:1, 69-73, 1998.

Cortical plasticity is not limited to young and developing animals but is also very present in the adult. For example, the digits of the hand are normally represented discontinuously in the adult monkey somatosensory cortex [5]. After connecting the skin of adjacent digits, the normal discontinuity between the cortical representations of adjacent fingers was shown to have disappear 3-8 months later. These findings suggests that maps in adult cortex can be altered by modifying the temporal coincidence of the inputs to these maps through life experiences.

In humans, such plasticity has also been observed using magnetoencephalography. Two adults were studied before and after surgical separation of webbed fingers. Whereas before surgery, the maps displayed shrunken and non-somatotopic hand representation, within weeks following surgery, cortical reorganization was evident and correlated with the new functionality of the separated digits [18]. A recent human study even demonstrated that the improved performance and threshold sensitivity in sensory discrimination task could be correlated with the degree of cortical reorganization after training [22].

Nevertheless, early exposure to activities in life may have an advantage. An imaging study has shown that in humans the cortical representation of the digits of the left hand of string players was larger than in controls. Interestingly, the amount of reorganization was correlated with the age at which the musicians started playing [6].

Another powerful example, is the putative remapping that has been observed after the tragic event of limb loss. Subjects have reported, for example, that scratching parts of their face relieve itching sensations in their lost or "phantom" limb [2] [26] [25]. An explanation suggests that the face responsive area in cortex, typically adjacent to the arm responsive area, takes over or expand into the area previously innervated by the lost limb. As a final example, a recent study has shown that subjects with paralysis in one limb, in some for up to 16 years, caused by a stroke or other brain damage, were able to recover partial and useful control of their limb after only six weeks of gradual training. The training included constraining the better limb to force usage of the enfeebled one. Magnetic resonance imaging (MRI) has shown that some brain areas followed a complex patterns of activation and deactivation. Some areas became increasingly active with training, whereas some areas started decreasing with further training and some stopped to be active after control recovery of the limb. One interpretation is that given that the regular pathway controlling the limb has been damaged, the brain must explore to find and construct a new pathway. This extend of exploration and pathfinding is apparently driven by the usage experience of the enfeebled limb. Once a new connecting path has been found, further training will decrease brain activity in some areas to concentrate it along the newly found pathway.

These types of experiments demonstrate that even after development, in adulthood, the brain remains plastic and indicates that its functionality is very much dependent on experience.

9.3.1 Experience Enrichment and Deprivation

Hippocampus and Environment

It is interesting to investigate the participation of the environment to brain plasticity. This has lead to surprising discoveries in the hippocampus in particular. Researchers have investigated the role of enriched environments on the plasticity in the brain; different degrees of enrichment for laboratory rats are illustrated in figure 9.4. Such studies have shown that the environment affects the biochemical parameters, increases angiogenesis (the genesis of new blood vessels), augments the dendritic arborization, synaptogenesis (the genesis of new neural connections), improves learning, increases gliogenesis (glial cells, that are the supporting cells in the brain) and even neurogenesis. Contrary to common beliefs, the birth or creation of new neurons in the brain appears to be a regular process that continues even into old age and in humans as well. A study found new neurons in the hippocampus of Swedish cancer patients [7]. Before they died of their disease, these patients had volunteered for a study that labeled any newborn cells in their bodies with a bright green dye. Results showed that new neurons had been born recently in a patient who was 62 years old. The intriguing question is what in the environment is responsible for the generation of new neurons in the brain?

Neurogenesis and the Environment

Another study at the Salk Institute [32] investigated which component in an environmental enrichment was responsible for an increase in the new formation of neurons in the hippocampus. For this purpose, they submitted mice to various conditions: water-maze learning (learner), swimming (swimmer), voluntary wheel running (runner) as well as enriched (enriched) and standard housing (control) groups (figure 9.4). They found that neither the maze learner nor the swimmer had any increased neurogenesis. However, running alone (runners) accounted for similar increase in animals living in enriched conditions. They concluded that voluntary exercise is sufficient for explaining the enhanced neurogenesis in enriched environments!

It is rather interesting that it is running alone and not swimming that benefits neurogenesis. One point to notice is that these laboratory animals are typically water aversive animals and do not swim at leisure as they do wheel running. Their level, or type of stress during

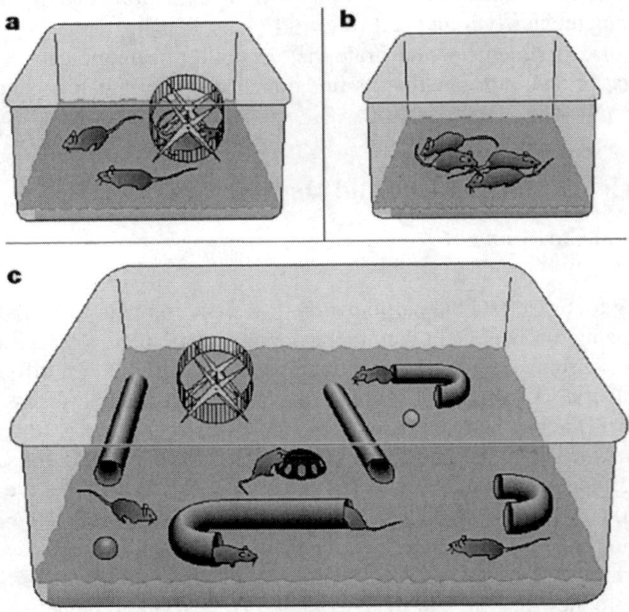

Figure 9.4: There is a significant difference in cognitive functioning in rats compared on the stimulation found in their environment. Living conditions in different experimental groups. a) A cage containing a running wheel for voluntary physical exercise (48 x 26 cm). b) A standard housing cage (30 x 18 cm). c) Cage for an enriched environment (86 x 76 cm). Enrichment consisted of social interaction (14 mice in the cage), stimulation of exploratory behavior with objects such as toys and a set of tunnels, and a running wheels for exercise. Reproduced with permission from van Praag, Henriette *et al. Nat Rev Neurosci.* 2000 Dec;1(3):191-8.

the exercise may therefore be partly responsible for the difference. Interestingly, in female national athletes, an increase was noted in the level of cortisol in the saliva of handball players after exercise whereas swimmer athletes did not show the effect compared to a sedentary group [8]. This indicates that the type of exercise influence the cortisol response although the level of performance is also a factor. Whether any correspondence can be drawn between the observations in rodent and humans remains to be seen.

Benefits of Enriched Environments

New neurons are therefore added continuously to certain areas of the adult brain, and in increased number after exercise. Their role and function are slowly being elucidated. Previous studies in mice had found that physical activity facilitated recovery from injury [14] and improved cognitive functions [9]. A following study has actually shown that running mice display increased synaptic plasticity and better performance in learning in a water-maze [33]. Whether the new neurons participate directly in these improvements remains to be seen, since other factors such as increased serotonin levels with running may exert multiple effects, influencing learning, synaptic plasticity and even neurogenesis.

In general, enrichment has beneficial effects on conditions such as strokes, epilepsy, and aging (see the review paper [34] and references therein). A recent paper reported that, in rats, three weeks of enrichment prevented the pharmacological induction of motor seizure and reduced apoptosis, or *programmed cell death*, by 45% in the hippocampus. Previous studies have shown that pre and postoperative enrichment or wheel running facilitated the recovery of brain lesions. In rats, even a short enrichment, e.g. 2h each day, as been shown to be as effective for certain tasks as continuous exposure. Even when applied with a delay, enrichment can facilitate recovery from brain damage. Rats transferred to an enriched cage 15 days after ligation of a cerebral artery showed, seven weeks later, motor improvement compared to rats kept in standard cages. Interestingly, pre-operative voluntary wheel running has been shown to provide benefits against induced ischaemia in gerbils, decreasing hippocampal damages as well as mortality from 55% to 10%. Note, however, that not all populations may show the similar benefits. For example, spontaneously hypertensive rats, do not show improved recovery from running wheel exercises after similar induced ischaemia.

Genetics and the Environment

In addition to pathologies, as the ones mentioned above, enrichment may also benefit populations with genetic abnormalities. Memory deficits in mice associated with a disruption of a neural receptor in the hippocampus could be rescued by exposure to an enriched environment for three hours daily for two months. In mice with the Huntington's disease transgene, enrichment delays the onset of behavioral deficits, such as loss of motor coordination even though the neural symptoms of the disease are still apparent. Moreover, enrichment improved learning and increased neurogenesis in mouse strains that are known as poor learners. These findings, taken together, suggest that some genetic constraints may be overridden by an adequate enriched environment.

Many beneficial effects have therefore been reported in enriched environment studies. However it is not entirely clear how long the effects last and what happens when enrichment is discontinued. Initial studies reported that the observed changes in neural structures and biochemistry revert to normal when animals are returned to regular housing. However, a recent study showed no differences in learning between a group of mice that was removed from an enriched environment after about two months and a group that remained in this environment for the entire duration of six months. Interestingly, it is the former group that showed increased cell proliferation in the hippocampus, although neurogenesis remained identical for both groups. It is perhaps the novelty rather than the continued exposure to complex stimuli that elicited the environmental effects on adult hippocampal neurogenesis. Nevertheless, another study lasting twice as long and with twice as many learning trials per day, reported increased learning, density of receptors and nerve growth factor in rats raised in an enriched environment. Moreover, brain changes appear more persistent after enrichment lasting 80 days than 30 days. Although the benefits of an enriched environment seem to depend on inveterate exposure to enrichment, further studies are needed to better describe all the parameters at play during enrichment protocols.

Blame it on your Upbringing

Fascinating elements are coming to light regarding the repercussions in adult life of situations that newborns have experienced. For example, adult rats that have been handled by humans caretakers briefly for 15 minutes each day during the first three weeks of life have significantly reduced stress responses to various stressful situations. These rats also display reduced neuron loss in the hippocampus and cognitive impairments associated with aging. Note how this situation is consistent with the hypothesis that we mentioned earlier and that suggests that stress hormones increase the vulnerability of neurons to age-related damage. Indeed, these rats have increased expressions of glucocorticoid receptors, e.g. cortisol receptors, that alter the regulation of the hormonal syntheses in response to stress.

Recent findings suggests that mother-offspring interactions may be decisive in defining the behavioral and hormonal responses to stress, whereas maternal behavior is also crucial for cognitive development. Increased gene expression of receptors, neuromodulators and neural factors in the hippocampus are correlated with the level of maternal licking and grooming during the first ten days of life. The transfer of offsprings from attentive mothers (high levels of licking and grooming) to less attentive ones, and vice versa, showed that these effects were the results of maternal behavior. Furthermore, improved learning in water mazes was observed with the offsprings of these attentive mothers.

Conversely, maternal deprivation has ill consequences on responses to stress, on cognitive development and susceptibility to disease. For example, two hours of maternal separation daily during the first two weeks after birth increased stress hormonal response to stressful situations in rats. Moreover, deprivation of maternal contact for one hour or more caused significant decrease in serum growth hormone.

9.4 Having Control over the Environment

A new hypothesis suggests that the neurogenesis in the hippocampal formation may be an important factor involved in the precipitation and recovery from depression [13]. In laboratory animals, exposure to inescapable shock leads to effects reminiscent of depression. Such shock has been linked to marked changes in endocrine activity and central nervous system neurochemistry, suppressed immunological function, reduced activity, weight loss, decreased aggression and lower dominance status, and even induced analgesia. Most of these effects can be improved when the animals have the possibility of controlling the aversive events [31].

Moreover, learning deficits and reduced plasticity in the hippocampus (long-term potentiation or LTP[1]) are observed after exposure to inescapable shock. Most interestingly, these deficits and plasticity improve when the animals are permitted to exert control.

In a study, two groups of rats were submitted to the same duration of low-intensity electric shock every minute for thirty minutes [31]. The first group of rats could not escape, but the second could escape by running through an archway and trigger a switch that shut off the current to both groups simultaneously. This ensure that both groups received the same electric shocks. After some time, the group of *escapees* could reduce the shock duration from four seconds to 1.5 seconds of which, 75% of the responses were less than 1.5 seconds. Plasticity in the hippocampus (LTP) was 82% of control potentiation for the escapable group whereas it was only 59% for the inescapable group.

This study indicates that the controllability of the situation affects the neural plasticity in the hippocampus at the cellular and synaptic level and that the impairment on plasticity is principally due to the lack of control, hence due to a *psychological* factor rather than to the shock itself.

Interestingly, note, however, that acute stress has a differential effect on male and female rats. It has recently been observed that whereas acute stress impairs a form of learning (classical conditioning) in female rats, the same stressor actually facilitates learning in males [28] [36]. These results indicate that even though the same aversive event is experienced, the induced behavioral responses can be opposite in males versus females. The differences in associative learning and emotional responding implicate estrogen in the underlying neuronal mechanism [36].

9.5 Relationships to Learning and Education

The studies presented here provide some good news for learning and education. The brain is plastic and to some extend is shaped by the experiences that we live, even in adult age. This suggests that perseverance in any enterprise may pay off, at least until our brain has been given the time to adapt to the new environment or to the new situation and possibly process the new informations more effectively. The experiments suggest that physical activity and a

[1]LTP, an instance of Hebb postulate of plasticity or *Hebbian learning*, is currently at the basis of many models of learning and memory formation [30].

diversified and changing environment appears to enhance the generation of neural synthesis. Hence, our experiences and our environments can drive the brain to generate new neurons even in old age, and we know that these neurons participate actively in the formation of new memories [29].

The Effect of Stress on Learning

One aspect that is clearly demonstrated in many studies is that chronic exposure to stress is detrimental and leads to destruction of brain cells and reduced cognitive abilities. This suggests that, for example, social and familial stress level may not only have a negative psychological effect on academic performances at school, but such sustained stressful environment as for the flight attendants, may cause in parallel physical brain damages that may impair learning. Provided that such damages are reversible and much evidence points to this possibility, it may still take a substantial amount of time for subjects once removed from their stressful environment to return to their normal level of performance. Hence, a reversal effect may require years of proper support and environment and there may not be quick remedies.

An Enriched Environment for Learning

As the experiments suggest, there may be more benefits than usually praised to exercising. It may, indeed, helps in keeping the brain healthy and less prone to damages. Moreover, studies on the effect of moderate exercise on host protection and immune function have shown, for example, that brisk walking nearly every day reduced the number of sickness days by half compared to inactivity over a period of 12 to 15 weeks. Surprisingly, this also occurs without changes in resting immune function[2][19].

It appears important for education to provide us with an *enriched environment* in which one must be an active participant to harvest all the benefits. Moreover, active participation in physical activities at intervals throughout the day may not only release tension and stress at many levels, but it may enhance neurological processes necessary for effective learning and memory. This strongly suggests that the trends to reduce physical activities in schools or, in some cases, to go as far as to eliminate them totally to facilitate supervision and reducing the numbers of injuries on school property is very wrong. Can the rise in psychological medication given to children be correlated with such factors as poor richness of the environments and low level of physical activities in children's life? The neurophysiological results certainly suggest that some experiences, some as simple as running, may have very important quantitative effects on the brain. This reminds us that we still know very little about the brain, and especially about the relationship of the neural substrate with psychology, and with the mind. Nevertheless, it also demonstrates that the best results are not always obtained by the most complex recipes.

More than the Fun of the Games

[2]Note, however, that intense exercise, or "severe physical stress", does reduce the immune response for a brief period from 3 to 72 hours after exercise, depending on the immune measure [20][21]. Even though there is lowering of immune function, the athletes don't seem to get sick more often than others [19]. Moreover, this decrease in immune response is smaller when endurance athletes use carbohydrate beverages before, during and after prolonged and intense exertion. Nevertheless, the link between consumption and their effects on endocrine and immune systems have not yet been elucidated [20].

A new avenue for learning and education might be found in the tremendously popular computer games. The games get our motivation and attention almost for free. Couldn't they be used as a vehicle of world and educational knowledge, not only about academic subjects typically linked to reasoning: physics, chemistry, biology, but also more interestingly about *emotional intelligence*? [11] Emotional intelligence includes abilities that better our social interactions and ourselves and that surprisingly are not part of the educational curriculum. It includes self-awareness, by which one recognizes and understands moods, emotions and drives and their effects on others, self-regulation, which is the control or redirection of disruptive impulses and moods that helps us think before acting. It includes social skills, motivation and empathy, which helps us understand the makeup of others and to treat people in accordance with their emotions.

In fact, practical psychology could really be a part of the basic curriculum in our educational systems. Topics such as biology, mathematics, and physics help us understand the biological and physical world around us, there should also be topics on basic aspects of understanding ourselves, our behaviors and reactions and our social dynamics. Aspects such as the ones included in Bowen theory and others [10][15], which include essential ideas such as triangling, emotional fusion, and intergenerational transmission, are easy to grasp and could be introduced early on. Having such concepts would provide us with better sets of tools to understand the social and psychological matrix that is part of our environment. Since understanding a situation is the first step towards taking control and possibly changing it for the best, being able to read social interactions, and understand the motivations or drives behind the actions of people around us is crucial. Because one possible cause of depression is apparently the inability or sense of inability to have control over our environment, or over ourself or future, such emotional intelligence skills may have wide benefits in society. Isn't the ultimate role of education to provide to our youngs the abilities to blossom at their fullest potential and to allow them to make their best contribution to our societies and to themselves?

Coming back to computer games, they could become a real vehicle for learning and education, by including much knowledge about all subjects in the play. The benefits that they provide, and could do in the future to a much more sophisticated level, include the personalization of what is being learned and the very powerful interactive sessions that they offer where the learner/player cannot remain passive. In a very near future, high-band technology could connect anyone to anyone in the globe in interactive sessions, perhaps for a common project, play or cause. And where the latest artificial intelligence algorithms could be used effectively as an interactive tutor to suggest paths of efficient learning during play, perhaps through intrigue and motivation by monitoring emotional and intellectual state of the individual.

Computer games could benefit us even more by moving them away from the computer and into the world. This means to allow the game to take place, not at a desk, but in the house, in the park, or in the woods near by. Such ability would improve the richness of our environments and experiences at the same time as providing us with physical activity that appears so beneficial to us at many levels.

Before reaching any final conclusions on improving learning methodology, one should appreciate that there may be sex differences as the ones that have been observed in experiments in the behavioral responses and their underlying neuronal mechanisms. Nevertheless, the educational methods of the future will not only be adapted or adaptive along sex differences, but also to the specificity of the individual's mechanisms in learning. Taking for example what can be considered an extreme case to illustrate the point, synaesthetic[3] indi-

[3]"Synaesthesia is a rare phenomenon in which a sensory stimulus in one modality can trigger sensory ex-

viduals may benefit from different types of associations in learning than non-synaesthetes would[27] [24]. The technology of the future may be able to reveal, possibly by inference from indirect observations, the specific mechanisms of learning of a particular individual and adapt the educational methodology for that individual. The benefits could include better attention, interest, retention, subject relevance and might just be fun at the same time.

---

perience in other modalities. For example, hearing a word (the 'inducer') might cause a synaesthete to see a particular colour (the 'concurrent'). Although there are many forms of synaesthesia involving different combinations of sensory inducer and concurrent, the most common consists of specific colours being elicited by written or spoken digits, letters or words."[27]

Bibliography

[1] Bienenstock EL, Cooper LN, Munro PW. Theory for the development of neuron selectivity: orientation specificity and binocular interaction in visual cortex, *J Neurosci.*, 1982 Jan;2(1):32-48

[2] Borsook, D and Becerra, L and Fishman, S and Edwards, A and Jennings, CL and Stojanovic, M and Papinicolas, L and Ramachandran, VS and Gonzalez, RG and Breiter, H., Acute plasticity in the human somatosensory cortex following amputation. *Neuroreport.* 1998 Apr 20;9(6):1013-7.

[3] Cho, Kwangwook and Ennaceur, A. and Cole, Jon C. and Suh, Chang Kook, Chronic Jet Lag Produces Cognitive Deficits, *Journal of Neuroscience*, 20:RC66(1-5), 2000.

[4] Cho, Kwangwook, Chronic 'jet lag' produces temporal lobe atrophy and spatial cognitive deficits, *Nature Neuroscience*, 4:6, 567-8, June 2001.

[5] Clark SA, Allard T, Jenkins WM, Merzenich MM., Receptive fields in the body-surface map in adult cortex defined by temporally correlated inputs. *Nature*, 1988 Mar 31;332(6163):444-5.

[6] Elbert, T and Pantev, C and Wienbruch, C. and Rockstroh, B and Taub, E., Increased cortical representation of the fingers of the left hand in string players, *Science*, Oct 13; 270(5234):305-7, 1995.

[7] Eriksson, PS and Perfilieva, E and Bjork-Eriksson, T and Alborn, AM and Nordborg, C and Peterson, DA and Gage, FH. Neurogenesis in the adult human hippocampus. *Nat Med.* 1998 Nov;4(11):1313-7, with comments in Nat Med. 1998 Nov;4(11):1207.

[8] Filaire, E and Duche, P and Lac, G and Robert, A. Saliva cortisol, physical exercise and training: influences of swimming and handball on cortisol concentrations in women. *Eur J Appl Physiol Occup Physiol.* 1996;74(3):274-8

[9] Fordyce, D.E. and Wehner, J.M., Brain Res., 619, 111-119, 1993.

[10] Gilbert, Roberta. Extraordinary Relationships: A New Way of Thinking About Human Interactions, 240 pages 1 edition (December 6, 1992), John Wiley & Sons, New York.

[11] Goleman, Daniel. Emotional Intelligence. Bantam Books, July 1997, New York 352 pp.

[12] Hebb, D O,Organization of behavior, Wiley, 1949, New York.

[13] Jacobs, BL and Praag, H and Gage, FH. Adult brain neurogenesis and psychiatry: a novel theory of depression. *Mol Psychiatry.* 2000 May;5(3):262-9. Review.

[14] Johansson, B.B. and Ohlsson, A, Exp. Neurol. 129, 322-327, 1997.

[15] Michael E. Kerr, Murray Bowen (Contributor). Family Evaluation : An Approach Based on Bowen Theory. 400 pages (October 1988). W W Norton & Company.

[16] Lupien, S.J. and de Leon, Mony and de Santi, Susan and Convit, Antonio and Tarshish, Chaim and Nair, N.P.V. and Thakur, Mira and McEwen, Bruce S. and Hauger, Richard L. and Meaney, Michael J., Cortisol levels during human aging predict hippocampal atrophy and memory deficits, *Nature Neuroscience*, 1:1, 69-73, 1998.

[17] McEwen, Bruce S., Stress and hippocampal plasticity, *Annu. Rev. Neurosci.*, 22:105-22, 1999.

[18] Mogilner, A and Grossman, JA and Ribary, U and Joliot, M and Volkmann, J and Rapaport, D and Beasley, RW and Llinas RR, Somatosensory cortical plasticity in adult humans revealed by magnetoencephalography, *Proc Natl Acad Sci U S A*, 1993 Apr 15;90(8):3593-7.

[19] Nieman, D. C. and Pedersen, B. K., Exercise and immune function. Recent developments. *Sports Med* 1999 Feb; 27(2):73-80.

[20] Nieman, DC. Nutrition, exercise, and immune system function. *Clin Sports Med.* 1999 Jul;18(3):537-48. Review.

[21] Pedersen, BK and Hoffman-Goetz, L. Exercise and the immune system: regulation, integration, and adaptation. *Physiol Rev.* 2000 Jul;80(3):1055-81. Review.

[22] Pleger, B and Dinse, HR and Ragert, P and Schwenkreis, P and Malin, JP and Tegenthoff M., Shifts in cortical representations predict human discrimination improvement, *Proc Natl Acad Sci U S A*, 2001 Oct 9;98(21):12255-60.

[23] Porter, N.M and Landfield, P.W., Stress hormones and brain aging: adding injury to insult?, *Nature Neuroscience*, 1:1,3-4, 1998.

[24] Ramachandran, VS and Hubbard, EM. Psychophysical investigations into the neural basis of synaesthesia. Proc R Soc Lond B Biol Sci. 2001 May 7;268(1470):979-83.

[25] Ramachandran, VS and Rogers-Ramachandran, D., Phantom limbs and neural plasticity. *Arch Neurol.* 2000 Mar;57(3):317-20.

[26] Ramachandran, V.S. and Blakeslee, Sandra, Phantoms in the brain : probing the mysteries of the human mind, New York : William Morrow, 1998, 1st ed, 328 p.

[27] Rich, AN and Mattingley, JB. Anomalous perception in synaesthesia: a cognitive neuroscience perspective. Nat Rev Neurosci. 2002 Jan;3(1):43-52. Review.

[28] Shors TJ. Acute stress rapidly and persistently enhances memory formation in the male rat. *Neurobiol Learn Mem.* 2001 Jan;75(1):10-29.

[29] Shors, TJ and Miesegaes, G and Beylin, A and Zhao, M and Rydel, T and Gould, E. Neurogenesis in the adult is involved in the formation of trace memories. *Nature.* 2001 Mar 15;410(6826):372-6..

[30] Shors, TJ and Matzel, LD. Long-term potentiation: what's learning got to do with it? *Behav Brain Sci.* 1997 Dec;20(4):597-614; discussion 614-55. Review.

[31] Shors, TJ and Seib, TB and Levine, S and Thompson, RF. Inescapable versus escapable shock modulates long-term potentiation in the rat hippocampus. *Science*. 1989 Apr 14;244(4901):224-6.

[32] van Praag, Henriette, Running increases cell proliferation and neurogenesis in the adult mouse dentate gyrus, *Nature Neuroscience*, 2:3, 266-270, March 1999.

[33] van Praag, Henriette and Christie, Brian R. and Sejnowski, Terrence J. and Gage, Fred H., Running enhances neurogenesis, learning and long-term potentiation in mice, *PNAS*, 96:23, 13427-13431, 1999.

[34] van Praag, Henriette and Kempermann, Gerd and Gage, Fred H. Neural consequences of environmental enrichment. *Nat Rev Neurosci.* 2000 Dec;1(3):191-8. Review.

[35] Wiesel TN, Hubel DH., Comparison of the effects of unilateral and bilateral eye closure on cortical unit responses in kittens, *J. Neurophysiol.*, 28(6):1029-40, Nov 1965.

[36] Wood, GE and Shors, TJ. Stress facilitates classical conditioning in males, but impairs classical conditioning in females through activational effects of ovarian hormones. *Proc Natl Acad Sci U S A*. 1998 Mar 31;95(7):4066-71.

Group Discussion 9
The Motivated Brain

Emotional Intelligence

Tokoro : When you talk about emotional intelligence, is it correct to understand it as a chemical state or even better, as a relation between the chemical state and the development or structure of the brain?

Coenen : I think that emotional intelligence is very complex and like with regular intelligence, it would be very speculative at this point to try to identify how it functions in the brain. On the other hand, we're starting to accumulate evidence on how emotions can affect development, plasticity and function of the brain by studying how different emotions change the level of neuromodulators and hormones present. This means that emotions do change the "chemical state" of the brain, which may affect in some global manner the structure or development of the brain as well as its plasticity and the level of activities in different areas.

Tokoro : Everybody talks about the joy of learning or enjoyable learning. Whereas in the traditional schooling system neither the teachers nor the students are in a mood for learning. Neither are they enjoying it. So it is very interesting to know how the whole learning process evolves in our brain. The emotional level starts off from chemical things in our brain, the chemical connections have an effect on our emotions and so on.

Coenen: We also know that the limbic system has a lot of interactions and is very broad. It can even interact on reinforcement signals which go all over the brain and we know that a lot of these reinforcement signals are involved in learning processes. We know that there are neuron modulators that can actually change the level of learning at a particular synapse. Im pretty sure that emotional states can change the system and the ability to learn but I didnt investigate that personally. One thing we know though is that if you see someone happy, smiling, we know that it affects the brain areas that are usually involved in smiling When I smile, I light up some areas in my brain and just the fact that I see someone smiling or being happy actually triggers those areas in my brain, so it is more likely that it will make me happy as well. And if I just smile without meaning to be happy, it also increases that activity a bit even more and so again the physical action is often interlinked with an actual state in the brain. And you can actually manipulate that. But it is one of the things that should be studied more: How emotion affects learning, as well as motivation.

Steels: Some methods have been proposed where people can cognitively control their emotions (or have their emotions be controlled) so that their brain gets in a more positive state.

Coenen: Indeed, you are capable teaching people how to recognize and understand their moods. People can be angry or get in a bad mood. Then you can introspect to see whether you had a good reason or not to be in that mood. And if you realise that you dont have good reasons and that youre making up reasons for it, then you may relativize your reasons, do something about it and change it. The hardest step is basically to realise something. And only then you can actually work on the changes. This counts for many other brain activities as well. If youre confronted with a physics problem or studying physics, and there is something you dont understand, you first have to realise that you dont understand, then you can do something about that. But if you dont realise this, then you dont have a handle on it. So when talking about emotions, you have to find out in retrospect what are they, what are the drives? What makes you happy? Why are you happy? Why are you sad? Think about the effect that you may have on others. Or others onto you. So maybe if someone is in a bad mood or depressed, theyll make you depressed. But do you have to be depressed because somebody else is depressed? No. But you should realise that this might actually be happening to you.

Tokoro: Yes, but if you explain that in a more systematic way, how do you do that? Because it is an interaction between neurons anyhow. What does emotional mean? Why do you use the word emotional instead of just intelligence? Like when you concentrate on something it might free some adrenaline, that is chemical, and it may affect the growth of neurons.

Coenen: Emotional intelligence refers to a person's ability to monitor and control his emotions as well as being able to read the emotional state and hence better connect or empathize with a person. It is taking into account the emotional state of a person and even transform it during personal and social interactions. These abilities are therefore quite different than the ones usually referred by regular "intelligence".

Steels: Another difference is probably that at least basic emotions stay at a subconscious non-cognitive level, whereas intelligence often involves conscious manipulation of cognitive representations, particularly symbolic representations. For example, if you need to think up a plan to get home from here, it will not come in a flash. There are goals and subgoals and preconditions for each step, and potential difficulties to be resolved, etc.

Coenen: Emotions are complex dynamical states that involve both physiological and neural states. An emotion involves the activation of many specific brain areas, as well as the activation of diffuse neural modulatory systems in the brain and hormonal responses that can affect both the brain and physiological system of the body (heart rate, sweeting glands, etc.). Both of these systems, neuromodulatory and hormonal, are diffuse systems that affect the responses of brain areas, and can modulate their plasticity. Therefore, emotional states can affect learning, retention and many other processes, by changing the level of neuromodulators and hormones present in the brain.

Impact of Depression

Coenen: In the study I presented, the flight attendants that did not have time to recover from jet lag caused by crossing multiple time zones had long term exposure to a high level of cortisol. Cortisol is a stress hormone that has beneficial effects for the organism with short term exposure. It allows the release of energy and increases the metabolism of many reactions in the organism to allow it to handle an accute current situation. As we saw, long term exposure to cortisol has also negative consequences: The temporal lobe of the brain of these attendants was reduced in volume, and, in addition, the attendants' reaction time was slower and their cognitive abilities was reduced.

Mogi: These flight attendants spend quite some time in a small place. Does the brain react to stress or to the fact of being confined?

Coenen: They differentiate between short term recovery and long term recovery. The short term recovery team actually flies exactly the same amount of hours as the other ones, but they only do flights that had less than 3 hours time difference. So they should less undergo the effect of being confined.

Nevejan: Im actually very pleased and shocked at the same time in hearing the story about the flight attendants. I have been dealing with the problem of teachers for the last few years. I come from a culture where there is a lot of energy in the people but the teachers are a huge depressed group. And it is becoming an almost general problem in a lot of countries in Europe.

Coenen: Why are the teachers depressed?

Nevejan: Well, the educational policies of the last decades which imposes all sorts of rules on teachers but gives them all the time fewer resources, are such that the teachers feel they have no control at all over their situation. If you know that these people run classes of 30 children, it is not astonishing. Really, they lack control over their environment, over the evaluation system, the rhythm, the curriculum. So they are all stuck within a system where they cannot control any of the parameters. But if I say this it is as if Im stigmatising a whole group and of course cannot do that, but still I think it is an issue. Olivier Coenens research show clearly what can happen when you get depressed. Without any control over their own situation, you get people who cannot listen anymore, who cannot sing with the children any more, who miss every motivation. This is one of the main problems that we are faced with in education these days and it has nothing to do with a better training.

Coenen: If you have a group of teachers who are pretty depressed, who are not motivated, they wont be able to play a motivating role and are bad examples.

Nevejan: Exactly. They keep saying: Teachers cannot teach anymore. But your research on how people learn, or when they cannot learn anymore, clearly shows what goes wrong.

Punset : This coincides with the findings of Professor Richard Boyatzis, a Human Ressources Consultant and writer. He said that if somebody is ill-tempered, he is like toxic, he is contaminating other people. And there is no way that in that kind of state of mind you can learn anything.

Chapter 10

Mass Media and Science

by Eduardo Punset

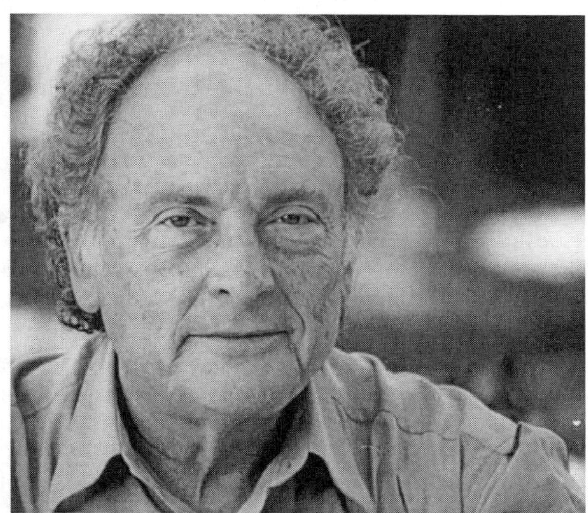

Eduardo Punset is Professor of Economic Policy at the Chemical Institute or Rmon Llull University, Barcelona. He was Chairman of the Bull Technological Institute, Professor of Innovation at Madrid University, and IMF Representative in the Caribbean. He actively participated in the Spanish political transition to democracy as Minister for Relations with the European Union and Member of the European Parliament. He is Director of REDES, a popular programme on Science. His latest book is "A Field Guide to Survive in the 21st Century."

This essay is based on a statement by Eduardo Punset at the Workshop

A few years ago Spanish Public Television asked me to do a program on economics. I said no. I prefered to do a program on the public understanding of science. They accepted and came up with the name "net" - REDES in Spanish, which also means " nets " for fishing. The Television Authority argued six years ago that audiences would think of nets for fishing, rather than the Web when confronted with the word Net. They were wrong.

My main interest is the language of science. How can we communicate science, and not just to children ? I care very much about children, but in our societies there are fewer and fewer of them, so the big need now is for adults. When I say communicating about science I do not mean the classroom style transfer of knowledge, but mass communication with hundreds of thousands of people at the same time. I used to write a column for *El Pais*, one of the journals in Spain, sometimes also for the New Herald Tribune. But when I started doing television I stopped this because if you can reach 300,000 people in Spain and 3 million more in Latin America every week for an hour, why would I continue wasting my time writing an article that would be read by 100,000 people at the most?

In this essay I want to talk about my experiences in making this program. What the obstacles to mass communication are about science, and what new developments can help us.

10.1 Obstacles to Scientific Understanding

Let me start by analysing the difficulties of finding a language to talk about science. The first difficulty is that our human language did not originate for science but evolved to support cooperation among human beings for better survival. In " The Mating Mind ", anthropologist Geoffrey Miller [2] argued that language was essentially fabricated for sexual seduction. Women want to go to bed with men that are brilliant and clever, and vice versa. And language is one way in which you can show your intellect. I do not know how serious all this is, but in any case the rigidity of language is a first obstacle. We have to communicate science with a language that was meant to be used for seduction.

The second obstacle, much more important I think, is that human language has been used mainly to articulate common sense and divine revelation, both of which are anti-science. This is very obvious if you look at the history of countries like Spain. Most scientific experiments are fascinating. They are even so fascinating that they seem mysterious and more difficult to believe than the idea of Moses saying something from the top of a hill. When you try to explain the creation of matter, the disintegration of atoms, or when you try to tell people that in an atom the distance from the electron to the nucleus of the atom is the same proportion as the distance from the earth to the moon, they do not understand what you are talking about. It goes against common sense.

The third obstacle is the limitation of our brain. A friend of mine who is the head of the National Council for Scientific Research, and a physicist, thinks that there are possibly cases where this evolutionary brain cannot understand some things, like quantum physics, and I agree with him. Perhaps it is impossible to understand our own brain or self-consciousness. In evolution, our brain learned how to deal with dinosaurs, Predators and other humans, but we never had to deal with atoms. We do not have to worry about this too much because we have technology. Technology can make things that we cannot see visible, slow down processes that go too fast to observe, perform enormously complex calculations which humans cannot do by hand, etc.

There are of course barriers for communicating science in addition to language. I just visited a remote village in Tarragona in Spain. I spent my infancy there, the first 12 years of my life. It was a nice place, built by the Arabs but now very poor. It has vineyards which were too costly to be maintained and so they were abandoned. There were some specialists, oenologues that came and knew how to revive the vineyards and now they sell the wine more expensively than French cuves! I talked to a farmer who had experienced the earlier period first hand, and asked him whether he was happy. He disagreed, saying that what goes up must come down. I told him that it is different now and not comparable ; that they have a brand now and another way of doing it. But people still keep thinking in the old way. They are not used to think in terms of geometrical changes or exponential growth. Their brains are not ready for it, and are not trained for it. So if you try to tell them that things are changing in an exponential way, they do not understand.

A final important obstacle in my view is the multi-disciplinarity of science. We live instead in a world that is monothematic. People like to have a single, definite, unique view on things, whereas interdisciplinarity assumes that many points of view are posssible each highlighting different aspects of a complex problem. There is not necessarily a single 'true' answer but the different viewpoints have to be weighed against each other. Our minds are not used to this kind of flexibility.

10.2 Improving scientific communication

These are some of the obstacles to communicate about science, but I am optimistic, particularly because there are a number of developments which help to overcome them.

Science as Culture

The first one is the turbulent irruption of science in culture. This is what really marks the new millenium for me. It is not the results of science but the method, the gradual acceptance of the scientific method. Science is this fantastic universal method to deepen knowledge of things, to get at well-founded knowledge. The method says: as long as you put in all these safeguards, as long as you prove every step and gather all the appropriate evidence, you will increase your understanding and get closer to the truth. At the same time it is very important that you are ready to abandon your beliefs at any time. If somebody presents other proof and other evidence, I must be ready to change the whole thing and accept the opposite of what I was saying before.

The scientific method is really a torpedo against most eastern and western thinking. It is very modest in a way but it is a torpedo questioning the way people were thinking and communicating to each other. If you take countries like Spain or Latin America, language and communication is really baroque, it is literary. I remember when I was a child and we sat in the streets on the sidewalks in the evening and we tortured our minds about where we came from, where would we go, who we were and all that kind of stuff, we never mentioned any science, any electron, any atom. We talked about Sartre, or Camus, that was knowledge to us. That was were we went when we were looking for answers.

Two years ago some 2000 youngsters gathered in a jazzclub in Munich. There was a stage and you know who was going to be on that stage? Richard Dawkins, Steven Pinker, Daniel Dennett. They were like actors. But they were talking about the origins of the world, and about when the stars will disappear and this was thrilling, because afterwards people in the streets were discussing what Dawkins said. I am not saying that people everywhere in the world are discussing now what Dawkins said last week, but it might come to that. Cultural changes are, as we know, the slowest changes you can imagine.

Yves Coppens is an anthropologist who was involved in finding Lucy, the first 3 million years old fossil. Lucy was tiny, very nice and had a much bigger brain that we thought she might have. She was a lady and had a much bigger brain than a chimp. She was really the first human. So Coppens told me you have two kinds of paleonthologists, you have the academics, like S.J. Gould - the most brilliant of them all, who has just died - nd then you have people like him, experimenting, scavenging. You have to have some of both. He said that when you start excavating, the first thing you discover is a biological novelty. The capacity of the brain has increased or a finger can be moved in a new way. Some years later you find the technological change linked to this biological change. For example, Lucy and their friends started to experiment with new tools. You see the relationship immediately. But sometimes you have to wait one hundred million years for the cultural change linked to this technological change to show up : organisationship, relationships with God, interpersonal relationships. If you sometimes despair, then do not, because we are traffickers of cultural change. And it takes a long time.

The objective of politics should be to synchronize the rhythms or to help people assimilate the fact that we live in the 21st century technology wise, in the 18th or 19th century socially and institutionally, and in the Middle Ages or Roman Empire culturally. These adjustments cost enormous efforts. Consider Spain for instance, I checked my e-mail last night and there were a lot of protests about a program of mine on the question of why so many women are assassinated by their husbands in Spain at this moment : 70 in 2001, and some 400,000 women ill-treated. For me this is a symptom of " decalage ". Women can work, they can divorce, they have their own income, but men, many men, continue to believe that women are their property. Just as some women think the same way about their children. You see that when you walk in the streets. There are mothers and noisy children and children are being hit. All this will change but it is a cultural thing. In the same way, it will take time before the general culture absorbs science and scientific method, but it will happen.

Impact of New Media

What else is happening? Well, a fantastic thing! The explosion of the Internet. Every week I talk about a different subject in my programs: the cosmos, schizophrenia next week, etc. It would be impossible if my researchers, journalists, and scientists had to travel around libraries, looking for books and information. They would never be able to build an hour program without the internet. People from everywhere have the same facilities. When they want to find out about something, they now have this fantastic resource available.

The Internet is part of the general audio-visual revolution. It is now easy to record, transmit and view (moving) images. The brain loves it. When I say apple, you all think of an apple, with a little shade here or there, some green, some red, some yellow, maybe a leaf. You think in terms of an image. It's incredible the way humans assimilate images. So now at last we have technology to massively use images in science communication within reach of many people and this will only increase.

The importance of images and metaphorical mappings between abstract domains and images is undisputed. When teaching economics I remember there was always something that the students never understood well: which was how monetary authorities control the monetary supply. Year after year they did not understand, and hence this year I tried it with a metaphorical mapping. It was fabulous. They got it! The base money became a heart and the money supply was all the other things around it.

Impact of Neuroscience

The third important development for me is the neuroscience revolution. What is this revolution revealing to us? Many things, but I just want to point out two of them.

The first finding is that the brain works in a very slow way for some things. To establish a new relationship with somebody, to learn a new capacity or a new ability is a very complex process. That is one of the dangers I see in enterprises, in companies, in a world when you are being told that you will change your profession five or six times. It takes a lot for the brain to change that many times because the processes are very complex and slow. This is often underestimated by the advocates of continuous change and lifelong learning.

The other thing which is relevant is the dominance of the subconsciousness, of the amygdala, over the neocortex. The position of Joseph Ledoux in New York is that the amygdala, or the premordial brain, inundates the neocortex and the neocortex can hardly fight back [1]. So we cannot forget this in human resource management in a firm, or in classrooms or anywhere else. The amygdala is always there. Emotion plays an enormous role in learning.

Lessons from the Media

Finally there are a few things you should not do when using multimedia to communicate with the rest of the world about science. First of all do not try to teach. You have to suggest, to open scenarios, to excite people, but do not try to teach because people come home, are tired and they do not want to be taught by television. I tried subtitles at one point but people do not want to read subtitles.

The second thing is the importance of the first 20 seconds. Not even the first minute, no the first 20 seconds. I have seen studies on the reactions of students to different speakers. The way they evaluated the teachers was based on the first five minutes. On closer examination these first five minutes coincided with the first 20 seconds. So this time period is enormously important. In the first 20 seconds the harm can already be done.

The third thing is that science is basically a dense subject, but you have to compensate for this. In my program Redes, I try to compensate for this with a very dynamic format that could be anything: interviews, reportages, the use of 3-D, studiowork, etc. The whole program is continuously jumping from one thing to the other. You are explaining science but you have to entertain as well. If you do all that, you cannot fail.

10.3 Conclusions

I have two concluding thoughts: for me science is a new religion. We will have a pope and cardinals, and the whole show. My main maxim is: do not be bored, do not let them bore you, and do not bore other people. The new audio-visual technologies and Internet are perfect tools to make science fun. When we talked about learning in the past, we were talking about learning history, about great warriors and writers. These are local or national heroes. But science has a planetary value. It is the same everywhere. If you have a marvellous method for learning but you are teaching silly things, outdated things, things that are not useful for the future, then you do not serve your purpose. Hence even though the learning process might not be very perfect, WHAT we will be learning through this learning process must be different from what we were learning before.

Bibliography

[1] Ledoux, J. (1996) The Emotional Brain. The Mysterious Underpinnings of Emotional Life. Simon and Schuster, New York.

[2] Miller, G. (2000) The Mating Mind: How Sexual Choice Shaped the Evolution of Human Nature. Doubleday, New York, 1999.

Group Discussion 10
Mass Media and Science

How Can Learning be Made Fun?

Nevejan : I just did an experiment with teachers and artists in England where everybody had to tell about their best learning experience. It proved soon that the cited experiences all captured an important emotional moment in life. Whether it was learning to swim or learning a language, they were all connected to feeling and emotion.

Allien: To learn you have to be emotionally involved.

Steels: The learners should be given the resilience to fail. According to me that is an absolute condition to be able to enjoy learning.

Hedegaard: Its very close to motivation, another essential part of the teaching-learning process.

Nevejan: Learning implicates a combination of emotions and survival. Its more than just emotions alone. The whole sensitive layer moves in. It has a lot to do with sensitivity, much less with cognitive aspects.

Punset: So be sure to make learning fun! Although science is eminent and most fascinating, we succeed in making it boring. The fun aspect is a priority, and thats why I like the Aibo robot so much. Its fun. Its nice. No wonder its a success with almost every child that can put its hands on it. They trust Aibo much more than their teacher. We must learn him how to teach. Maybe not. But we should make sure not to bore the planet any longer.

Allien: Exactly. Although we nowadays have incredible multi-media possibilities, 70 percent of the learning content on the Internet is still text-based and linear. Neither are we using the challenging potential of computers for graphics and imaging. The computers themselves are not guilty but the content providers will have to instigate a revolution...

Nevejan: I think a problem is the lack of stimulation from the educational authorities. I made this computer program Demi Dubbel for kids and they really love it. Its a timemachine on the Internet through which the children of two different classrooms each collect their part of the data about history and art to complete the project together offline. This is the fourth year that the program runs in most of the primary schools in Amsterdam. The teachers love it, the children love it and still there is an enormous resistance from the official educational policymakers. They are not convinced of the quality of the program and keep saying: "I dont have any problem with the children's motivations, but what do they learn?" Whereas in a week time these kids learned about Andy Warhol, about Brueghel and other artists. When you ask art historians, they acknowledge: "Yes, of course, these kids have learned a lot". The irony is that from the moment you can really motivate the kids, the policymakers start getting suspicious. If you create fun in schools, youre a dangerous creature.

Allien: Youre very dangerous to the teacher unions, thats for sure. They are in some countries counterproductive in the evolution of new learning processes.

Dautenhahn: There is a tension between teaching and exploration. We need a teacher. What is the function of a teacher, how should the teacher interact with the children or adults?

I think we all agree upon the idea that learning should be fun, that children should be allowed to explore, that they should not be restricted to a linear sequence of information but must be active, playful learners. On the other hand, you can play without learning. You can use these shooting computer games for hours and hours and you might learn sensitive motor control, and hands-and-eye coordination, how to press buttons, but that is not what we want if we think about creativity. So Im very interested in the tension between the learner on the one hand and the development of technology on the other.

The Importance of Science Education

Punset: In a decade the word science will no longer be used. All knowledge will be scientific knowledge and so will be the process of learning. Which needs not to be boring but deeply exciting. To overcome the historical deflection or non-scientific vocation of language, communication will concentrate on very powerful short time continuous impacts running through interactive audio-visual channels targeted to the whole of the population instead of just the school age group. Thats what I foresee.

Caroline: But talking about values, will children be able to figure out the distinction between good and bad?

Punset: For the distinction of values I think we will need more science education than there is now. With a scientific background, we will at least be able to put technology into a right perspective. What is in danger, is the preservation of the local culture. I find it difficult to imagine a world in which evolution applies to a physical world and not to world of culture and ideas. I may be absolutely wrong but the ideas and culture which currently enable us to adapt to new environments will disappear from the general pool of genes, of cultural genes. I wouldnt be to much worried about that. I am even willing to pay more taxes to keep up some very local almost extinct culture. Because in the end only those ideas and culture that are adapted will survive on a global level. The science business is another thing. When we look at schools now, we dont see television. Neither do we see science which has erupted as a storm in the world culture although I believe there is some urgency to do so. At the moment we transmit only this baroque localised culture. Thats the only thing we really know how to teach. And that is what we are still teaching.

Coenen: I was really happy to see that you take into account the process of emotion, of self esteem and intuition in this problem of learning. I know that science is a very good tool and will become very important in the future but I must say that Im a little hesitant to make it the exclusive source of knowledge. It doesnt include a lot of empirical knowledge cultures have taken thousands of years to accumulate. Through that process they probably accumulated empirical knowledge that may actually turn out to be found exact through a scientific method as well. The empirical knowledge they arrived at may result from an enormously complex set of rules that interact with one another. By simply applying a scientific method which seeks simple interactions first, we might not be able to find these rules. Im thinking about Chinese medicine or so. Or Indians art of eating. Maybe they took into account a lot of interactions in our body that we dont understand yet. Suppose you have kidney stones and your doctor says it is due to too much calcium. It could be true but it could also be due to an interaction in your body which is triggered by having not enough calcium. The first scientific hypothesis doesnt always work out.

Punset: Very often we find that only intuitive reasoning allows you to find shortcuts. We use a different strategy than the one you follow in the usual scientific process of trying to prove that every alternative hypothesis is wrong. You jump but you cant do this unless there is a lot of subconscious information. I think it was Picasso who said something like "Im not looking for something, je trouves". But actually it is not true. He actually found things because he devoted a lot of time researching

Allien : There is never a spontaneous generation of knowledge. Edgar Morin is working on the fact that "cogito" is important, but "computo" or "computare" remains the basic food. We have to compute a lot to have a good intuition. And it is not important whether it is conscious or not, which is important is to compute.

Nevejan : How do you learn students to find there way in this overflow of information? Make sure they know a lot!

Allien : So computo permits cogito, it permits to have direct knowledge or as Olivier said : shortcuts.

Punset : One of the things we learn from biology that without energy the life inside the membrane cell its false. Life means its a mistake it means that thanks to a lot of energy you manage to maintain some order for a few years, a few day in the case of a mosquito, a few years in the case of a rat, so without this effort, without this energy, without this computo, there is no intuition, there is no order, there is no life. So we should tell children its nice this intuition but its no excuse not to get into computo.

Allien : To integrate, we need a lot of input. Like when children riding bicycles, they are not thinking they are riding bicycles but they are making a lot of complex tasks. There is a lot of knowledge integrated unconsciously and quite complex that is more difficult to debrief upon or to recuperate in the conscious sense.

Chapter 11

Stimulating Brain Power

by Bernard Allien

Bernard Allien is President of Franklin Research Center, a philosopher and an Information Sciences expert. Working in media and new media strategies, he is currently involved in a large-scale SONY project using the web for the circulation of various cultural and knowledge resources (KEY). This project is currently in a pilot phase in Hong Kong. It informs us how the web can be used as an educational medium which touches a broad community of learners.

Developments in technology, new approaches to the psychology of learning, and recent discoveries in neuroscience all herald a revolution in our traditional ways of thinking about education. This is just as well, since current socio-economic trends highlight the importance of life-long learning, while the problems facing humanity as a whole have never been more complex, and the need to develop thinking, creative and problem-solving skills has never been more urgent.

A new attitude is required. Many educators and learning philosophers are calling for a learner-centred approach. We feel that individuals should be approached as " learner-researchers " in a "knowledge network society". Technology is not the center but an essential peripheral in this necessary mutation. It helps to promote exchange between individuals (Ego) and between groups (Eco - okos is Greek for home, and by extension, the " home " that is our planet). The exchange of information is only the first part of the process, and Information Technologies (IT) must become Knowledge Technologies (KT). We need to use technology in association with other methods if we are to enable the brain to develop its full intuitive and creative power.

11.1 The need for change

In our view, a revolution in education is preferable to a gradual reform of the institutions of education. Many students today feel that they are being inadequately served by institutional education. One reason is that institutions have traditionally required individuals to adapt to uniform, teacher-centered methods of transmitting knowledge. As a result, many students have experienced boredom, lack of motivation, and even disgust with the school system, based on their bad experience or lack of success. Outside the institutions, other more sophisticated and enjoyable methods of transmitting knowledge, through media, games and entertainment compete with traditional education. The contrast between the resources of new technologies and traditional teaching programmes is extremely marked, and makes the latter seem boring.

Taking into account the latest research in neuroscience, new interconnected interactive technologies and new learning theories, it should be possible to develop an original approach to education, where learning is not in opposition to enjoyment but each is allowed to feed into and stimulate the other. This approach should take us beyond the twin extremes of mindless fun and tedious study that now confront the student, and stimulate creativity and self-expression at a time when concern with educational standards has forced these vital aspects of human endeavor off the agenda. As a new model of learning, electronic learning or E-learning could complement existing methods. In particular, it could address topics and domains not covered by traditional education. E-learning could focus on enhancing the whole personality and encouraging people to identify and use all of their talents. It would help them to decide what is worth learning, and see problems from many points of view

11.2 Attitude in Learning

Learning philosopher Guy Claxton points out: " There is much attention being paid, at present, to the facilitation of learning. But unless we understand equally the dynamics of engagement, which enables learners to commit themselves and their learning resources wholeheartedly to the process of learning, and of disinhibition, which enables learners to avoid or overcome tendencies to defend or withdraw unnecessarily, then our attempts at facilitation are always likely to founder. " Claxton:1996, p.7.

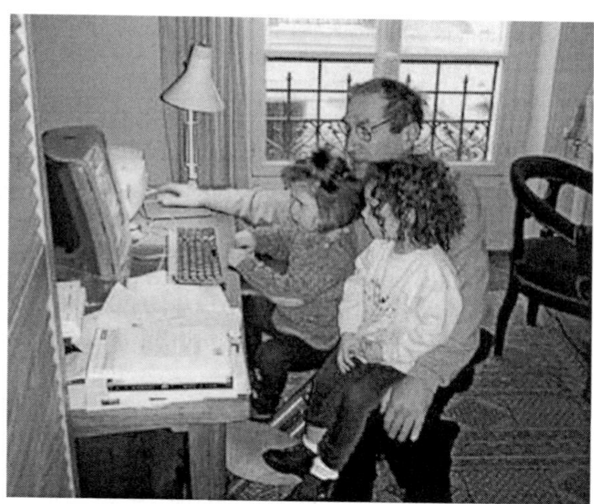

Figure 11.1: Everybody can get involved in educational processes from the early stages onwards. Information technology can be integrated without ignoring social interaction. (fp)

No one disagrees that motivation is hugely important in successful learning. Instead of merely decrying students'lack of motivation, we should attempt to understand its origins and develop ways of overcoming it. For example, one reason for lack of motivation may be that students have no faith that what they are being asked to learn is worth their efforts, and sometimes this assessment may be justified.

Alternatively, people may disengage because of a perceived threat to their self-esteem. Thinking they will fail, they protect their self-image by not trying. Patterns in behaviour such as low resilience to criticism or failure tend to be set in childhood, and so we need to design strategies to help children develop resilience and generate a generally positive attitude to learning. They need to see learning as fun now as well as profitable in the long term. This is the problem with many schools today. Children are told that they will need to acquire knowledge and skills for a future which seems very remote to them and which they may well regard with some anxiety. It is therefore not surprising that they are more likely to take the faster routes to pleasure and a sense of achievement, like watching an entertaining TV program or playing computer games rather than taking pains to learn to read and write. This is not to say that they are learning nothing while they are watching TV. But they are not learning the survival skills they will need as learners: how to deal with frustration and impatience, and how to develop robust self-confidence. This only comes with the awareness from their own experience that there are rewards to be had from persistent engagement in the face of difficulty.

Emotions in learning

Learning tasks involve emotions, in spite of the traditional emphasis on calm impassivity as a prerequisite for the successful learner. These emotions cover a range between anxiety, excitement and interest. Anxious and stressed people will probably be in the wrong emotional state for effective learning. When people are stressed, their brains no longer operate at a high level. Primitive survival instincts take over. Positive anxiety is a different matter: this is often stimulated by video and computer games for example, when players struggle to survive in a chaotic, dangerous world. It is this kind of stimulation and arousal that makes people enjoy such games. As they are not really at risk, and know that " it is only a Game ", their anxiety becomes excitement.

Positive excitement is a tremendous spur to learning. Psychologist Mihaly Csikszentmihalyi refers to the state of total concentration and excitement as flow. In the state of flow, self-consciousness, irrelevant considerations and concern with success or failure all disappear. This is one of the most rewarding and pleasurable states that people can experience. Good students are often people who are able to experience the state of flow while they are studying; children absorbed in play may also be said to enter this state.

A new approach to intelligence

Howard Gardner's concept of Multiple Intelligences has usefully extended the field of what we refer to as intelligence. The " promotion " of such aptitudes as athletic skill to what he calls " bodily-kinesthetic intelligence " is an important step forward. However, we still need to develop General Intelligence, not in the traditional sense of the term, but taken here in Montaigne's sense of the " well-made mind ". Specialization, although vital, is not enough on its own. People need to become generalists as well.Those with high General Intelligence, in our sense, have the ability to see across disciplinary boundaries. They can orchestrate their multiple intelligences and make them work together. This allows them to explore problems from many points of view. We need to facilitate the matching of domains but also suggest spaces of interconnectivity. The great thinkers of the past were not constrained by disciplinary boundaries. Leonardo da Vinci would have laughed at the idea that he could not be both a scientist and an artist. There is no reason why this kind of thinker can only exist in the past. Many scientists are good musicians; many writers are good at drawing (e.g. Victor Hugo), or are good photographers; good directors are often good actors, and the reverse is also true. There have even been good politicians who have also been good philosophers. It is essential to encourage this kind of multi-creativity.

11.3 Stimulating brain power

Brain power is a potentially subversive and revolutionary force, designed to handle the uncertainty of the future and to provide the motor for self-expression, creativity, power of play and tolerance. Ongoing educational experiments (like the educational practices discussed by Carla Rinaldi with pre-school children in Reggio, Italy - see chapter 3) suggest ways of stimulating brain power. An approach focused on stimulating brain power will also draw upon recent research in neuroscience and apply its discoveries and technology to the improvement of healthy brains. Neuroscience tells us that every experience and every conversation actually physically sculpts the brain. Lack of adequate mental stimulation is one of the major causes of inequality. This inequality increases with age. People working in repetitive jobs with low creativity are allowing their brains to decay. Depression also greatly reduces activity in the frontal lobe, which undermines the ability to pay attention. The flexibility acquired in the mental gymnasium provided by the new learning context will make subjects capable of jumping laterally from one domain to the next, or vertically within a chosen domain.

Figure 11.2: The enjoyment experienced in play must somehow be carried over to learning activities. (mw)

How can we use our brains more effectively? We will focus here on the need to develop ingenuity, intuition and creativity, and generally ensure that our brains remain flexible and in continual evolution - so that we do not allow them to "seize up" and close down to new ideas. That is, we will pay less attention to the kind of conscious, explicit, rational " hard thinking " that is traditionally regarded as the best kind of human thought. This attitude is still evident in the work of learning theorists such as Howard Gardner, who insist on the importance of explicit, communicable understanding of what has been learned [3]. However, when we examine our own experience, we can probably all find examples of times when our unconscious, unarticulated knowledge of something allowed us to perform more effectively. For example, many habitually conscious thinkers find it difficult to speak foreign languages. They are too busy thinking about what they are doing to speak fluently and effectively. If you keep thinking about the rules you have learned, you will have difficulty keeping up with any conversation in a foreign language. " Hard " thinking ignores the unconscious and is directly linked to the ego. When we are worried about our appearance and performance, we feel anxious and under pressure. This stress has demonstrably negative effects on the capacity to find innovative solutions. One of the reasons for Gardner's focus on conscious thinking is that he is interested in improving students' ability to transfer what has been learned outside the classroom. If we cannot articulate the rules, he says, we are in danger of regressing to infantile theories, superstitions and so on when faced with a real-life problem. However, in unusual situations, the best policy may be to question our usual rules. If we stick to rules too rigidly, we will undermine our capacity for creative thought.

Another problem with conscious thinking is that the focus of attention is deliberately restricted to exclude anything that is prejudged to be irrelevant. This reduces the likelihood of spotting a creative solution. The process of selection it implies is also liable to lead us back to our own expectations and inclinations, including the sort of regression mentioned by Gardner and, in this way too, it weakens our receptivity. We must recognize that individual maturation is a progressive process. The aim should be to stimulate the different layers of accumulated development, in order to promote creativity and a liberating form of self-expression. All registers can be usefully drawn upon; of particular importance is the flexibility that allows these registers to be linked to one another.

Figure 11.3: Learning and play cannot be opposed. Particularly for young children, both activities are strongly integrated and there needs to be enough unstructured time to allow for them.(fp)

The power of play

Creative, ingenious thinking requires a certain amount of time and space. These days, parents are very conscious of the need to keep up with the school curriculum and make sure their children are kept busy with " activities " every minute of the day. But child psychologists argue that it is important to leave children time to play. As we may remember from our own experience as children, it is often when we are not being attended to, when we are not being constantly distracted by fresh stimulation, that we begin to play most absorbingly. The child psychiatrist Sebastian Kraemer actually argues that boredom is the basis for creativity. We need to learn to tolerate frustrating situations and apparently dead time. Otherwise we will never learn to wait patiently for an answer. If we consistently react too quickly, we will become rigid in our behavior.

The view of learning as hard and deliberate means that play is seen as " mere fun ". But we do ourselves a great injustice by opposing learning and play. Cognitive scientist Andy Clark and developmental psychologist Annette Karmiloff-Smith have shown that children have an innate tendency to seek greater coherence and flexibility in what they have already learned [1], [4]. They do this by playing. In play, they explore and often undo something they have just learned. They may even seem to be regressing to an earlier, less competent state while they are doing this. Instead, they are seeking out connections between this new skill and other areas of expertise in the brain. Through play, they are learning to create interconnections in the mind which allow know-how from different domains to be linked. Failed experiments may teach them as much as successful ones in this kind of play. But they must be allowed the time, space and lack of interference in which to do it. Child learners are considered by Carla Rinaldi to be intuitive and empirical "researchers". We must ensure that we do not get in their way.

The role of intuition

Many people have forgotten how to listen to the voices of intuition. An intuition may be a physical feeling (a gut feeling that this is the right or wrong decision). It may be an insight, the old light-bulb flashing on, something which seems to burst in on us from outside (we ask ourselves: where did that come from?). We might have hunches we are not sure are correct, but which may have a sound basis. There is even an aesthetic dimension to intuitions: Francis Crick wrote of his discovery of DNA that a structure this pretty just had to exist'. It is important to facilitate concentric or direct access to intuitions, whether they are viewed by the subject with an a priori attitude of trust or suspicion. Intuitions are in any case useful associations for the discovery of probable truths. Selecting which intuitions to discard and which to follow is performed a posteriori.

In the traditional view, this kind of thinking might be seen as sloppy, fuzzy, childish or lazy. But the Cartesian view of man as a conscious, articulate, rational being, which remains the basis for institutional education, is demonstrably flawed. In this view, the unconscious simply gets in the way of learning, by allowing emotions to disrupt rational thought. Butthe unconscious can also be a cognitive resource. As philosopher Edgar Morin has pointed out, Homo is not just sapiens but demens; and it is by using the resources of both our conscious and unconscious minds that we will best be able to tap into our own ingenuity. The new educational methods should not only seek to address the acquisition of direct knowledge. They should aim to stimulate the " computo " (that which is computed now) and the " cogito " (the reflection which comes later on the basis of prior computations).

The capacity to switch off rational, deliberate thinking is linked to the ability to gain access to flows of intuition and experience what we call " knowledge leap-frogging ". This happens when learners "leap" spontaneously and pleasurably from one level of knowledge to the next, stimulated by their desire to know more. Individuals derive great satisfaction from such acceleration in their speed of thought, and in seeing truths liberated from the constraints of linear reasoning.

Immediate profitability should not be the motivation for acquiring new information or assessing what has been acquired. We need to identify what will give greater benefit in the long term. We have to weave our associations of thoughts and intuitions into a complex knowledge fabric.

11.4 "Soft" thinking and creativity

Creative people in all domains have often insisted on the importance in their work of avoiding conscious thinking. Cezanne said: " If I think, everything is lost. " We can stimulate creativity by allowing individuals to draw on and develop this mental attitude or tendency as a complement to rational analytical thinking.

Psychologists Haber and Eredlyi have shown that creativity entails improved access to memories and that this happens when subjects are in a relaxed state. Other experiments, like those of Kenneth Bowers and his colleagues at the University of Waterloo in Canada, have shown that paying heed to our guesses and intuitions gives us access to the unconscious machinations of our minds. So we should design online tools that enable the emergence of unconscious and spontaneous waves of " direct knowledge ".

The new focus on creativity

Much more attention is being paid these days to the importance of creativity in all areas of life. Politicians, psychologists and educators are arguing that creativity is good for the economy, good for individuals, good for society and good for education. The first of these 'goods' provides what is seen as the strongest argument. Politicians who argue that creativity should take a central place within the school curriculum usually focus on its utilitarian aspect, its importance to the economic health of the nation.

Alan Greenspan, chairman of the US Federal Reserve Board, speaking at Harvard University in June 1999, remarked on the advantages of a liberal education: " Specifically, the broadening of one's world view that is acquired through a liberal education almost surely contributes to an understanding of the interrelationship of different fields of endeavor. Important new knowledge is very often the result of interdisciplinary observation. The broader the context that an inquiring mind brings to a problem, the greater will be the potential for creative insights that, in the end, contributes to a more productive economy. "

In the past, the study of creativity was usually based on exceptional individuals displaying high-order creativity, such as Mozart or Leonardo da Vinci. Creative people were those who produced something original and of value in the public realm, and their creativity was measured and recognized through this work. Furthermore, creativity was a characteristic expressed in one particular sphere rather than a general ability. A highly creative musician was not expected to show the same skill in painting.

One vital way of fostering creativity is by taking a wider view of what it is. If the definition of creativity is outstanding innovation within a field, leading to a break with past understandings or perspectives, then we are referring to an ability displayed by only a handful of exceptional individuals. However, outstanding creativity is not the only kind worth talking about. Anyone is capable of being creative given the right conditions. Creativity may involve innovation for the individual, not necessarily leading to a paradigm shift in the public sphere. Creative activity is possible in all subjects at school, all domains of knowledge and all areas of life. It is not confined to any particular domain, and it is not only found in the so-called 'creative arts'. Creativity is also expressed in the resourcefulness and agency of ordinary people in the way they lead their lives.

Adaptability and flexibility are basic life-skills in the new age of uncertainty. Creative thinking is possibility thinking, seeing more than is initially evident. It implies a 'can-do' attitude, an openness to the possibilities that might develop, an ability to deploy a range of ways of looking at a situation. It will, therefore, be increasingly important in the future, both as a marketable skill and as an aid in selecting one's paths in life. In an aging society, creative activity is an excellent way of promoting mental fitness and flexibility.

Encouraging creativity in organizations not only enhances market share, but makes employees more committed and less frustrated, giving them a sense of agency and a rise in self-esteem. Creativity also involves problem identification as well as problem-solving. If you are able to ask the right questions, you may be able to find a way around a problem or a blockage. Creativity draws upon all of our intelligences and makes them work together. But it draws upon intuitive, non-conscious processes as well as rational and/or conscious ones.

Creativity does need practice. People who are able to enter voluntarily into the realm of fantasy have been found to be more creative than people who cannot. The former have often been cultivating their powers of imagination since childhood. They are able to fall into a state of reverie where imagery becomes more vivid and fluid. They have a receptive, non-censoring attitude to the activities of their own minds. Creative thinkers can " let go " of mental control.

People need to learn to exercise their imagination rather than simply cramming to do well in tests, but curriculum requirements and job pressures may not leave children and adults sufficient time. This is why we need to make sure they are provided for outside school and work.

11.5 Conclusion

The revolution in education I am calling for should be an attempt to stimulate a holistic, instinctive, intuitive, creative, synoptic and systemic view of knowledge. We should shy away from turning children and adults into living encyclopaedias, and instead focus on activities that link together the pleasure of living and the pleasure of learning. This could lead to a culture where knowledge is a pleasure and where there is a new focus on the art of living well.

Bibliography

[1] Clark, A. (1997) Being There: Putting brain, body and world together again. The MIT Press, Bradford Books, Cambridge Ma.

[2] Claxton, G. (1996) Liberating the Learner: Lessons for Professional Development in Education. Routledge, London and NY.

[3] Gardner, H. (1993) Multiple Intelligences: The Theory in Practice. Basic Books, New York.

[4] Karmiloff-Smith, A. (1992) Beyond Modularity: A Developmental perspective on Cognitive Science. The MIT Press, Cambridge, Mass.

Group Discussion 11
Unleashing the Creative Mind

The New Role of Teachers

Punset : I agree about the importance of intuitive reasoning, but like to stress that there is always the hard work before intuition can work. Yes, you jump, but you cant do this unless there is a lot of subconscious information. I think it was Picasso who said something like "Im not looking for something, je trouves". But actually it is not true. He found things because he devoted a lot of time on research.

Allien : There is never a spontaneous generation of knowledge. Edgar Morin has written on the fact that "cogito" is important, but "computo" or "computare" remains the basic food. We have to compute a lot to have a good intuition. And it is not important whether it is conscious or not, what is important is to compute.

Nevejan : How do you learn students to find there way in the overflow of information available on the web? Make sure they know a lot!

Allien : So computo permits cogito, it permits to have direct insight or as Olivier said: to have shortcuts.

Punset : One of the things we learn from biology is that without energy life inside the membrane cell does not exist. Thanks to a lot of energy you manage to maintain some order for a few years, a few day in the case of a mosquito, a few years in the case of a rat. So without this effort, without this energy, without this computo, there is no intuition, there is no order, there is no life. So we should tell children its nice these direct intuitions, but there is no excuse not to get into computo.

Steels: I suppose all this means that learner-centered learning is central, but we must still take our responsibilities as teachers to transmit existing relevant know how and make sure that students go through the hard work that is the basis of intuition.

Allien : To integrate, we need a lot of input. But it is like children riding bicycles, they are not thinking they are riding bicycles but they are doing nevertheless a complex task. There is a lot of knowledge integrated unconsciously and it is very difficult to debrief it later or to recuperate it in a conscious sense.

Punset : What we should try to avoid is to apply rational decisions to automate the learning process. We dont need your bloody logic, the human mind can go very well by itself. Let these automatic and unconscious processes flow because most of what we think comes naturally anyhow.

Alternatives

Nevejan: You argue for a radical revolution in education. I believe that alternatives will emerge. But we will always need a balance in society. To maintain democracy is not easy. To take care of others or to protect others, is not always fun. But it is necessary and causes good life. Public schools may not be cheap and they dont make money but they will remain important. Of course there are certain values that you cannot address that way. And we will have to come up with solutions because otherwise it will ruin civilisation.

Steels: We have to free teachers from educational bureaucracy and unions or whatever that restrains them. The power has to go back to the teachers.

Dautenhahn: I think about evolution in education as a kind of spiral thing, rather than a revolution, because the relation between technology and human cognition. The frontiers are constantly changing and we always have to try and keep up with them, look beyond, try to predict what will happen. One of the terms that I really hate is "added value". What is the difference between using your robot with children as opposed to NOT using your robot? As opposed to what, using a dog? Or a human being? Or have the children interact with each other? Let us try to find out what is possible, push technology and see what comes out. Of course you also have to ask what do we want, what are the goals and how can we maybe change technology so that we have these goals. To make things even more complex there is this fact that the brain is itself a complex adaptive system. So our target is actually a moving target. Technologies will change human beings: how we perceive the world, how we interact with others, how we learn, and this will induce new generations of researchers to build new learning environments.

Wynants: The visions of the philosopher Ivan Illich who wrote Deschooling Society in 1971, still stand out as a valuable reflection on learning through an institutional organisation. And especially on the assessments and transmission of values:

> Universal education through schooling is not feasible. It would be no more feasible if it were attempted by means of alternative institutions built on the style of present schools. Neither new attitudes of teachers toward their pupils nor the proliferation of educational hardware or software (in classroom or bedroom), nor finally the attempt to expand the pedagogue's responsibility until it engulfs his pupils' lifetimes will deliver universal education. The current search for new educational funnels must be reversed into the search for their institutional inverse: educational webs which heighten the opportunity for each one to transform each moment of his living into one of learning, sharing, I believe that most of the research now going on about the future tends to advocate further increases in the institutionalization of values and that we must define conditions which would permit precisely the contrary to happen. We need research on the possible use of technology to create institutions which serve personal, creative, and autonomous interaction and the emergence of values which cannot be substantially controlled by technocrats.

Allien: We are enriched not only by theories or by scientific deduction, but by utilisation, by experiments at school or at home. It is important to be open to the different experiences in the world, and trying not to be trapped by a specific theory, that after a while will anyhow be destroyed by reality, in the school itself for instance. Children are always disturbing our adult order, our adult rationality and its good to be on the borderline of chaos and rationality. Therefore we should always reconsider existing principles, not trying to destroy them but to test them.

Theme VI

A Peek into the Future

Ezrabot. Ezra, age 10

Let's try to imagine what will become possible.

Ken Mogi

Chapter 12

Brains at Play

by Marleen Wynants

Marleen Wynants is an independent journalist from Belgium. She graduated in linguistics and communication sciences from the University of Leuven and has written a large number of articles and columns tracking the development of ICT technologies and their impact on society. Her most recent book is "Does your child's school have a future?"

Figure 12.1: Prototype of a device for communicating information through tiles, developed by Jun Rekimoto. The tiles are put on a sensor-enhanced flat panel display. A tile on which a picture is displayed can be connected to a map to show where it has been taken and then connected to a clock to know the time in that location.

2058. We Take a peek in the World Wide Clubhouse, a learning community of toddlers, young kids, adults and elder citizens, located in Futureville, on the outskirts of Paris. Did you notice the bright mosaic mural in the Play Hall when you entered? Every month, this mural changes, according to the themes that the kids are working on. The kids who contributed to the mural can transfer it to an electronic timebox - an archive of things accomplished, kept from early childhood. They can look and change their timebox by manipulating active tiles. The Play Hall has no central meeting point, but several nooks with different sized coloured chairs and even some reclining chairs to take a little nap. From the Play Hall you can reach the different Studios: the Music Studio, the Self-Discovery Studio, the Creative Studio and the Eco Studio.

> *"People move slower now", Myra (84), a lawyer, says. "They look more around them, are more attentive, more alert. When I was younger, you couldn't stop them rushing from one place to another. We lost a lot of energy there. And every time you felt like you were winning, somebody else changed the rules of the game. So we ended up in a collective paralysis. It was a puzzle, but the pieces didn't fit. Until we had this global vision about an organic planet, living systems called cities and the urge to make them enjoyable.*

The Eco studio is a physical learning environment where contact with nature and the study of the earth are explored in many ways. This is the place where teams of different generations take turns in maintaining the vegetable garden and cooking well-balanced food. The younger kids are eager to play outside and get dirty hands. They participate in planting or harvesting vegetables and fruit, they also learn about nutritional and ecological values from the teachers and older volunteers. They marvel at the colors of the crossbred flowers and are perplexed by the sizes and shapes of the crossbred peas. Some of them leave it at that. They indulge in picking fruit, in taking care of the small poultry community or in just roaming around in the orchard, chasing each other and enjoying the many swings that hang in the trees. Others are puzzled by the whole growing process and participate actively in the genetic experiments that the older kids are performing.

There's a lot of activity going on today in the vegetable garden. The sun is out and so are the kids. Most of the excitement seems to come from the greenhouse. At the suggestion of the biology teacher, last years' pea harvest was separated in large and tiny varieties of peas. They crossbred them and the offspring resulted again in large peas and small peas. The next step was to cross the tall peas with other tall peas and the small peas with the small ones. Some children have started collecting the harvest of the tall ones, and they notice to their amazement that one quarter of them is short! Whilst the offspring of the small peas turns out to be small, with no exception.

"How is that possible!" Billie exclaims. She holds up a tiny pea and compares it to a tall one. "They're from the same tall parents", she says "and still, such a difference!" "Look at your brother", the gardener says. Billie looks at her older brother who is collecting the shells of the peas for compost. "What about my brother?" she asks. "Marcus come over here, please!", the biology teacher waves Marcus over to the group of children that gathers around Billie. "Go stand over here", the teacher says. Marcus stands close to his sister. "Now, what do you see?" The teacher asks. "Billie is already taller than Marcus," says one of the kids. "So what?" Billie asks. "It means that you will probably end up taller than me anyway" Marcus says. Billie forgets to close her mouth. "Now I see," she says. "It's about the same principle, isn't it? My father is really tall, my mother is much shorter, so again any length is possible." "And what do we probably get if both parents are short?" the teacher asks. "Short children" a boy answers, at least if the length of people goes the same way as the length of peas. "Welcome to genetics", the biology teacher says and they all start giggling. "What will happen when we continue crossbreeding?" Marcus asks. "Do you want to find that out?" The teacher asks. "Yes!" The whole group nods very convincingly. "Alright" says the gardener "let's get to work then!" "Who's in?" he asks and heads into the direction of the greenhouse. The whole group starts following him.

The biology teacher frowns. "Alright", he says to himself, "we'll get to the theory later on this week." He turns around and bounces into a girl with her hands full of leaves from the fruittrees. "How are things going?" He asks. "Great," the girl says. "I think we have less pollution than last year." She belongs to a group of children working on a project about air pollution. Some kids can be seen collecting grass and leaves from the orchard or small clothes items that have been exposed to the open air for a few days, some a few weeks. They label the items and take pictures. Under the guidance of the chemistry teacher, they will run tests on the items to see what kinds of pollution can be detected. And what the degree is.

Later on that week, they will exchange their findings around one of the large tables in the Play Hall. The younger kids will make an illustrated report on causes of air pollution, the older ones will try to predict the evolution of the local situation using mathematical models. The final report will be presented to the whole learning community of Futureville just before their the next fieldtrip to the countryside during which new data will be collected by everybody to continue the project on a larger scale. They plan to meet with other school communities to launch a common multi media report in order to come to a long term and

Figure 12.2: Schools of the future will in many ways be very much like today's schools, where children can enjoy nature and physical play. (mw)

more global evaluation of the pollution problem.

> *For ages people couldn't move away from the sit-still-and-listen attitude in schools, says Leon (84), a teacher. We were not allowed to eat while listening, or to knead a ball to calm down some nerves, not even to make drawings. And then around the turn of the century they brought in computers. My kids had to spend hours in front of a screen, gazing at texts and exercises and clicking their own intelligence away. It was pretty mutilating in a way, yes.*

Let's get back to the Play Hall. Over there is the Book Nook. There are magazines and books on brightly coloured bookshelves and some are lingering on a table. One of them is Alice in Wonderland and two kids of about 5 years old are making a collage with images of all the animals that appear in the story which was read to them by the advanced readers, a group of children of different ages sharing the same reading level. The Book Nook is situated in the southern corner of the Play Hall, the warmest of them all. In that corner you most likely find an Aiball, a cute ball-like robot on wheels, always looking for the warmest spot in the area. When an Aiball gets picked up, it senses when a person does not feel happy and starts making funny noises. When put down too roughly, you might hear "Gosh!" or the sound of breaking glass, depending on how the kids in the Creative Studio programmed it. The Aiball has a pen that it can lower onto the floor to make drawings. The kids play around with this toy making triangles, circles, and learning about computational geometry as they go.

Hush now, let's take a look in the Creative Studio. It has a wall to wall broadband screen on the left side and to the right there is a mezzanine. The mezzanine serves as the media center of the learning community but also of other communities of Transville. That is why the mezzanine usually buzzes like the newsroom in a historic movie... Here some teachers and older kids are composing an electronic newspaper and a final report on the so-called Transit project. The project started from the fact that about 60older. So Pip and Johnny figured that interviewing the oldest people in their community might learn them a lot about the former century. Teachers enthusiastically supported the project because the interview would allow reflections on the future, on the present and on the past.

> *Some things cost only one third of the things they cost in the old days, says Robin (79), a shopkeeper. We thought recycling started and ended at putting things in a black, blue or yellow plastic bags . At the time we never thought about buying less. Before becoming a global holiday, the buy-nothing-today day was just a gimmick from some alternative people.*

Hey, what is all the fuss on the Creative Studio floor? Apparently one of the Aiballs needs some fine tuning. On one of the broadband screens a kid from Tokyo is showing exactly where one of the sensors should be fixed. The girl holding the Aiball nods. "You'll have to re-boot it" the boy on the other side of the broadband screen says. His Japanese is being automatically translated. "All right", the girl sighs and reboots the robot. She puts him on the floor again and he rolls off with a squeaky sound that makes everybody shiver. "Maybe we need another sound," says Pip who steps down from the mezzanine. "It's all yours!" the girl says. "I have to prepare things for the sports training this afternoon. Is that OK with you?" "Fine" Pip says. "See you later! Hi Tai!" she waves at the boy on the screen and picks up the Aiball. She looks up at the mezzanine. "Johnny? Can you help us out here." "What sound do you have in mind?" Johnny says. "Some whistling birds?" "We can do better than that" Rita says. Rita is Johnny's mother and she comes in assisting the teachers two days a week. "What about Britney Spears?" "That old tart!" Rita shrieks. "Can't we recycle something less

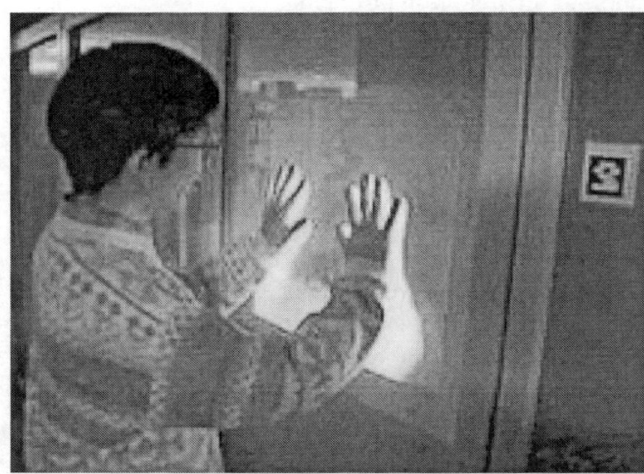

Figure 12.3: Prototype of a holowall, developed by Jun Rekimoto. Interaction is possible by touching a large see-through screen on which remote images can be displayed through a broadband network.

intrusive?" "What are your favourite sounds?" Pip asks Tai. Tai comes closer to the screen. He takes his wearable, points at the room and they get a list of self-drawn icons at the side of the screen. Johnny touches the first one, a kind of beetle, and the studio is filled with the sound of a million crickets. "I like listening to that before I go to sleep" Tai says. "What is that?" Pip asks. Johnny points to the second icon, a kind of monorail car. Some cheerful clinging resounds. "I like that!" Pip exclaims. "Me too", Johnny says. "It's the sound of a train entering Gotanda station in Tokyo in 1996" Tai says. "My grandmother recorded this with her first digital camera", whereupon he launches a video showing the train entering the station. "Wow", Rita says. "I had to wait for my first digital camera until 2002". "Didn't you have pictures before?" Pip asks. "Yes, sure", Rita says, "We had video too but you could not transmit it to other people just by pointing at it. It was the cable-age, remember?". "Sounds really old ..." Johnny says. "Did people still wear wigs at that time?" "C'mon!" Rita exclaims. "We'll spend some time together in the Time Machine this afternoon, just to refresh your memory. So, we go for the subway sound?" They all nod. Tai smiles broadly.

> *We thought broadband would bring us zillions of channels of music from all over the world, or an endless catalogue of pay-per-film, says Lim (85), a journalist. I never imagined it would become the favourite medium in the communication with my grandchildren. I talk or listen to them while eating breakfast at least two times a week. They see me move around, making another toast and when they head for the fridge, I quickly add an extra layer of cream cheeseŁ I can see them rub their eyes and check their teeth in the mirror, hoping that that will do for their daily hygiene. So when we don't activate the screens later that day, I leave them the audiovisual message where I stick up an old-fashioned broom: Don't forget to brush your teeth! It has become our private joke.*

Let's move a bit further down the hall to The Self- Discovery Studio which has been reserved by some teachers preparing the upcoming fieldtrip at Titisee, a lake in the Black

Forest area of Germany. Everybody in the learning community will retreat for a week in a log cabin near the Lake. Most of the time will be dedicated to social and outside activities and this needs a lot of practical planning and pedagogical expertise. The broadband screen in The Self-Discovery Studio links the teachers directly with Elvis, the janitor of the log cabin. They are almost done with the practical arrangements when Rita pops in. “Sorry”, she says, “but we’re all ready for a break with tea and cake in the Playhall.” “Want some?” she asks Elvis and shows him a plate full of appetizing homemade cakes that come directly from the Eco Studio. Elvis smacks his lips. “You know what would be really revolutionary?” he says. “A teleportation! I only have to point at the cakes and I get them right from this screen. But in the meantime, we’re fine. I guess the meeting is over? See you tomorrow!” He pats his belly, then taps on his active tattoo and disappears from the screen, provoking an outburst of giggles from the women.

Ting-ting-ting-ting... An Aiball rolls by and installs itself right in the middle of a weak beam of sunlight. Johnny runs after it, stops in the doorway and pulls up his shoulders. “It works”, he says proudly. “Can I skip tea?” “Take some cake with you”, Rita says and hands him a slice on a napkin. “I really need to work on my Cool Collections,” Johnny says. “The deadline is next week, you see.” “I know,” Rita says. “Did you get the pictures of my skeleton collection of small animals?” “Yeah¡‘ Johnny says. ”A true masterpiece! Wish I had collected them. Do I inherit these¿‘ Rita hesitates. ”...I think I threw them out in a black plastic bag.“ she says. ”Still thanks for the digital traces, mum¡‘ Johnny blows her a kiss and runs off while crumbs of cake leave a distinct trail after him. Some things will never change...

List of authors

Bernard Allien
Franklin Research Center LTD
184 Turney Road
Dulwich, London SE2 1JL
UNITED KINGDOM

Olivier Coenen
Sony CSL Paris
6, rue Amyot
75005 Paris
FRANCE

Kerstin Dautenhahn
Adaptive Systems Research Group
The University of Hertfordshire,
Department of Computer Science
College Lane, Hatfield
Hertfordshire AL10 9AB
UNITED KINGDOM

Mariane Hedegaard
Institute of Psychology
University of Aarhus
Asylvej 4
Risskov
DENMARK

Mark Johnson
MRC Scientist, Director,
Centre for Brain and Cognitive Development
School of Psychology
Birkbeck College, University of London
Malet Street
London WC1E 7HX
UNITED KINGDOM

Ken Mogi
Sony Computer Science Labs Inc
Takanawa Muse Building
3-14-13 Higashi-Gotanda, Shinagawa-Ku
Tokyo 141
JAPAN

Caroline Nevejan
Hogeschool van Amsterdam
Nieuwe Amstelstraat 59
1011 PL Amsterdam
THE NETHERLANDS

Eduardo Punset
Agencia Planetaria, S.A.
Rambla Catalunya, 74 2
08007 Barcelona
SPAIN

Carla Rinaldi
Reggio Children srl
Piazza Della Vittoria, 6
42100 Reggio Emilia
ITALY

Luc Steels
VUB AI laboratory, Brussels, and
Sony Computer Science Laboratory
6, rue Amyot
75005 Paris
FRANCE

Mario Tokoro
Sony Computer Science Labs Inc
Takanawa Muse Building
3-14-13 Higashi-Gotanda, Shinagawa-Ku
Tokyo 141
JAPAN

Subject Index